THE 100 MOST INFLUENTIAL
INVENTORS
OF ALL TIME

THE BRITANNICA GUIDE TO THE WORLD'S MOST INFLUENTIAL PEOPLE

THE 100 MOST INFLUENTIAL
INVENTORS
OF ALL TIME

EDITED BY ROBERT CURLEY, MANAGER, SCIENCE AND TECHNOLOGY

Britannica®
Educational Publishing

IN ASSOCIATION WITH

ROSEN
EDUCATIONAL SERVICES

Published in 2010 by Britannica Educational Publishing
(a trademark of Encyclopædia Britannica, Inc.)
in association with Rosen Educational Services, LLC
29 East 21st Street, New York, NY 10010.

First Edition

Britannica Educational Publishing
Michael I. Levy: Executive Editor
Marilyn L. Barton: Senior Coordinator, Production Control
Steven Bosco: Director, Editorial Technologies
Lisa S. Braucher: Senior Producer and Data Editor
Yvette Charboneau: Senior Copy Editor
Kathy Nakamura: Manager, Media Acquisition
Robert Curley: Manager, Science and Technology

Rosen Educational Services
Hope Lourie Killcoyne: Senior Editor and Project Manager
Nelson Sá: Art Director
Matthew Cauli: Designer
Introduction by Stephanie Watson

Library of Congress Cataloging-in-Publication Data

The 100 most influential inventors of all time / edited by Robert Curley.—1st ed.
        p. cm.—(The Britannica guide to the world's most influential people)
"In association with Britannica Educational Publishing, Rosen Educational Services."
Includes index.
ISBN 978-1-61530-003-7 (library binding)
1. Inventors—Biography—Popular works. 2. Inventions—History—Popular works.
I. Curley, Robert, 1955– II. Title: One hundred most influential inventors of all time.
T39.A14 2010
609.2'2—dc22

                                                                        2009027248

Manufactured in the United States of America

Cover photo: David Joel/Photographer's Choice RF/Getty Images

CONTENTS

25

directional nozzle

steam exhaust
causes sphere
to spin

pivot

steam rises
through tubes

water vaporized
in heated kettle

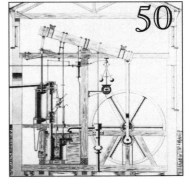

50

66

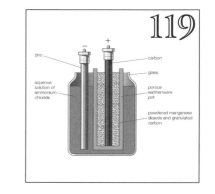

INTRODUCTION

Just a few hundred years ago, life was far different than it is today. When people wanted to travel or communicate, they had to go on foot or horseback. A journey of just a few miles by this method could be a long, arduous process. Whatever people owned—from clothing to tools—had to be made by hand. Work was manual, laborious, and often tedious. Illness was a constant threat; diseases rapidly spread through unsanitary conditions and were difficult to treat with the rudimentary medicines available.

Today, life in the United States and other developed countries is about ease and convenience. Communication is global and instantaneous. Transportation can carry people across states, countries, and even entire continents in a matter of hours. Industry has been automated, providing people with plenty of time outside of work to enjoy leisure pursuits. Modern medical treatments have enabled people to stay healthy well into their eighth, ninth, or even tenth decade.

Life has been transformed over the years through the efforts of the men and women who had the brilliance, diligence, and creativity to come up with new and better ways of doing things. As detailed throughout these pages, their inventions spawned many more inventions, speeding up the pace of progress even further. Alexander Graham Bell's fascination with the idea of sending sound down a wire from the speaker to the listener gave birth to the telephone, which ultimately led to the cell phone, fax machine, modem, and a communication system that now links the entire globe.

These inventions, like many others, have clearly improved life by keeping people healthier, helping them to communicate and work more efficiently, and allowing them to travel farther. X-rays allowed doctors to look inside the human body to treat disease and injury. The electric light illuminated the darkness so people could work (and play) at night. Braille made it possible for blind people to read.

However, some inventions, while having their obvious benefits, have also had their pitfalls. Before Eli Whitney invented the cotton gin in 1793, separating cotton lint from its seeds was a 10-hour, labour-intensive ordeal. Whitney's invention transformed cotton production into a rapid process that for the first time made cotton farming a highly profitable business. Yet the cotton gin also prolonged slavery, as cotton plantations needed a larger labour force to keep up with increased production demands.

Other inventions were controversial because of their potential for destruction. Edward Teller, father of the hydrogen bomb, was described by one scientist as being one of the "most thoughtful statesmen of science." However, another contemporary referred to Teller as "a danger to all that's important," and claimed that the world would have been better off without him. In 1948, Paul Hermann Müller received a Nobel Prize for discovering the toxic effects on insects of the chemical compound known as DDT, a pesticide that efficiently wiped out the insects that carry deadly diseases such as malaria, yellow fever, and typhus. DDT was initially hailed as a "miracle" pesticide. Yet by the early 1970s it had been banned from public use in the United States. Health officials had discovered that while DDT was killing insects, it was also accumulating in other wildlife, notably falcons and eagles, and dangerously lowering their reproduction rate.

Even the most groundbreaking and world-changing inventions were not always recognized as such when they were introduced to the public. When Rutherford B. Hayes saw a demonstration of Alexander Graham Bell's telephone in 1876, the president's response was less than enthusiastic. "That's an amazing invention, but who would ever want to use one of them?" he scoffed. In 1968, the audience attending a computer conference at the San Francisco Civic Auditorium likely didn't know what to make of Douglas Engelbart's invention—a small wooden box with a button that moved a cursor on an attached machine. His "mouse," so named for its tail-like cable, now enables virtually every home and business computer user to navigate around their computer screens.

Inventors themselves have sometimes been skeptical about the ability of their own creations to endure. Despite the public excitement that greeted their Cinèmatographe motion picture machine when it was released in 1895, the Lumière brothers felt that their invention was just a fad. In fact, Louis Lumière referred to the cinema as "an invention without a future." In spite of the Lumière brothers' initial cynicism, film endures as one of the most popular art forms today.

WHAT INSPIRES INVENTION?

The old saying, "Necessity is the mother of invention," couldn't be more true. Inventors have had a knack for recognizing a need or problem in society and then discovering a way to fill that need or solve that problem.

In the 15th century, as the number of universities in Europe grew and public literacy spread, a more efficient method was needed for reproducing books—a demand that was met by Johannes Gutenberg's printing press.

Sometimes it was the inventor's own necessity that gave birth to invention. Frustrated at having to change pairs of glasses whenever he switched from reading to viewing objects at a distance, Benjamin Franklin invented a new type of glasses—bifocals—that could easily accommodate both views.

Intelligence and curiosity are unquestionably important assets for inventors, but having an advanced degree—or even a formal education—has never been a prerequisite. Thomas Edison studied at home with his mother. Orville and Wilbur Wright never finished high school. George Washington Carver, who began life as a slave, taught himself to read from the only book he possessed—*Webster's Elementary Spelling Book*.

What ultimately fueled the spark of discovery and led inventors to their "eureka" moment was unique to each person. Dr. Robert H. Goddard, who pioneered the first rocket-powered spacecraft, became fascinated with the idea of space flight after reading H.G. Wells's science fiction novel *The War of the Worlds*. Decades before Henry Ford introduced the Model T automobile and designed the moving assembly line, he became fascinated with the inner workings of clocks and watches. When Steve Wozniak, inventor of the Apple II computer, was 11 years old, he built a computer so that he could play tic-tac-toe.

Often inventors were inspired by one another. Orville and Wilbur Wright became interested in aviation after reading about German aviation engineer Otto Lilienthal's experiments with gliders. In turn, the Wright Brothers' famous 1903 flight at Kitty Hawk, N.C., inspired a teen-aged Russian boy named Igor Sikorsky to later invent the world's first single-rotor helicopter.

Some inventions throughout history have occurred purely by accident. In 1796, in an effort to find an inexpensive way to print his own plays, Austrian actor and playwright Alois Senefelder stumbled across the promising potential of using fine-grained stone instead of copper plate, thereby inventing the process of lithography. In 1839, businessman Charles Goodyear was looking for a way to make natural rubber more pliable, when he accidentally spilled some rubber mixed with sulfur on a hot stove. He discovered that instead of melting, the rubber became more elastic. Thus was the vulcanization process born, and with it a whole range of uses for rubber.

For other inventions, however, the process was painstakingly slow and required many hours of trial and error. Thomas Edison experimented with 6,000 different materials before finally discovering a filament (carbonized thread) that would stay lit for many hours inside a bulb without burning up. It's no wonder that the famous quote "Genius is 99 percent perspiration and 1 percent inspiration" is attributed to him.

Despite the hard work that was often required to produce an invention, money was not always the impetus for the inventors in this book. In fact, before the 18th century, inventors had no guarantee that their ideas would not be stolen. The design of Eli Whitney's cotton gin was so basic that manufacturers throughout the South began to copy it, and Whitney was never able to profit from his own invention.

However, the introduction of the U.S. Patent system in 1790 meant that inventors could for the first time prevent others from copying their work. (Thomas Edison was issued some 1,093 U.S. patents during his prolific career.) With the protection that patents afforded often came huge profits. When Henry Ford died in 1947, his estimated net worth was around $600 million.

Money was just one of the benefits awarded to those who came up with a successful invention. Inventors also earned fame, recognition, and a place in history. Some received what is thought to be the highest honour—the Nobel Prize. (The man responsible for establishing this prize, Alfred Nobel, is himself included in the pages of this book for his invention of dynamite.) In 1909, Guglielmo Marconi received the Nobel Prize in Physics for developing the first practical radio. English biochemist

Frederick Sanger was awarded the Nobel Prize in Chemistry twice: once in 1958 and again in 1980 (shared with Paul Berg and Walter Gilbert) for his pioneering work unraveling the mysteries of DNA.

THE INVENTORS

This book recognizes not only the inventors whose work changed the course of human life, but also those whose ideas paved the way for future generations of inventors. In the mid 1800s, mathematician Charles Babbage developed a model for an automatic computing engine, but he never built his device. A century later, Babbage's idea that a machine could perform scientific computations reemerged, and today the computer is recognized as one of the most revolutionary inventions in history.

The vast majority of the inventors who have been included in these pages lived during the 19th and 20th centuries, which should come as no surprise considering that this was the time period in which the modern scientific age began. However, that is not to say that the many inventors who came before that period were any less important. Cro-Magnons' stone tools were a technological feat. The Archimedes screw water pump, invented in the 3rd century BCE, is still in use today. Recorded history would not have been possible without Cai Lun's invention of paper in 105 CE.

There was no lack of invention before the 19th century; it was just the pace of invention that sped up significantly after that time. When Charles Duell, head of the U.S. Patent Office, famously declared, "Everything that can be invented has been invented," in 1899, how wrong he was. In 2008 alone, the U.S. Patent and Trademark Office granted more than 185,000 patents for new inventions.

Some of these inventions may never make headlines or revolutionize the world, but they will all have an effect (however subtle) on people's lives.

The speed of invention today is so rapid that the world can literally change during the course of one individual's lifetime. Someone who was born in the early part of the 20th century will have witnessed the invention of the television, computer, Internet, microwave oven, helicopter, penicillin, and dozens of other innovations that have transformed the way in which people live.

One of the fields where invention has made the greatest strides is in medical science. At the turn of the 20th century, doctors were able to look inside the human body without cutting it open (thanks to Wilhelm Röntgen's X-rays). By the end of the century, they had unraveled the entire genetic code and discovered the minute changes that lead to disease. Looking ahead into the next century, new therapies might be developed that could reprogram human DNA, changing the course of an individual's medical history before he or she is even born.

So many inventors have made important contributions that to mention them all here would far exceed the space limitations of this book. The 100 men and women who have been included are among the greatest and most prolific inventors of all time. They were selected because their inventions have altered the course of people's lives and have left an indelible stamp on human history.

CRO-MAGNON

C ro-Magnon was a population of early *Homo sapiens* dating from the Upper Paleolithic Period (*c.* 40,000 to *c.* 10,000 years ago) in Europe. In their ancient cave habitations they left behind traces of ingenious stone tools, carved statuettes and figurines, and painted scenes of striking beauty that are considered to be among the greatest treasures of human creativity.

In 1868, in a shallow cave at Cro-Magnon near the town of Les Eyzies-de-Tayac in the Dordogne region of southwestern France, a number of obviously ancient human skeletons were found. The cave was investigated by the French geologist Édouard Lartet, who uncovered five archaeological layers. The human bones found in the topmost layer proved to be between 10,000 and 35,000 years old. The prehistoric humans revealed by this find were called Cro-Magnon and have since been considered, along with Neanderthals (*H. neanderthalensis*), to be representative of prehistoric humans.

Cro-Magnons were robustly built and powerful and are presumed to have been about 5 feet 5 inches to 5 feet 7 inches (about 166 to 171 cm) tall. The body was generally heavy and solid, apparently with strong musculature. The forehead was straight, with slight browridges, and the face short and wide. Cro-Magnons were the first humans (genus *Homo*) to have a prominent chin. The brain capacity was about 100 cubic inches (1,600 cc), somewhat larger than the average for modern humans. It is thought that Cro-Magnons were probably fairly tall compared with other early human species.

It is still hard to say precisely where Cro-Magnons belong in recent human evolution, but they had a culture that produced a variety of sophisticated tools such as retouched blades, end scrapers, "nosed" scrapers, the chisel-like tool known as a burin, and fine bone tools. They also seem to have made tools for smoothing and scraping leather. Some Cro-Magnons have been associated with the Gravettian industry, or Upper Perigordian industry, which is characterized by an abrupt retouching technique that produces tools with flat backs. Cro-Magnon dwellings are most often found in deep caves and in shallow caves formed by rock overhangs, although primitive huts, either lean-tos against rock walls or those built completely from stones, have been found. The rock shelters were used year-round; the Cro-Magnons seem to have been a settled people, moving only when necessary to find new hunting or because of environmental changes.

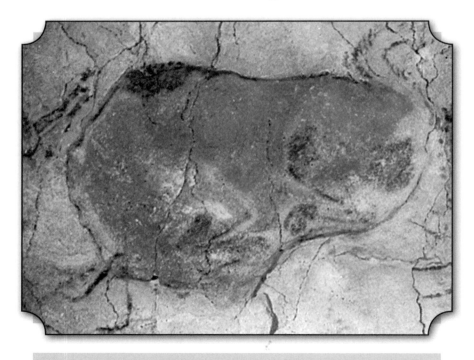

Magdalenian cave painting of a bison, Altamira, Spain. A. Held/J.P. Ziolo, Paris

Like the Neanderthals, the Cro-Magnon people buried their dead. The first examples of art by prehistoric peoples are Cro-Magnon. The Cro-Magnons carved and sculpted small engravings, reliefs, and statuettes not only of humans but also of animals. Their human figures generally depict large-breasted, wide-hipped, and often obviously pregnant women, from which it is assumed that these figures had significance in fertility rites. Numerous depictions of animals are found in Cro-Magnon cave paintings throughout France and Spain at sites such as Lascaux, Les Eyzies-de-Tayac, and Altamira, and some of them are surpassingly beautiful. It is thought that these paintings had some magic or ritual importance to the people. From the high quality of their art, it is clear that Cro-Magnons were not primitive amateurs but had previously experimented with artistic mediums and forms. Decorated tools and weapons show that they appreciated art for aesthetic purposes as well as for religious reasons.

It is difficult to determine how long the Cro-Magnons lasted and what happened to them. Presumably they were gradually absorbed into the European populations that came later. Individuals with some Cro-Magnon character-istics, commonly called Cro-Magnoids, have been found in the Mesolithic Period (8000 to 5000 BCE) and the Neolithic Period (5000 to 2000 BCE).

IMHOTEP

(b. 27th century BCE, Memphis, Egypt)

Imhotep (Greek: Imouthes) was a vizier, sage, architect, astrologer, and chief minister to Djoser (reigned 2630–2611 BCE), the second king of Egypt's third dynasty, who was later worshipped as the god of medicine in Egypt and in Greece, where he was identified with the Greek god of medicine, Asclepius. He is considered to have been the architect of the step pyramid built at the necropolis of Ṣaqqārah in the city of Memphis. The oldest extant monument of hewn stone known to the world, the pyramid consists of six steps and attains a height of 200 feet (61 metres).

Although no contemporary account has been found that refers to Imhotep as a practicing physician, ancient documents illustrating Egyptian society and medicine during the Old Kingdom (c. 2575– c. 2130 BCE) show that the chief magician of the pharaoh's court also frequently served as the nation's chief physician. Imhotep's reputation as the reigning genius of the time, his position in the court, his training as a scribe, and his becoming known as a medical demigod only 100 years after his death are strong indications that he must have been a physician of considerable skill.

Not until the Persian conquest of Egypt in 525 BCE was Imhotep elevated to the position of a full deity, replacing Nefertem in the great triad of Memphis, shared with his mythological parents Ptah, the creator of the universe, and Sekhmet, the goddess of war and pestilence. Imhotep's cult reached its zenith during Greco-Roman times, when his temples in Memphis and on the island of Philae (Arabic: *Jazīrat Fīlah*) in the Nile River were often crowded with sufferers who prayed and slept there with the conviction that the god would reveal remedies to them in their dreams. The only Egyptian mortal besides the 18th-dynasty sage and minister Amenhotep to attain the honour of total deification, Imhotep is still held in esteem by physicians who, like the eminent 19th-century British practitioner Sir William Osler, consider him "the first figure of a physician to stand out clearly from the mists of antiquity."

ARCHIMEDES

(b. *c.* 290–280 BCE, Syracuse, Sicily [now in Italy]—d. 212/211 BCE, Syracuse)

The most famous mathematician of ancient Greece, Archimedes is especially important for his discovery of the relation between the surface and volume of a sphere and its circumscribing cylinder and for his formulation of a hydrostatic principle (known as Archimedes' principle). As an inventor he is known for various ingenious (and perhaps mythical) optical and mechanical devices, including a device for raising water, still used in developing countries, known as the Archimedes screw.

Archimedes probably spent some time in Egypt early in his career, but he resided for most of his life in Syracuse, the principal Greek city-state in Sicily, where he was on intimate terms with its king, Hieron II. Archimedes published his works in the form of correspondence with the principal mathematicians of his time, including the Alexandrian scholars Conon of Samos and Eratosthenes of Cyrene. He played an important role in the defense of Syracuse against the siege laid by the Romans in 213 BCE by constructing war machines so effective that they long delayed the capture of the city. When Syracuse eventually fell to the Roman general Marcus Claudius Marcellus in the autumn of 212 or spring of 211 BCE, Archimedes was killed in the sack of the city.

Far more details survive about the life of Archimedes than about any other ancient scientist, but they are largely anecdotal, reflecting the impression that his mechanical genius made on the popular imagination. Thus, he is credited with inventing the Archimedes screw, and he is supposed to have made two "spheres" that Marcellus took back to Rome—one a star globe and the other a device (the details of which are uncertain) for mechanically representing the motions of the Sun, the Moon, and the planets. The story that he determined the proportion of gold and silver in a wreath made for Hieron by weighing it in water is probably true, but the version that has him leaping from the bath in which he supposedly got the idea and running naked through the streets shouting "Heurēka!" ("I have found it!") is popular embellishment. Equally apocryphal are the stories that he used a huge array of mirrors to burn the Roman ships besieging Syracuse; that he said, "Give me a place to stand and I will move the Earth"; and that a Roman soldier killed him because he refused to leave his mathematical diagrams — although all are popular reflections of his real interest in catoptrics (the branch of optics dealing with the reflection of light from mirrors, plane or curved), mechanics, and pure mathematics.

According to Plutarch (*c.* 46–119 CE), Archimedes had so low an opinion of the kind of practical invention at which he excelled and to which he owed his contemporary fame that he left no written work on such subjects. While it is true that — apart from a dubious reference to a treatise, "On Sphere-Making" — all of his known works were of a theoretical character, his interest in mechanics nevertheless deeply influenced his mathematical thinking. Not only did he write works on theoretical mechanics and hydrostatics, but his treatise *Method Concerning Mechanical Theorems* shows that he used mechanical reasoning as a heuristic device for the discovery of new mathematical theorems.

CAI LUN

(b. 62? CE, Guiyang [now Leiyang, in present-day Hunan province], China — d. 121, China)

Cai Lun (courtesy name [zi] Jingzhong) was a Chinese court official who is traditionally credited with the invention of paper.

Cai Lun was a eunuch who entered the service of the imperial palace in 75 CE and was made chief eunuch under the emperor Hedi (reigned 88–105/106) of the Dong (Eastern) Han dynasty in the year 89. About the year 105 Cai conceived the idea of forming sheets of paper from the macerated bark of trees, hemp waste, old rags, and fishnets. The paper thus obtained was found to be superior in writing quality to cloth made of pure silk (the principal writing surface of the time), as well as being much less expensive to produce and having more abundant sources.

Cai reported his discovery to the emperor, who commended him for it. Important improvements were subsequently made to Cai's papermaking process by his apprentice, Zuo Bo, and the process was rapidly adopted throughout China, from which it eventually spread to the rest of the world. Cai himself was named a marquess in 114.

HERON OF ALEXANDRIA

(fl. c. 62 CE, Alexandria, Egypt)

Heron (or Hero) of Alexandria was a Greek geometer and inventor whose writings preserved for posterity a knowledge of the mathematics and engineering of Babylonia, ancient Egypt, and the Greco-Roman world.

Heron's most important geometric work, *Metrica*, was lost until 1896. It is a compendium, in three books, of geometric rules and formulas that Heron gathered from a variety of sources, some of them going back to ancient Babylon, on areas and volumes of plane and solid figures. Book I enumerates means of finding the area of various plane figures and the surface areas of common solids. Included is a derivation of Heron's formula (actually, Archimedes' formula) for the area A of a triangle,

$$A = \sqrt{s(s-a)(s-b)(s-c)}$$

in which a, b, and c are the lengths of the sides of the triangle, and *s* is one-half the triangle's perimeter. Book I also contains an iterative method known by the Babylonians (*c.* 2000 BCE) for approximating the square root of a number to arbitrary accuracy. (A variation on such an iterative method is frequently employed by computers today.) Book II gives methods for computing volumes of various solids, including the five regular Platonic solids. Book III treats the division of various plane and solid figures into parts according to some given ratio.

Other works on geometry ascribed to Heron are *Geometrica, Stereometrica, Mensurae, Geodaesia, Definitiones*, and *Liber Geëponicus*, which contain problems similar to those in the *Metrica*. However, the first three are certainly not by Heron in their present form, and the sixth consists largely of extracts from the first. Akin to these works is the *Dioptra*, a book on land surveying; it contains a description of the diopter, a surveying instrument used for the same purposes as the modern theodolite. The treatise also contains applications of the diopter to measuring celestial distances and describes a method for finding the distance between Alexandria and Rome from the difference between local times at which a lunar eclipse would be observed at the two cities. It ends with the description of an odometer for measuring the distance a wagon or cart travels. *Catoptrica* ("Reflection") exists only as a Latin translation of a work formerly thought to be a fragment of Ptolemy's *Optica*. In *Catoptrica* Heron explains the rectilinear propagation of light and the law of reflection.

Of Heron's writings on mechanics, all that remain in Greek are *Pneumatica, Automatopoietica, Belopoeica*, and *Cheirobalistra*. The *Pneumatica*, in two books, describes a menagerie of mechanical devices, or "toys": singing birds, puppets, coin-operated machines, a fire engine, a water organ, and his most famous invention, the aeolipile, the first steam-powered engine. This last device consisted of

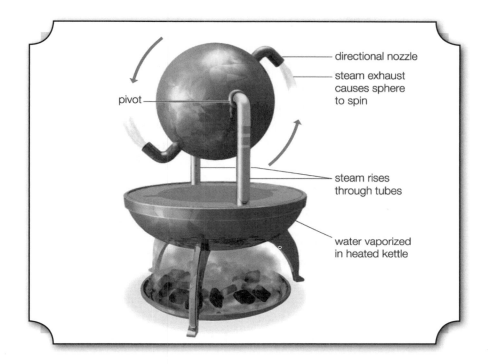

directional nozzle

steam exhaust causes sphere to spin

pivot

steam rises through tubes

water vaporized in heated kettle

Heron of Alexandria fashioned the first known "steam engine," though he only used it to power toys and amuse visitors. Encyclopædia Britannica, Inc.

a hollow sphere mounted so that it could turn on a pair of hollow tubes that provided steam to the sphere from a cauldron. The steam escaped from the sphere from one or more bent tubes projecting from its equator, causing the sphere to revolve. The aeolipile is the first known device to transform steam into rotary motion. Like many other machines of the time that demonstrated basic mechanical principles, it was simply regarded as a curiosity or a toy and was not used for any practical purpose.

The *Belopoeica* ("Engines of War") purports to be based on a work by Ctesibius of Alexandria (fl. *c.* 270 BCE). Heron's *Mechanica*, in three books, survives only in an Arabic translation, somewhat altered. This work is cited by Pappus of Alexandria (fl. 300 CE), as is also the *Baroulcus* ("Methods of Lifting Heavy Weights"). *Mechanica*, which is closely based on the work of Archimedes, presents a wide range of engineering principles, including a theory of motion, a theory of the balance, methods of lifting and transporting heavy objects with mechanical devices, and how to calculate the centre of gravity for various simple shapes. Both *Belopoeica* and *Mechanica* contain Heron's solution of the problem of two mean proportionals—two quantities, x and y, that satisfy the ratios $a{:}x = x{:}y = y{:}b$, in which a and b are known—which can be used to solve the problem of constructing a cube with double the volume of a given cube.

Only fragments of other treatises by Heron remain. One on water clocks is referred to by Pappus and the philosopher Proclus (410–485 CE). Another, a commentary on Euclid's *Elements*, is often quoted in a surviving Arabic work by Abu'l-'Abbās al-Faḍl ibn Ḥātim al-Nayrīzī (c. 865–922).

JOHANNES GUTENBERG

(b. 14th century, Mainz [now in Ger.]—d. probably Feb. 3, 1468, Mainz)

Johann Gensfleisch zur Laden zum Gutenberg was a German craftsman and inventor who originated a method of printing from movable type that was used without important change until the 20th century. The unique elements of his invention consisted of a mold, with punch-stamped matrices (metal prisms used to mold the face of the type) with which type could be cast precisely and in large quantities; a type-metal alloy; a new press, derived from those used in wine making, papermaking, and bookbinding; and an oil-based printing ink. None of these features existed in Chinese or Korean printing, or in the existing European technique of stamping letters on various surfaces, or in woodblock printing.

LIFE

Gutenberg was the son of a patrician of Mainz. What little information exists about him, other than that he had acquired skill in metalwork, comes from documents of financial transactions. Exiled from Mainz in the course of a bitter struggle between the guilds of that city and the patricians, Gutenberg moved to Strassburg (now Strasbourg, France) probably between 1428 and 1430. Records put his presence there from 1434 to 1444. He engaged in such crafts as gem cutting, and he also taught crafts to a number of pupils.

Some of his partners, who became aware that Gutenberg was engaged in work that he kept secret from them, insisted that, since they had advanced him considerable sums, they should become partners in these activities as well. Thus, in 1438 a five-year contract was drawn up between him and three other men: Hans Riffe, Andreas Dritzehn, and Andreas Heilmann. It contained a clause whereby in case of the death of one of the partners, his heirs were not to enter the company but were to be compensated financially.

INVENTION OF THE PRESS

When Andreas Dritzehn died at Christmas 1438, his heirs, trying to circumvent the terms of the contract, began a lawsuit against Gutenberg in which they demanded to be made partners. They lost the suit, but the trial revealed that Gutenberg was working on a new invention. Witnesses testified that a carpenter named Conrad Saspach had advanced sums to Andreas Dritzehn for the building of a wooden press, and Hans Dünne, a goldsmith, declared that he had sold to Gutenberg, as early as 1436, 100 guilders' worth of printing materials. Gutenberg, apparently well along the way to completing his invention, was anxious to keep secret the nature of the enterprise.

After March 12, 1444, Gutenberg's activities are undocumented for a number of years, but it is doubtful that he returned immediately to Mainz, for the quarrel between patricians and guilds had been renewed in that city. In October 1448, however, Gutenberg was back in Mainz to borrow more money, which he received from a relative. By 1450 his printing experiments had apparently reached a considerable degree of refinement, for he was able to persuade Johann Fust, a wealthy financier, to lend him 800 guilders—a very substantial capital investment, for which the tools and equipment for printing were to act as securities. Two years later Fust made an investment of an additional 800 guilders for a partnership in the enterprise. Fust and Gutenberg eventually became estranged, Fust, apparently, wanting a safe and quick return on his investment, while Gutenberg aimed at perfection rather than promptness.

Fust won a suit against him, the record of which is preserved, in part, in what is called the *Helmaspergersches Notariatsinstrument* ("the Helmasperger notarial instrument"), dated Nov. 6, 1455, now in the library of the University of Göttingen. Gutenberg was ordered to pay Fust the total sum of the two loans and compound interest (probably totaling 2,020 guilders). Traditional historiography suggested that this settlement ruined Gutenberg, but more recent scholarship suggests that it favoured him, allowing him to operate a printing shop through the 1450s and maybe into the 1460s.

PRINTING OF THE BIBLE

There is no reason to doubt that the printing of certain books (*werck der bucher*, specifically mentioned in the

This engraving shows a printing press in 1498 and is from a book printed in that year. The Bridgeman Art Library/Getty Images

record of the trial, refers to the Forty-two-Line Bible that was Gutenberg's masterpiece) was completed, according to Gutenberg's major biographers, in 1455 at the latest. It has been estimated that the sale of the Forty-two-Line Bible alone would have produced many times over the sum owed Fust by Gutenberg, and there exists no explanation as to why these tangible assets were not counted among Gutenberg's property at the trial.

After winning his suit, Fust gained control of the type for the Bible and for Gutenberg's second masterpiece, a Psalter, and at least some of Gutenberg's other printing equipment. He continued to print, using Gutenberg's materials, with the assistance of Peter Schöffer, his son-in-law, who had been Gutenberg's most skilled employee and a witness against him in the 1455 trial. The first printed book in Europe to bear the name of its printer is a magnificent Psalter completed in Mainz on Aug. 14, 1457, which lists Johann Fust and Peter Schöffer.

The Psalter is decorated with hundreds of two-colour initial letters and delicate scroll borders that were printed using a most ingenious technique based on multiple inking on a single metal block. Most experts are agreed that it would have been impossible for Fust and Schöffer alone to have invented and executed the intricate technical equipment necessary to executed this process between Nov. 6, 1455, when Gutenberg lost control of his printing establishment, and Aug. 14, 1457, when the Psalter appeared. It was Gutenberg's genius that was responsible for the Psalter decorations. In the 1960s it was suggested that he may also have had a hand in the creation of copper engraving, in which he may have recognized a method for producing pictorial matrices from which to cast reliefs that could be set with the type, initial letters, and calligraphic scrolls. It is at present no more than a hypothesis, but Gutenberg's absorption in both copper engraving and the Psalter decorations would certainly have increased Johann Fust's impatience and vindictiveness.

A number of other printings used to be attributed to Gutenberg. They are now considered the work of other minor printers; among these is a Thirty-six-Line Bible printed in Bamberg, a typographic resetting of the Forty-two-Line Bible. Attributed to Gutenberg himself is a *Türkenkalender*, a warning against the impending danger of Turkish invasion after the fall of Constantinople in 1453, printed December 1454 for 1455 use, some letters of indulgence, and some school grammars. The identity of the printer of a *Missale Speciale Constantiense* is still not established, but it was probably produced about 1473 in Basel, Switzerland.

In January 1465 the archbishop of Mainz pensioned Gutenberg, giving him an annual measure of grain, wine, and clothing and exempting him from certain taxes. His financial status in his last years has been debated but was probably not destitute.

CHRISTIAAN HUYGENS

(b. April 14, 1629, The Hague, Neth. — d. July 8, 1695, The Hague)

Christiaan Huygens (or Christian Huyghens) was a Dutch mathematician, astronomer, and physicist who founded the wave theory of light, discovered the true shape of the rings of Saturn, and made original contributions to the science of dynamics — the study of the action of forces on bodies. He was responsible for the practical application of the pendulum as a time controller in clocks.

Huygens was from a wealthy and distinguished middle-class family. His father, Constantijn Huygens, a diplomat, Latinist, and poet, was the friend and correspondent of many outstanding intellectual figures of the day, including the scientist and philosopher René Descartes. From an early age, Huygens showed a marked mechanical bent and a talent for drawing and mathematics. Some of his early efforts in geometry impressed Descartes, who was an occasional visitor to the Huygens' household. In 1645 Huygens entered the University of Leiden, where he studied mathematics and law. Two years later he entered the College of Breda, in the midst of a furious controversy over the philosophy of Descartes. Although Huygens later rejected certain of the Cartesian tenets including the identification of extension and body, he always affirmed that mechanical explanations were essential in science, a fact that later was to have an important influence on his mathematical interpretation of both light and gravitation.

In 1655 Huygens for the first time visited Paris, where his distinguished parentage, wealth, and affable disposition gave him entry to the highest intellectual and social circles. During his next visit to Paris in 1660, he met Blaise Pascal, with whom he had already been in correspondence on mathematical problems. Huygens had already acquired a European reputation by his publications in mathematics, especially his *De Circuli Magnitudine Inventa* of 1654, and by his discovery in 1659 of the true shape of the rings of Saturn—made possible by the improvements he had introduced in the construction of the telescope with his new method of grinding and polishing lenses. Using his improved telescope, he discovered a satellite of Saturn in March 1655 and distinguished the stellar components of the Orion nebula in 1656. His interest, as an astronomer, in the accurate measurement of time then led him to his discovery of the pendulum as a regulator of clocks, as described in his *Horologium* (1658).

In 1666 Huygens became one of the founding members of the French Academy of Sciences, which granted him a pension larger than that of any other member and an apartment in its building. Apart from occasional visits to Holland, he lived from 1666 to 1681 in Paris, where he made the acquaintance of the German mathematician and philosopher Gottfried Wilhelm Leibniz, with whom he remained on friendly terms for the rest of his life. The major event of Huygens's years in Paris was the publication in 1673 of his *Horologium Oscillatorium*. That brilliant work contained a theory on the mathematics of curvatures, as well as complete solutions to such problems of dynamics as the derivation of the formula for the time of oscillation of the simple pendulum, the oscillation of a body about a stationary axis, and the laws of centrifugal force for uniform circular motion. Some of the results were given without proof in an appendix, and Huygens's complete proofs were not published until after his death.

The treatment of rotating bodies was partly based on an ingenious application of the principle that in any system of bodies the centre of gravity could never rise of its own accord above its initial position. Earlier Huygens had applied the same principle to the treatment of the problem of collisions, for which he had obtained a definitive solution in the case of perfectly elastic bodies as early as 1656, although his results remained unpublished until 1669.

The somewhat eulogistic dedication of the *Horologium Oscillatorium* to Louis XIV brought to a head murmurs against Huygens at a time when France was at war with Holland, but in spite of this he continued to reside in Paris. Huygens's health was never good, and he suffered from recurrent illnesses, including one in 1670 which was so serious that for a time he despaired of his own life.

A serious illness in 1681 prompted him to return to Holland, where he intended to stay only temporarily. But the death in 1683 of his patron, Jean-Baptiste Colbert, who had been Louis XIV's chief adviser, and Louis's increasingly reactionary policy, which culminated in the revocation (1685) of the Edict of Nantes, which had granted certain liberties to Protestants, militated against his ever returning to Paris.

Huygens visited London in 1689 and met Sir Isaac Newton and lectured on his own theory of gravitation before the Royal Society. Although he did not engage in public controversy with Newton directly, it is evident from Huygens's correspondence, especially that with Leibniz, that in spite of his generous admiration for the mathematical ingenuity of the *Principia*, he regarded a theory of gravity that was devoid of any mechanical explanation as fundamentally unacceptable. His own theory, published in 1690 in his *Discours de la cause de la pesanteur* ("Discourse on the Cause of Gravity"), though dating at least to 1669, included a mechanical explanation of gravity based on Cartesian vortices. Huygens's *Traité de la Lumière (Treatise on Light)*, already largely completed by 1678, was also published in 1690. In it he again showed his need for ultimate mechanical explanations in his discussion of the nature of light. But his beautiful explanations of reflection and refraction—far superior to those of Newton—were entirely independent of mechanical explanations, being based solely on the so-called Huygens's principle of secondary wave fronts.

As a mathematician Huygens had great talent rather than genius of the first order. He sometimes found difficulty in following the innovations of Leibniz and others, but he was admired by Newton because of his love for the old synthetic methods. For almost the whole of the 18th century his work in both dynamics and light was overshadowed by that of Newton. In gravitation his theory was never taken seriously and remains today of historical interest only. But his work on rotating bodies and his contributions to the theory of light were of lasting importance. Forgotten until the early 19th century, these latter appear today as some of the most brilliant and original contributions to modern science and will always be remembered by the principle bearing his name.

The last five years of Huygens's life were marked by continued ill health and increasing feelings of loneliness and melancholy. He made the final corrections to his will in March 1695 and died after much suffering later that same year.

ANTONIE VAN LEEUWENHOEK
(b. Oct. 24, 1632, Delft, Neth.—d. Aug. 26, 1723, Delft)

A ntonie van Leeuwenhoek was a Dutch microscopist who was the first to observe bacteria and protozoa. His researches on lower animals refuted the doctrine of spontaneous generation, and his observations helped lay the foundations for the sciences of bacteriology and protozoology.

Little is known of Leeuwenhoek's early life. When his stepfather died in 1648, he was sent to Amsterdam to become an apprentice to a linen draper. Returning to Delft when he was 20, he established himself as a draper and haberdasher. In 1660 he obtained a position as chamberlain to the sheriffs of Delft. His income was thus secure and sufficient enough to enable him to devote much of his time to his all-absorbing hobby, that of grinding lenses and using them to study tiny objects.

Leeuwenhoek made microscopes consisting of a single, high-quality lens of very short focal length; at the time, such simple microscopes were preferable to the compound microscope, which increased the problem of chromatic aberration. Although Leeuwenhoek's studies lacked the organization of formal scientific research, his powers of careful observation enabled him to make discoveries of fundamental importance. In 1674 he began to observe bacteria and protozoa, his "very little animalcules," which he was able to isolate from different sources, such as rainwater, pond and well water, and the human mouth and intestine, and he calculated their sizes.

In 1677 he described for the first time the spermatozoa from insects, dogs, and man, though Stephen Hamm probably was a codiscoverer. Leeuwenhoek studied the structure of the optic lens, striations in muscles, the mouthparts of insects, and the fine structure of plants and discovered parthenogenesis in aphids. In 1680 he noticed that yeasts consist of minute globular particles. He extended Marcello Malpighi's demonstration in 1660 of the blood capillaries by giving (in 1684) the first accurate description of red blood cells. In his observations on rotifers in 1702, Leeuwenhoek remarked that "in all falling rain, carried from gutters into water-butts, animalcules are to be found; and that in all kinds of water, standing in the open air, animalcules can turn up. For these animalcules can be carried over by the wind, along with the bits of dust floating in the air."

A friend of Leeuwenhoek put him in touch with the Royal Society of England, to which, from 1673 until 1723, he communicated by means of informal letters most of his discoveries and to which he was elected a fellow in 1680. His discoveries were for the most part made public in the society's *Philosophical Transactions*. The first representation of bacteria is to be found in a drawing by Leeuwenhoek in that publication in 1683.

His researches on the life histories of various low forms of animal life were in opposition to the doctrine that they could be produced spontaneously or bred from corruption. Thus, he showed that the weevils of granaries (in his time commonly supposed to be bred from wheat as well as in it) are really grubs hatched from eggs deposited by winged insects. His letter on the flea, in which he not only described its structure but traced out the whole history of its metamorphosis, is of great interest, not so much for the exactness of his observations as for an illustration of his opposition to the spontaneous generation of many lower organisms, such as "this minute and despised creature." Some theorists asserted that the flea was produced from sand, others from dust or the like, but Leeuwenhoek proved that it bred in the regular way of winged insects.

Leeuwenhoek also carefully studied the history of the ant and was the first to show that what had been commonly reputed to be ants' eggs were really their pupae, containing the perfect insect nearly ready for emergence, and that the true eggs were much smaller and gave origin to maggots, or larvae. He argued that the sea mussel and other shellfish were not generated out of sand found at the seashore or mud in the beds of rivers at low water but from spawn, by the regular course of generation. He maintained the same to be true of the freshwater mussel, whose embryos he examined so carefully that he was able to observe how they were consumed by "animalcules," many of which, according to his description, must have included ciliates in conjugation, flagellates, and the *Vorticella*. Similarly, he investigated the generation of eels, which were at that time supposed to be produced from dew without the ordinary process of generation.

The dramatic nature of his discoveries made him world famous, and he was visited by many notables—including Peter I the Great of Russia, James II of England, and Frederick II the Great of Prussia.

Leeuwenhoek's methods of microscopy, which he kept secret, remain something of a mystery. During his lifetime he ground more than 400 lenses, most of which were very small—some no larger than a pinhead—and usually mounted them between two thin brass plates, riveted together. A large sample of these lenses, bequeathed to the

Royal Society, were found to have magnifying powers of between 50 and, at the most, 300 times. In order to observe phenomena as small as bacteria, Leeuwenhoek must have employed some form of oblique illumination, or other technique, for enhancing the effectiveness of the lens, but this method he would not reveal. Leeuwenhoek continued his work almost to the end of his long life of 90 years.

Leeuwenhoek's contributions to the *Philosophical Transactions* amounted to 375 and those to the *Memoirs of the Paris Academy of Sciences* to 27. Two collections of his works appeared during his life, one in Dutch (1685–1718) and the other in Latin (1715–22); a selection was translated by S. Hoole, *The Select Works of A. van Leeuwenhoek (1798–1807)*.

BENJAMIN FRANKLIN

(b. Jan. 17 [Jan. 6, Old Style], 1706, Boston, Mass. [now in U.S.]—d. April 17, 1790, Philadelphia, Pa., U.S.)

Benjamin Franklin was an American printer and publisher, author, inventor and scientist, and diplomat. One of the foremost of the Founding Fathers, Franklin helped draft the Declaration of Independence and was one of its signers, represented the United States in France during the American Revolution, and was a delegate to the Constitutional Convention. He made important contributions to science, especially in the understanding of electricity, and is remembered for the wit, wisdom, and elegance of his writing.

EARLY LIFE

Ben Franklin was born the 10th son of the 17 children of a man who made soap and candles, one of the lowliest of the artisan crafts. In an age that privileged the firstborn son, Franklin was, as he tartly noted in his *Autobiography*, "the youngest Son of the youngest Son for five Generations back." He learned to read very early and had one year in grammar school and another under a private teacher, but his formal education ended at age 10. At 12 he was apprenticed to his brother James, a printer. His mastery of the printer's trade, of which he was proud to the end of his life, was achieved between 1718 and 1723. In the same period he read tirelessly and taught himself to write effectively.

His first enthusiasm was for poetry, but, discouraged with the quality of his own, he gave it up. Prose was another matter. Young Franklin discovered a volume of *The Spectator*—featuring Joseph Addison and Sir Richard Steele's famous periodical essays, which had appeared in England in 1711–12—and saw in it a means for improving his writing. He read these *Spectator* papers over and over, copied and recopied them, and then tried to recall them from memory. He even turned them into poetry and then back into prose. Franklin realized, as all the Founders did, that writing competently was such a rare talent in the 18th century that anyone who could do it well immediately attracted attention. "Prose writing" became, as he recalled in his *Autobiography*, "of great Use to me in the Course of my Life, and was a principal Means of my Advancement."

In 1721 James Franklin founded a weekly newspaper, the *New-England Courant*, to which readers were invited to contribute. Benjamin, now 16, read and perhaps set in type these contributions and decided that he could do as well himself. In 1722 he wrote a series of 14 essays signed "Silence Dogood" in which he lampooned everything from funeral eulogies to the students of Harvard College. For one so young to assume the persona of a middle-aged woman was a remarkable feat, and Franklin took "exquisite Pleasure" in the fact that his brother and others became convinced that only a learned and ingenious wit could have written these essays.

Late in 1722 James Franklin got into trouble with the provincial authorities and was forbidden to print or publish the *Courant*. To keep the paper going, he discharged his younger brother from his original apprenticeship and made him the paper's nominal publisher. New indentures were drawn up but not made public. Some months later, after a bitter quarrel, Benjamin secretly left home, sure that James would not "go to law" and reveal the subterfuge he had devised.

YOUTHFUL ADVENTURES

Failing to find work in New York City, Franklin at age 17 went on to Quaker-dominated Philadelphia, a much more open and religiously tolerant place than Puritan Boston. One of the most memorable scenes of the *Autobiography* is the description of his arrival on a Sunday morning, tired and hungry. Finding a bakery, he asked for three pennies' worth of bread and got "three great Puffy Rolls." Carrying one under each arm and munching on the third, he walked up Market Street past the door of the Read family, where stood Deborah, his future wife. She saw him and "thought I made, as I certainly did, a most awkward ridiculous Appearance."

A few weeks later he was rooming at the Reads' and employed as a printer. By the spring of 1724 he was enjoying the companionship of other young men with a taste for reading, and he was also being urged to set up in business for himself by the governor of Pennsylvania, Sir

William Keith. At Keith's suggestion, Franklin returned to Boston to try to raise the necessary capital. His father thought him too young for such a venture, so Keith offered to foot the bill himself and arranged Franklin's passage to England so that he could choose his type and make connections with London stationers and booksellers. Franklin exchanged "some promises" about marriage with Deborah Read and, with a young friend, James Ralph, as his companion, sailed for London in November 1724, just over a year after arriving in Philadelphia. Not until his ship was well out at sea did he realize that Governor Keith had not delivered the letters of credit and introduction he had promised.

In London Franklin quickly found employment in his trade and was able to lend money to Ralph, who was trying to establish himself as a writer. The two young men enjoyed the theatre and the other pleasures of the city, including women. While in London, Franklin wrote *A Dissertation on Liberty and Necessity, Pleasure and Pain* (1725), a Deistical pamphlet inspired by his having set type for William Wollaston's moral tract, *The Religion of Nature Delineated*. Franklin argued in his essay that since human beings have no real freedom of choice, they are not morally responsible for their actions. This was perhaps a nice justification for his self-indulgent behaviour in London and his ignoring of Deborah, to whom he had written only once. He later repudiated the pamphlet, burning all but one of the copies still in his possession.

By 1726 Franklin was tiring of London. He considered becoming an itinerant teacher of swimming, but, when Thomas Denham, a Quaker merchant, offered him a clerkship in his store in Philadelphia with a prospect of fat commissions in the West Indian trade, he decided to return home.

Achievement of Security and Fame

Denham died, however, a few months after Franklin entered his store. The young man, now 20, returned to the printing trade and in 1728 was able to set up a partnership with a friend. Two years later he borrowed money to become sole proprietor.

His private life at this time was extremely complicated. Deborah Read had married, but her husband had deserted her and disappeared. One matchmaking venture failed because Franklin wanted a dowry of £100 to pay off his business debt. A strong sexual drive, "that hard-to-be-govern'd Passion of Youth," was sending him to "low Women," and he thought he very much needed to get married. His affection for Deborah having "revived," he "took her to Wife" on Sept. 1, 1730. At this point Deborah may have been the only woman in Philadelphia who would have him, for he brought to the marriage an illegitimate son, William, just borne of a woman who has never been identified. Franklin's common-law

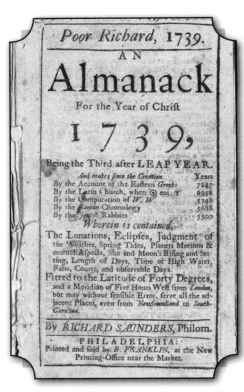

Title page for Poor Richard's almanac for 1739, *written, printed, and sold by Benjamin Franklin.* Rare Book and Special Collections Division, Library of Congress, Washington, D.C.

marriage lasted until Deborah's death in 1774. They had a son, Franky, who died at age four, and a daughter, Sarah, who survived them both. William was brought up in the household and apparently did not get along well with Deborah.

Franklin and his partner's first coup was securing the printing of Pennsylvania's paper currency. Franklin helped get this business by writing *A Modest Enquiry into the Nature and Necessity of a Paper Currency* (1729), and later he also became public printer of New Jersey, Delaware, and Maryland. Other moneymaking ventures included the *Pennsylvania Gazette*, published by Franklin from 1729 and generally acknowledged as among the best of the colonial newspapers, and *Poor Richard's almanac*, printed annually from 1732 to 1757. Despite some failures, Franklin prospered. Indeed, he made enough to lend money with interest and to invest in rental properties in Philadelphia and many coastal towns. He had franchises or partnerships with printers in the Carolinas, New York, and the British West Indies. By the late 1740s he had become one of the wealthiest colonists in the northern part of the North American continent.

As he made money, he concocted a variety of projects for social improvement. In 1727 he organized the Junto, or Leather Apron Club, to debate questions of morals, politics, and natural philosophy and to exchange knowledge of business affairs. The need of Junto members for easier access to books led in 1731 to the organization of the Library Company of Philadelphia. Through the Junto, Franklin proposed a paid city watch, or police force. A paper read to the same group resulted in the organization of a volunteer fire company. In 1743 he sought an intercolonial version of the Junto, which led to the formation of the American Philosophical Society. In 1749 he published *Proposals Relating to the Education of Youth in Pennsilvania*; in

1751 the Academy of Philadelphia, from which grew the University of Pennsylvania, was founded. He also became an enthusiastic member of the Freemasons and promoted their "enlightened" causes.

Although still a tradesman, he was picking up some political offices. He became clerk of the Pennsylvania legislature in 1736 and postmaster of Philadelphia in 1737. Prior to 1748, though, his most important political service was his part in organizing a militia for the defense of the colony against possible invasion by the French and the Spaniards, whose privateers were operating in the Delaware River.

In 1748 Franklin, at age 42, had become wealthy enough to retire from active business. He took off his leather apron and became a gentleman, a distinctive status in the 18th century. Since no busy artisan could be a gentleman, Franklin never again worked as a printer; instead, he became a silent partner in the printing firm of Franklin and Hall, realizing in the next 18 years an average profit of over £600 annually. He announced his new status as a gentleman by having his portrait painted in a velvet coat and a brown wig; he also acquired a coat of arms, bought several slaves, and moved to a new and more spacious house in "a more quiet Part of the Town." Most important, as a gentleman and "master of [his] own time," he decided to do what other gentlemen did—engage in what he termed "Philosophical Studies and Amusements."

SCIENTIFIC STUDIES

In the 1740s electricity was one of these curious amusements. It was introduced to Philadelphians by an electrical machine sent to the Library Company by one of Franklin's English correspondents. In the winter of 1746–47, Franklin and three of his friends began to investigate electrical phenomena. Franklin sent piecemeal reports of his ideas and experiments to Peter Collinson, his Quaker correspondent in London. Since he did not know what European scientists might have already discovered, Franklin set forth his findings timidly. In 1751 Collinson had Franklin's papers published in an 86-page book titled *Experiments and Observations on Electricity*. In the 18th century the book went through five English editions, three in French, and one each in Italian and German.

Franklin's fame spread rapidly. The experiment he suggested to prove the identity of lightning and electricity was apparently first made in France before he tried the simpler but more dangerous expedient of flying a kite in a thunderstorm. But his other findings were original. He created the distinction between insulators and conductors. He invented a battery for storing electrical charges. He coined new English words for the new science of electricity— *conductor*, *charge*, *discharge*, *condense*, *armature*, *electrify*, and others. He showed that electricity was a single "fluid" with positive and negative or plus and minus charges and not, as traditionally thought, two kinds of fluids. And he demonstrated that the plus and minus charges, or states of electrification of bodies, had to occur in exactly equal amounts—a crucial scientific principle known today as the law of conservation of charge.

PUBLIC SERVICE IN LATER LIFE

Franklin was not only the most famous American in the 18th century but also one of the most famous figures in the Western world of the 18th century; indeed, he is one of the most celebrated and influential Americans who has ever lived. Although one is apt to think of Franklin exclusively as an inventor, as an early version of Thomas Edison, which he was, his 18th-century fame came not simply from his many inventions but, more important, from his fundamental contributions to the science of electricity. If there had been a Nobel Prize for Physics in the 18th century, Franklin would have been a contender. Enhancing his fame was the fact that he was an American, a simple man from an obscure background who emerged from the wilds of America to dazzle the entire intellectual world. Most Europeans in the 18th century thought of America as a primitive, undeveloped place full of forests and savages and scarcely capable of producing enlightened thinkers. Yet Franklin's electrical discoveries in the mid-18th century had surpassed the achievements of the most sophisticated scientists of Europe. Franklin became a living example of the natural untutored genius of the New World that was free from the encumbrances of a decadent and tired Old World—an image that he later parlayed into French support for the American Revolution.

Despite his great scientific achievements, however, Franklin always believed that public service was more important than science, and his political contributions to the formation of the United States were substantial. He had a hand in the writing of the Declaration of Independence, contributed to the drafting of the Articles of Confederation—America's first national constitution— and was the oldest member of the Constitutional Convention of 1787 that wrote the Constitution of the United States of America in Philadelphia. More important, as diplomatic representative of the new American republic in France during the Revolution, he secured both diplomatic recognition and financial and military aid from the government of Louis XVI and was a crucial member of the commission that negotiated the treaty by which Great Britain recognized its former 13 colonies as a sovereign nation. Since no one else could have accomplished all that he did in France during the Revolution, he can quite plausibly be regarded as America's greatest diplomat.

Equally significant perhaps were Franklin's many contributions to the comfort and safety of daily life, especially in his adopted city of Philadelphia. No civic project was too large or too small for his interest. In addition to his lightning rod and his Franklin stove (a wood-burning stove that warmed American homes for more than 200 years), he invented bifocal glasses, the odometer, and the glass harmonica (armonica). He had ideas about everything—from the nature of the Gulf Stream to the cause of the common cold. He suggested the notions of matching grants and Daylight Saving Time. Almost single-handedly he helped to create a civic society for the inhabitants of Philadelphia. Moreover, he helped to establish new institutions that people now take for granted: a fire company, a library, an insurance company, an academy, and a hospital.

Probably Franklin's most important invention was himself. He created so many personas in his newspaper writings and almanac and in his posthumously published *Autobiography* that it is difficult to know who he really was. Following his death in 1790, he became so identified during the 19th century with the persona of his *Autobiography* and the Poor Richard maxims of his almanac—e.g., "Early to bed, early to rise, makes a man healthy, wealthy, and wise"—that he acquired the image of the self-made moralist obsessed with the getting and saving of money. Consequently, many imaginative writers, such as Edgar Allan Poe, Henry David Thoreau, Herman Melville, Mark Twain, and D.H. Lawrence, attacked Franklin as a symbol of America's middle-class moneymaking business values. Indeed, early in the 20th century the famous German sociologist Max Weber found Franklin to be the perfect exemplar of the "Protestant ethic" and the modern capitalistic spirit. Although Franklin did indeed become a wealthy tradesman by his early 40s, when he retired from his business, during his lifetime in the 18th century he was not identified as a self-made businessman or a budding capitalist. That image was a creation of the 19th century. But as long as America continues to be pictured as the land of enterprise and opportunity, where striving and hard work can lead to success, then that image of Franklin is the one that is likely to endure.

JAMES WATT

(b. Jan. 19, 1736, Greenock, Renfrewshire, Scot.—d. Aug. 25, 1819, Heathfield Hall, near Birmingham, Warwick, Eng.)

James Watt was a Scottish instrument maker and inventor whose steam engine contributed substantially to the Industrial Revolution. He was elected fellow of the Royal Society of London in 1785.

EDUCATION AND TRAINING

Watt's father, the treasurer and magistrate of Greenock, ran a successful ship- and house-building business. A delicate child, Watt was taught for a time at home by his mother; later, in grammar school, he learned Latin, Greek, and mathematics. The source for an important part of his education was his father's workshops, where, with his own tools, bench, and forge, he made models (e.g., of cranes and barrel organs) and grew familiar with ships' instruments.

Deciding at age 17 to be a mathematical-instrument maker, Watt first went to Glasgow, where one of his mother's relatives taught at the university, then, in 1755, to London, where he found a master to train him. Although his health broke down within a year, he had learned enough in that time "to work as well as most journeymen." Returning to

Glasgow, he opened a shop in 1757 at the university and made mathematical instruments (e.g., quadrants, compasses, scales). He met many scientists and became a friend of Joseph Black, who developed the concept of latent heat. In 1764 he married his cousin Margaret Miller, who, before she died nine years later, bore him six children.

THE WATT ENGINE

While repairing a model Newcomen steam engine in 1764 Watt was impressed by its waste of steam. In May 1765, after wrestling with the problem of improving it, he suddenly came upon a solution—the separate condenser, his first and greatest invention. Watt had realized that the loss of latent heat (the heat involved in changing the state of a substance— e.g., solid or liquid) was the worst defect of the Newcomen engine and that therefore condensation must be effected in a chamber distinct from the cylinder but connected to it. Shortly afterward, he met John Roebuck, the founder of the Carron Works, who urged him to make an engine. He entered into partnership with him in 1768, after having made a small test engine with the help of loans from Joseph Black. The following year Watt took out the famous patent for "A New Invented Method of Lessening the Consumption of Steam and Fuel in Fire Engines."

Meanwhile, Watt in 1766 became a land surveyor; for the next eight years he was continuously busy marking out routes for canals in Scotland, work that prevented his making further progress with the steam engine. After Roebuck went bankrupt in 1772, Matthew Boulton, the manufacturer of the Soho Works in Birmingham, took over a share in Watt's patent. Bored with surveying and with Scotland, Watt immigrated to Birmingham in 1774.

After Watt's patent was extended by an act of Parliament, he and Boulton in 1775 began a partnership

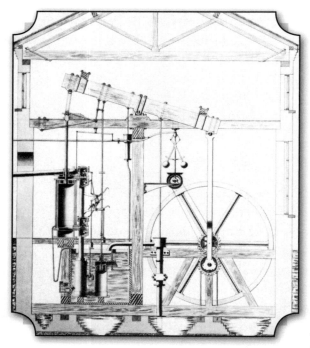

James Watt's rotative steam engine with sun-and-planet gear, original drawing, 1788. In the Science Museum, London. British Crown copyright, Science Museum, London

that lasted 25 years. Boulton's financial support made possible rapid progress with the engine. In 1776 two engines were installed, one for pumping water in a Staffordshire colliery, the other for blowing air into the furnaces of John Wilkinson, the famous iron-master. That year Watt married again—his second wife, Ann MacGregor, bore him two more children.

During the next five years, until 1781, Watt spent long periods in Cornwall, where he installed and supervised numerous pumping engines for the copper and tin mines, the managers of which wanted to reduce fuel costs. Watt, who was no businessman, was obliged to endure keen bargaining in order to obtain adequate royalties on the new engines. By 1780 he was doing well financially, though Boulton still had problems raising capital. In the following year Boulton, foreseeing a new market in the corn, malt, and cotton mills, urged Watt to invent a rotary motion for the steam engine, to replace the reciprocating action of the original. He did this in 1781 with his so-called sun-and-planet gear, by means of which a shaft produced two revolutions for each cycle of the engine. In 1782, at the height of his inventive powers, he patented the double-acting engine, in which the piston pushed as well as pulled. The engine required a new method of rigidly connecting the piston to the beam. He solved this problem in 1784 with his invention of the parallel motion—an arrangement of connected rods that guided the piston rod in a perpendicular motion—which he described as "one of the most ingenious, simple pieces of mechanism I have contrived." Four years later his application of the centrifugal governor for automatic control of the speed of the engine, at Boulton's suggestion, and in 1790 his invention of a pressure gauge, virtually completed the Watt engine.

Later Years

Demands for his engine came quickly from paper mills, flour mills, cotton mills, iron mills, distilleries, and canals and waterworks. By 1790 Watt was a wealthy man, having received £76,000 in royalties on his patents in 11 years. The steam engine did not absorb all his attention, however. He was a member of the Lunar Society in Birmingham, a group of writers and scientists who wished to advance the sciences and the arts. Watt experimented on the strength of materials, and he was often involved in legal proceedings to protect his patents. In 1785 he and Boulton were elected fellows of the Royal Society of London. Watt then began to take holidays, bought an estate at Doldowlod, Radnorshire, and from 1795 onward gradually withdrew from business.

With the approach of his retirement in 1800 and because that was also the year in which his patents and partnership would expire, Watt established in 1794 the new firm of Boulton & Watt, which built the Soho Foundry to manufacture steam engines more competitively. During this time Watt's son by his first marriage, James, gave him anxiety. A youthful sympathizer with the French Revolution, he had been criticized in Parliament for presenting in 1792 an address from the Manchester Constitutional Society to the Société des Amis de la Constitution in Paris. After being cleared of political suspicion on his return home two years later, however, he and Boulton's son, Matthew, took over the management of the new firm.

Watt's long retirement was saddened by the deaths of a son by his second marriage, Gregory, and of many of his close friends. Nevertheless, he travelled with his wife to Scotland and to France and Germany when the Peace of Amiens was signed in 1802 and continued to work in the garret of his house, which he had equipped as a workshop. There he invented a sculpturing machine with which he reproduced original busts and figures for his friends. He also acted as consultant to the Glasgow Water Company. His achievements were amply recognized in his lifetime: he was made doctor of laws of the University of Glasgow in 1806 and a foreign associate of the French Academy of Sciences in 1814 and was offered a baronetcy, which he declined.

JOSEPH AND ÉTIENNE MONTGOLFIER

respectively, (b. Aug. 26, 1740, Annonay, France—d. June 26, 1810, Balaruc-les-Bains); (b. Jan. 6, 1745, Annonay, France—d. Aug. 2, 1799, enroute from Lyon to Annonay)

The Montgolfier brothers, Joseph-Michel and Jacques-Étienne, were French pioneer developers of the hot-air balloon who conducted the first untethered flights. Modifications and improvements of the basic Montgolfier design were incorporated in the construction of larger balloons that, in later years, opened the way to exploration of the upper atmosphere.

Joseph and Étienne were 2 of the 16 children of Pierre Montgolfier, whose prosperous paper factories in the small town of Vidalon, near Annonay, in southern France, ensured the financial support of their balloon experiments. While carrying on their father's paper business, they maintained their interest in scientific experimentation.

In 1782 they discovered that heated air, when collected inside a large lightweight paper or fabric bag, caused the bag to rise into the air. (According to one, possibly apocryphal, story, the brothers took inspiration from watching

Jean-François Pilâtre de Rozier and François Laurent, marquis d'Arlandes, ascending in a Montgolfier balloon at the Château de la Muette, Paris, Nov. 21, 1783. © Photos.com/Jupiterimages

Joseph's wife's skirts as they billowed in the kitchen from the heat of a charcoal burner being used to dry laundry.) The Montgolfiers made the first public demonstration of their discovery on June 4, 1783, at the marketplace in Annonay. They filled their 35-foot- (10.5-metre-) diameter balloon with heated air by burning straw and wool under the opening at the bottom of the bag. The balloon rose into the air about 3,000 feet (1,000 metres), remained there some 10 minutes, and then settled to the ground more than a mile and a half from where it rose. The Montgolfiers traveled to Paris and then to Versailles, where they repeated the experiment with a larger balloon on Sept. 19, 1783, sending a sheep, a rooster, and a duck aloft as passengers. The balloon floated for about 8 minutes and landed safely about 2 miles (3.2 kilometres) from the launch site. On Nov. 21, 1783, the first manned untethered flight took place in a Montgolfier balloon with Pilatre de Rozier and François Laurent, marquis d'Arlandes, as passengers. The balloon sailed over Paris for 5.5 miles (9 kilometres) in about 25 minutes.

The two brothers were honoured by the French Académie des Sciences. They published books on aeronautics and continued their scientific careers. Joseph invented a calorimeter and the hydraulic ram, and Étienne developed a process for manufacturing vellum.

ALESSANDRO VOLTA

(b. Feb. 18, 1745, Como, Lombardy [now in Italy]—d. March 5, 1827, Como)

Alessandro Giuseppe Antonio Anastasio Volta (also known as Count Volta) was an Italian physicist whose invention of the electric battery provided the first source of continuous current.

In 1775 Volta's interest in electricity led him to invent the electrophorus, a device used to generate static electricity. He became professor of physics at the Royal School of Como in 1774 and discovered and isolated methane gas in 1778. One year later he was appointed to the chair of physics at the University of Pavia.

In 1780 Volta's friend Luigi Galvani discovered that contact of two different metals with the muscle of a frog resulted in the generation of an electric current. Volta had been studying how electricity stimulates the senses of touch, taste, and sight. When Volta put a metal coin on top of his tongue and another coin of a different metal under his tongue and connected their surfaces with a wire, the coins tasted salty. Like Galvani, Volta assumed that he was working with animal electricity until 1796 when he discovered that he could also produce a current when he substituted a piece of cardboard soaked in brine for his tongue. Volta correctly conjectured that the effect was caused by the contact between metal and a moist body. Around 1800 he constructed what is now known as a voltaic pile consisting of layers of silver, moist cardboard, and zinc, repeated in that order, beginning and ending with a different metal. When he joined the silver and the zinc with a wire, electricity flowed continuously through the wire. This rudimentary form of battery produced a smaller voltage than the Leyden jar, an earlier device for storing static electricity, but it was easier to use because it could supply a steady current and did not have to be recharged.

In 1801 in Paris, Volta gave a demonstration of his battery's generation of electric current before Napoleon, who made Volta a count and senator of the kingdom of Lombardy. The emperor of Austria made him director of the philosophical faculty at the University of Padua in 1815. The volt, a unit of the electromotive force that drives current, was named in his honour in 1881.

JOSEPH-MARIE JACQUARD
(b. July 7, 1752, Lyon, France — d. Aug. 7, 1834, Oullins)

Joseph-Marie Jacquard was the French inventor of an automatic loom that served as the impetus for the technological revolution of the textile industry. The Jacquard loom also demonstrated the concept of a programmable machine; for this reason it is frequently considered to be a precursor of the digital computer.

Jacquard first formed the idea for his loom in 1790, but his work was cut short by the French Revolution, in which he fought on the side of the Revolutionaries in the defense of Lyon. In 1801 Jacquard demonstrated an improved drawloom, for which he was awarded a bronze medal. He continued his work, and in 1804–05 he introduced an attachment that has caused any loom that uses it to be called a Jacquard loom. The loom worked by tugging various-coloured threads into patterns by means of an array of rods. By inserting a card punched with holes, an operator could control the motion of the rods and thereby alter the pattern of the weave. Moreover, the loom was equipped with a card-reading device that slipped a new card from a prepunched deck into place every time the shuttle was thrown, so that complex weaving patterns could be automated. In 1806 the loom was declared public property, and Jacquard was rewarded with a pension and a royalty on each machine.

His machine aroused bitter hostility among the silk weavers, who feared that its labour-saving capabilities would deprive them of jobs. The weavers of Lyon not only burned machines that were put into production but attacked Jacquard as well. Eventually, the advantages of the loom brought about its general acceptance, and by 1812 there were 11,000 in use in France. In 1819 Jacquard was awarded a gold medal and the Cross of the Legion of

Honour. The use of his loom spread to England in the 1820s and from there virtually worldwide.

The Jacquard loom was a marvel of the Industrial Revolution. A textile-weaving loom, it could also be called the first practical information-processing device. What was extraordinary about the device was that it transferred the design process from a labour-intensive weaving stage to a card-punching stage. Once the cards had been punched and assembled, the design was complete, and the loom implemented the design automatically. The Jacquard loom, therefore, could be said to be programmed for different patterns by these decks of punched cards.

For those intent on mechanizing calculations, the Jacquard loom provided important lessons: the sequence of operations that a machine performs could be controlled to make the machine do something quite different; a punched card could be used as a medium for directing the machine; and, most important, a device could be directed to perform different tasks by feeding it instructions in a sort of language—i.e., making the machine programmable. It is not too great a stretch to say that, in the Jacquard loom, programming was invented before the computer. The punched cards were adopted by the noted English inventor Charles Babbage as an input-output medium for his proposed Analytical Engine, which is generally considered to be the first computer.

JOHN LOUDON McADAM

(b. Sept. 21, 1756, Ayr, Ayrshire, Scot.—d. Nov. 26, 1836, Moffat, Dumfriesshire)

John Loudon McAdam was a Scottish inventor of the macadam road surface.

In 1770 he went to New York City, entering the countinghouse of a merchant uncle; he returned to Scotland with a considerable fortune in 1783. There he purchased an estate at Sauhrie, Ayrshire. McAdam, who had become a road trustee in his district, noted that the local highways were in poor condition. At his own expense he undertook a series of experiments in road making.

In 1798 he moved to Falmouth, Cornwall, where he continued his experiments under a government appointment. In 1815, having been appointed surveyor general of the Bristol roads, he put his theories into practice. McAdam had no use for the masonry constructions of his predecessors and contemporaries. Instead, he showed that traffic could be supported by a relatively thin layer of small, single-sized, angular pieces of broken stone placed and compacted on a well-drained natural formation and covered by an impermeable surface of smaller stones. Drainage was essential to the success of McAdam's method, and he required the pavement to be elevated above the surrounding surface. The structural layer of broken stone was 8 inches (20.32 cm) thick and used stone of 2 to 3 inches (5 to 8 cm) maximum size laid in layers and compacted by traffic—a process adequate for the traffic of the time. The top layer was 2 inches (5 cm) thick, using three-fourths- to 1-inch (2.5 cm) stone to fill surface voids between the large stones. Continuing maintenance was essential.

Although McAdam drew on the successes and failures of others, his total structural reliance on broken stone represented the largest paradigm shift in the history of road pavements. To document his work, McAdam wrote *Remarks on the Present System of Road-Making* (1816) and *Practical Essay on the Scientific Repair and Preservation of Roads* (1819).

As the result of a parliamentary inquiry in 1823 into the whole question of road making, McAdam's views were adopted by the public authorities, and in 1827 he was appointed Surveyor General of Metropolitan Roads in Great Britain. Macadamization of roads did much to facilitate travel and communication. The principles were quickly adopted in other countries, notably the United States, and are still used today.

NICÉPHORE NIÉPCE

(b. March 7, 1765, Chalon-sur-Saône, France—d. July 5, 1833, Chalon-sur-Saône)

Nicéphore Niépce was a French inventor who was the first to make a permanent photographic image.

The son of a wealthy family suspected of royalist sympathies, Niépce fled the French Revolution but returned to serve in the French army under Napoleon Bonaparte. Dismissed because of ill health, he settled near his native town of Chalon-sur-Saône, where he remained engaged in research for the rest of his life.

In 1807 Niépce and his brother Claude invented an internal-combustion engine, which they called the Pyréolophore, explaining that the word was derived from a combination of the Greek words for "fire," "wind," and "I produce." Working on a piston-and-cylinder system similar to 20th-century gasoline-powered engines, the Pyréolophore initially used lycopodium powder for fuel, and Niépce claimed to have used it to power a boat.

When lithography became a fashionable hobby in France in 1813, Niépce began to experiment with the then-novel printing technique. Unskilled in drawing, and unable to obtain proper lithographic stone locally, he sought a way to provide images automatically. He coated pewter with various light-sensitive substances in an effort to copy superimposed engravings in sunlight. From this he progressed in April 1816 to attempts at photography, which he called heliography (sundrawing), with a camera. He recorded a view from his workroom window on paper sensitized with silver chloride but was only partially able to fix the image. Next he tried various types of supports for the light-sensitive material bitumen of Judea, a kind of asphalt, which hardens on exposure to light. Using this material he succeeded in 1822 in obtaining a photographic copy of an engraving superimposed on glass. In 1826/27, using a camera, he made a view from his workroom on a pewter plate, this being the first permanently fixed image from nature. Metal had the advantage of being unbreakable and was better suited to the subsequent etching process to produce a printing plate, which was Niépce's final aim. In 1826, he had produced another heliograph, a reproduction of an engraved portrait, which was etched by the Parisian engraver Augustin-François Lemaître, who pulled two prints. Thus Niépce not only solved the problem of reproducing nature by light, but he invented the first photomechanical reproduction process. While on a visit to England in 1827, Niépce addressed a memorandum on his invention to the Royal Society, London, but his insistence on keeping the method secret prevented the matter from being investigated.

Unable to reduce the very long exposure times by either chemical or optical means, Niépce in 1829 finally gave in to the repeated overtures of Louis-Jacques-Mandé Daguerre, a Parisian painter, for a partnership to perfect and exploit heliography. Niépce died without seeing any further advance, but, building on his knowledge, and working with his materials, Daguerre eventually succeeded in greatly reducing the exposure time through his discovery of a chemical process for development of (making visible) the latent (invisible) image formed upon brief exposure.

ROBERT FULTON

(b. Nov. 14, 1765, Lancaster county, Pa. [now in U.S.]—d. Feb. 24, 1815, New York, N.Y.)

Robert Fulton was an American inventor, engineer, and artist who brought steamboating from the experimental stage to commercial success. He also designed a system of inland waterways, a submarine, and a steam warship.

Fulton was the son of Irish immigrants. When their unproductive farm was lost by mortgage foreclosure in 1771, the family moved to Lancaster, where Fulton's father died in 1774 (not 1786 as is generally written). Having learned to read and write at home, Fulton was sent at age eight to a Quaker school; later he became an apprentice in a Philadelphia jewelry shop, where he specialized in the painting of miniature portraits on ivory for lockets and rings.

After settling his mother on a small farm in western Pennsylvania in 1786, Fulton went to Bath, Va., to recover from a severe cough. There the paintings by the young man—tall, graceful, and an engaging conversationalist— were admired by people who advised him to study in Europe. On returning to Philadelphia, Fulton applied himself to painting and the search for a sponsor. Local merchants, eager to raise the city's cultural level, financed his passage to London in 1787.

Although Fulton's reception in London was cordial, his paintings made little impression; they showed neither the style nor the promise required to provide him more than a precarious living. Meanwhile, he became acquainted with new inventions for propelling boats: a water jet ejected by a steam pump and a single, mechanical paddle. His own experiments led him to conclude that several revolving paddles at the stern would be most effective.

Beginning in 1794, however, having admitted defeat as a painter, Fulton turned his principal efforts toward canal engineering. His *Treatise on the Improvement of Canal Navigation*, in 1796, dealt with a complete system of inland-water transportation based on small canals extending throughout the countryside. He included details on inclined planes for raising boats—he did not favour locks—aqueducts for valley crossings, boats for specialized cargo, and bridge designs featuring bowstring beams to transmit only vertical loads to the piers. A few bridges were built to his design in the British Isles, but his canal ideas were nowhere accepted.

Undaunted, he travelled in 1797 to Paris, where he proposed the idea of a submarine, the *Nautilus*, to be used in France's war with Britain; it would creep under the hulls of British warships and leave a powder charge to be exploded later. The French government rejected the idea, however, as an atrocious and dishonourable way to fight. In 1800 he was able to build the *Nautilus* at his own expense; he conducted trials on the Seine and finally obtained government sanction for an attack, but wind and tide enabled two British ships to elude his slow vessel.

In 1801 Fulton met Robert R. Livingston, a member of the committee that drafted the U.S. Declaration of Independence. Before becoming minister to France, Livingston had obtained a 20-year monopoly of steamboat navigation within the state of New York. The two men decided to share the expense of building a steamboat in Paris using Fulton's design—a side paddlewheel, 66-foot- (20-metre-) long boat, with an eight-horsepower engine of French design. Although the engine broke the hull, they were encouraged by success with another hull. Fulton ordered parts for a 24-horsepower engine from Boulton and Watt for a boat on the Hudson, and Livingston obtained an extension on his monopoly of steamboat navigation.

Returning to London in 1804, Fulton advanced his ideas with the British government for submersible and low-lying craft that would carry explosives in an attack. Two raids against the French using his novel craft, however, were unsuccessful. In 1805, after Nelson's victory at Trafalgar, it was apparent that Britain was in control of the seas without the aid of Fulton's temperamental weapons. In the same year, the parts for his projected steamboat were ready for shipment to the United States, but Fulton spent a desperate year attempting to collect money he felt the British owed him.

MAIDEN VOYAGE

Arriving in New York in December 1806, Fulton at once set to work supervising the construction of the steamboat that had been planned in Paris with Livingston. He also attempted to interest the U.S. government in a submarine, but his demonstration of it was a fiasco. By early August 1807 a 150-foot- (45-metre-) long *Steamboat*, as Fulton called it, was ready for trials. Its single-cylinder condensing steam engine (24-inch bore and four-foot stroke) drove two 15-foot-diameter side paddlewheels; it consumed oak and pine fuel, which produced steam at a pressure of two to three pounds per square inch. The 150-mile (240-km) trial run from New York to Albany required 32 hours (an average of almost 4.7 miles [7.6 km] per hour), considerably better time than the four miles per hour required by the monopoly. The passage was epic because sailing sloops required four days for the same trip.

After building an engine house, raising the bulwark, and installing berths in the cabins of the now-renamed *North River Steamboat*, Fulton began commercial trips in September. He made three round-trips fortnightly between New York and Albany, carrying passengers and light freight. Problems, however, remained: the mechanical difficulties, for example, and the jealous sloopboatmen, who through "inadvertence" would ram the unprotected paddlewheels of their new rivals. During the first winter season he stiffened and widened the hull, replaced the cast-iron crankshaft with a forging, fitted guards over the wheels, and improved passenger accommodations. These modifications made it a different boat, which was registered in 1808 as the *North River Steamboat of Clermont*, soon reduced to *Clermont* by the press.

In 1808 Fulton married his partner's niece, Harriet Livingston, by whom he had a son and three daughters.

In 1811 the Fulton-designed, Pittsburgh-built *New Orleans* was sent south to validate the Livingston–Fulton steamboat monopoly of the New Orleans Territory. The trip was slow and perilous, river conditions being desperate because of America's first recorded, and also largest, earthquake, which had destroyed New Madrid just below the confluence of the Ohio and Mississippi rivers. Fulton's low-powered vessel remained at New Orleans, for it could go no farther upstream than Natchez. He built three boats for Western rivers that were based at New Orleans, but none could conquer the passage to Pittsburgh.

Fulton was a member of the 1812 commission that recommended building the Erie Canal. With the English blockade the same year, he insisted that a mobile floating gun platform be built—the world's first steam warship—to protect New York Harbor against the British fleet. The *Demologos*, or *Fulton*, as the ship was alternately called, incorporated new and novel ideas: two parallel hulls, with paddlewheel between; the steam engine in one hull, and boilers and stacks in the other. It weighed 2,745 displacement tons and measured 156 feet (48 metres) in length; a slow vessel, its speed did not exceed 6 knots (6 nautical miles, or 11 km, per hour). Launched in October 1814, the heavily gunned and armoured steamship underwent successful sea trials but was never used in battle; when peace came in December, it was transferred to the Brooklyn Navy Yard, where it was destroyed by an accidental explosion in 1829.

By 1810 three of Fulton's boats served the Hudson and Raritan rivers. His steamboats also replaced the horse ferries that were used for heavily travelled river crossings in New York, Boston, and Philadelphia. He retained the typical broad double-ended hulls that needed no turning for the return passage. Manhattan's crosstown Fulton Street, named in 1816, was the principal thoroughfare connecting the two river terminals.

Fulton spent much of his wealth in litigations involving the pirating of patents relating to steamboats and in trying to suppress rival steamboat builders who found loopholes in the state-granted monopoly. His wealth was further depleted by his unsuccessful submarine projects, investments in paintings, and financial assistance to farmer kin and young artists. After testifying at a legal hearing in Trenton, early in 1815, he became chilled en route home to New York, where he died. His family made claims on the U.S. government for services rendered. A bill of $100,000 for the relief of the heirs finally passed the Congress in 1846 but was reduced to $76,300, with no interest.

A Hudson–Fulton Celebration in 1909 commemorated the success of the *North River Steamboat of Clermont* and the discovery in 1609 of the North River by the English navigator who was the first to sail upstream to Albany. A "Robert Fulton" commemorative stamp was issued in 1965, the bicentenary of his birth, and the two-story farmhouse, his birthplace, was acquired and restored by the Pennsylvania Historical and Museum Commission.

ELI WHITNEY

(b. Dec. 8, 1765, Westboro, Mass. [now in U.S.]—d. Jan. 8, 1825, New Haven, Conn., U.S.)

Eli Whitney was an American inventor, mechanical engineer, and manufacturer, best remembered as the inventor of the cotton gin but most important for developing the concept of mass production of inter-changeable parts.

Whitney's father was a respected farmer who served as a justice of the peace. In May 1789 Whitney entered Yale College, where he learned many of the new concepts and

Eli Whitney's cotton gin, shown here, revolutionized the cotton industry by making it much easier to separate the cotton from the seed. Getty/HultonArchive

experiments in science and the applied arts, as technology was then called. After graduation in the fall of 1792, Whitney was disappointed twice in promised teaching posts. The second offer was in Georgia, where, stranded without employment, short of cash, and far from home, he was befriended by Catherine Greene. Phineas Miller, a young man of Whitney's age, Connecticut-born and Yale-educated, managed Mulberry Grove, Greene's splendid plantation. Miller and Whitney became friends.

At a time when English mills were hungry for cotton, the South exported a small amount of the black-seed, long-staple variety. Though it could easily be cleaned of its seed by passing it through a pair of rollers, its cultivation was limited to the coast. On the other hand, a green-seed, short-staple variety that grew in the interior resisted cleaning; its fibre adhered to the seed. Whitney saw that a machine to clean the green-seed cotton could make the South prosperous and make its inventor rich. He set to work and constructed a crude model. Whitney's cotton gin had four parts: (1) a hopper to feed the cotton into the gin; (2) a revolving cylinder studded with hundreds of short wire hooks, closely set in ordered lines to match fine grooves cut in (3) a stationary breastwork that strained out the seed while the fibre flowed through; and (4) a clearer, which was a cylinder set with bristles, turning in the opposite direction, that brushed the cotton from the hooks and let it fly off by its own centrifugal force.

After perfecting his machine Whitney secured a patent (1794), and he and Miller went into business manu-facturing and servicing the new gins. However, the unwillingness of the planters to pay the service costs and the ease with which the gins could be pirated put the partners out of business by 1797.

The planters' ability to defeat lawsuits brought against them by Whitney for infringement of patent rights and their mounting wealth apparently induced a sense of guilt at denying the inventor any reward: in 1802 the state of South Carolina agreed to pay $50,000, half the sum asked by Miller & Whitney for the patent rights. The action was followed by similar settlements with North Carolina, Tennessee, and, finally and reluctantly, Georgia. Miller & Whitney grossed about $90,000; the partners netted practically nothing. When Congress refused to renew the patent, which expired in 1807, Whitney concluded that "an invention can be so valuable as to be worthless to the inventor." He never patented his later inventions, one of which was a milling machine.

Whitney learned much from his experience. He knew his own competence and integrity, which were acknowledged and respected. He redirected his mechanical and entrepreneurial talents to other projects in which his system for manufacturing gins was applicable. In 1797 the government, threatened by war with France, solicited 40,000 muskets from private contractors because the two national armories had produced only 1,000 muskets in three years. Twenty-six contractors bid for a total of 30,200. Like the government armories, they used the conventional method whereby a skilled workman fashioned a complete musket, forming and fitting each part. Thus, each weapon was unique; if a part broke, its replacement had to be especially made.

Whitney broke with this tradition with a plan to supply 10,000 muskets in two years. He designed machine tools by which an unskilled workman made only a particular part that conformed precisely, as precision was then measured, to a model. The sum of such parts was a musket. Any part would fit any musket of that design. He had grasped the concept of interchangeable parts. "The tools which I contemplate to make," he explained, "are similar to an engraving on copper plate from which may be taken a great number of impressions perceptibly alike."

But more than 10 years passed before Whitney delivered his 10,000 muskets. He constantly had to plead for time while struggling against unforeseen obstacles, such as epidemics and delays in supplies, to create a new system of production. Finally, he overcame most of the skepticism in 1801, when, in Washington, D.C., before President-elect Thomas Jefferson and other officials, he demonstrated the result of his system: from piles of disassembled muskets they picked parts at random and assembled complete muskets. They were the witnesses at the inauguration of the American system of mass production.

In 1817 Whitney married Henrietta Edwards, granddaughter of the Puritan theologian Jonathan Edwards. Of his four children, three survived, including Eli Whitney, Jr., who continued his father's arms manufactory in Hamden, Connecticut.

ALOIS SENEFELDER

(b. Nov. 6, 1771, Prague [now in the Czech Republic]—d. Feb. 26, 1834, Munich, Ger.)

Johann Nepomuk Franz Alois Senefelder was a German inventor of lithography.

The son of an actor at the Theatre Royal in Prague, Senefelder was unable to continue his studies at the University of Ingolstadt after his father's death and thus tried to support himself as a performer and author, but without success. He learned printing in a printing office, purchased a small press, and sought to do his own printing.

Desiring to publish plays that he had written but unable to afford the expensive engraving of printing plates, Senefelder tried to engrave them himself. His work on copper plates was not proving very successful when an accident led to his discovery of the possibilities of stone (1796). Senefelder records that one day he jotted down a laundry list with grease pencil on a piece of Bavarian limestone. It occurred to him that if he etched away the rest of the surface, the markings would be left in relief. Two years of experimentation eventually led to the discovery of flat-surface printing (modern lithography, from Greek *lithos*, "stone"). Senefelder closely held the secret of lithographic printing until 1818, when he documented his discovery in *Vollständiges Lehrbuch der Steindruckerey* (1818; *A Complete Course of Lithography*).

Senefelder later accepted an offer from a music publisher, Johann Anton André, to set himself up at Offenbach and train others in his lithographic process. In later years the king of Bavaria settled a handsome pension on Senefelder.

SIR WILLIAM CONGREVE

(b. May 20, 1772, London, Eng.—d. May 16, 1828, Toulouse, France)

Sir William Congreve was an English artillery officer and inventor, best known for his military rocket, which was a significant advance on earlier black-powder rockets. It provided the impetus for an early wave of enthusiastic utilization of rockets for military purposes in Europe.

Congreve based his rockets on those used by the Indian prince Hyder Ali against the British in 1792 and 1799 at Seringapatam. In 1805 he built a rocket 40.5 inches (103 cm) long, with a stabilizing stick 16 feet (4.9 m) long and a range of 2,000 yards (1.8 km). Congreve's rockets were used to bombard Boulogne, Copenhagen, and Danzig in the Napoleonic Wars and in the British attack on Fort McHenry, near Baltimore, in 1814, which inspired Francis

Scott Key to write in the "Star Spangled Banner" (now the U.S. national anthem): " . . . the rockets' red glare, the bombs bursting in air."

Congreve continued to improve his rockets' range and accuracy, leading many European countries to form rocket corps, usually attached to artillery units. Performance of the Congreve rockets was poor by modern standards because the only available propellant was black powder, which is not ideal for propulsion. They were made obsolete by improved artillery and ordnance, but they continued to find uses for flares and ship rescue.

Congreve is also usually considered the first modern inventor to propose plating warships with armour (1805) to protect against artillery fire. Upon the death of his father in 1814 (whose baronetcy he inherited), he became comptroller of the Royal Laboratory of Woolwich Arsenal. From 1818 until his death, Congreve was a member of Parliament for Plymouth, Devon.

RENÉ LAËNNEC

(b. Feb. 17, 1781, Quimper, Brittany, France—d. Aug. 13, 1826, Kerlouanec)

René-Théophile-Hyacinthe Laënnec was a French physician who invented the stethoscope and perfected the art of auditory examination of the chest cavity.

When Laënnec was five years old, his mother, Michelle Félicité Guesdon, died from tuberculosis, leaving Laënnec and his brother, Michaud, in the incompetent care of their father, Théophile-Marie Laënnec, who worked as a civil servant and had a reputation for reckless spending. In 1793, during the French Revolution, Laënnec went to live with his uncle, Guillaume-François Laënnec, in the port city of Nantes, located in the Pays de la Loire region of western France. Laënnec's uncle was the dean of medicine at the University of Nantes. Although the region was in the midst of counterrevolutionary revolts, the young Laënnec settled into his academic training and, under his uncle's direction, began his medical studies. His first experience working in a hospital setting was at the Hôtel-Dieu of Nantes, where he learned to apply surgical dressings and to care for patients. In 1800 Laënnec went to Paris and entered the École Pratique, studying anatomy and dissection in the laboratory of surgeon and pathologist Guillaume Dupuytren. Dupuytren was a bright and ambitious academic who became known for his many surgical accomplishments and for his work in alleviating permanent tissue contracture in the palm, a condition later named Dupuytren contracture. While Dupuytren undoubtedly influenced Laënnec's studies, Laënnec also received instruction from other well-known French anatomists and physicians, including Gaspard Laurent Bayle, who studied tuberculosis and cancer; Marie-François-Xavier Bichat, who helped establish histology, the study of tissues; and Jean-Nicolas Corvisart des Marets, who used chest percussion to assess heart function and who served as personal physician to Napoleon I.

Laënnec became known for his studies of peritonitis, amenorrhea, the prostate gland, and tubercle lesions. He graduated in 1804 and continued his research as a faculty member of the Society of the School of Medicine in Paris. He wrote several articles on pathological anatomy and became devoted to Roman Catholicism, which led to his appointment as personal physician to Joseph Cardinal Fesch, half brother of Napoleon and French ambassador to the Vatican in Rome. Laënnec remained Fesch's physician until 1814, when the cardinal was exiled after

Napoleon's empire fell. While Laënnec's embrace of Catholic doctrine was viewed favourably by royalists, many in the medical profession criticized his conservatism, which contradicted the views of many academicians. Nonetheless, Laënnec's restored faith inspired him to find better ways to care for people, especially the poor. From 1812 to 1813, during the Napoleonic Wars, Laënnec took charge of the wards in the Salpêtrière Hospital in Paris, which was reserved for wounded soldiers. After the return of the monarchy, in 1816 Laënnec was appointed as physician at the Necker Hospital in Paris, where he developed the stethoscope.

Laënnec's original stethoscope design consisted of a hollow tube of wood that was 3.5 cm (1.4 inches) in diameter and 25 cm (10 inches) long and was monoaural, transmitting sound to one ear. It could be easily disassembled and reassembled, and it used a special plug to facilitate the transmission of sounds from the patient's heart and lungs. His instrument replaced the practice of immediate auscultation, in which the physician laid his ear on the chest of the patient to listen to chest sounds. The awkwardness that this method created in the case of women patients compelled Laënnec to find a better way to listen to the chest. His wooden monoaural stethoscope was replaced by models using rubber tubing at the end of the 19th century. Other advancements include the development of binaural stethoscopes, capable of transmitting sounds to both ears of the physician.

In 1819 Laënnec published *De l'auscultation médiate* ("On Mediate Auscultation"), the first discourse on a variety of heart and lung sounds heard through the stethoscope. The first English translation of *De l'auscultation médiate* was published in London in 1821. Laënnec's treatise aroused intense interest, and physicians from throughout

Europe came to Paris to learn about Laënnec's diagnostic tool. He became an internationally renowned lecturer. In 1822 Laënnec was appointed chair and professor of medicine at the College of France, and the following year he became a full member of the French Academy of Medicine and a professor at the medical clinic of the Charity Hospital in Paris. In 1824 he was made a chevalier of the Legion of Honour. That same year Laënnec married Jacquette Guichard, a widow. They did not have any children, his wife having suffered a miscarriage. Two years later at the age of 45 Laënnec died from cavitating tuberculosis—the same disease that he helped elucidate using his stethoscope. Using his own invention, he could diagnose himself and understand that he was dying.

Because Laënnec's stethoscope enabled heart and lung sounds to be heard without placing an ear on the patient's chest, the stethoscope technique became known as the "mediate" method for auscultation. Throughout Laënnec's medical work and research, his diagnoses were supported with observations and findings from autopsies. In addition to revolutionizing the diagnosis of lung disorders, Laënnec introduced many terms still used today. For example, *Laënnec's cirrhosis*, used to describe micronodular cirrhosis (growth of small masses of tissue in the liver that cause degeneration of liver function), and *melanose* (Greek, meaning "black"), which he coined in 1804 to describe melanoma. Laënnec was the first to recognize that melanotic lesions were the result of metastatic melanoma, in which cancer cells from the original tumour site spread to other organs and tissues in the body. He is considered the father of clinical auscultation, and he wrote the first descriptions of pneumonia, bronchiectasis, pleurisy, emphysema, and pneumothorax. His classification of pulmonary conditions is still used today.

GEORGE STEPHENSON

(b. June 9, 1781, Wylam, Northumberland, Eng.—d. Aug. 12, 1848, Chesterfield, Derbyshire)

George Stephenson was an English engineer and principal inventor of the railroad locomotive.

Stephenson was the son of a mechanic who operated a Newcomen atmospheric-steam engine that was used to pump out a coal mine at Newcastle upon Tyne. The boy went to work at an early age and without formal schooling; by age 19 he was operating a Newcomen engine. His curiosity aroused by the Napoleonic war news, he enrolled in night school and learned to read and write. He soon married and, in order to earn extra income, learned to repair shoes, fix clocks, and cut clothes for miners' wives, getting a mechanic friend, the future Sir William Fairbairn, to take over his engine part-time. His genius with steam engines, however, presently won him the post of engine wright (chief mechanic) at Killingworth colliery.

Stephenson's first wife died, leaving him with a young son, Robert, whom he sent to a Newcastle school to learn mathematics; every night when the boy came home, father and son went over the homework together, both learning. In 1813 George Stephenson visited a neighbouring colliery to examine a "steam boiler on wheels" constructed by John Blenkinsop to haul coal out of the mines. In the belief that the heavy contraption could not gain traction on smooth wooden rails, Blenkinsop had given it a ratchet wheel running on a cogged third rail, an arrangement that created frequent breakdowns. Stephenson thought he could do better, and, after conferring with Lord Ravensworth, the principal owner of Killingworth, he built the *Blucher*, an engine that drew eight loaded wagons carrying 30 tons of coal at 4 miles (6 km) per hour. Not satisfied, he sought to improve his locomotive's power and introduced the "steam blast," by which exhaust steam was redirected up the chimney, pulling air after it and increasing the draft. The new design made the locomotive truly practical.

Over the next few years, Stephenson built several locomotives for Killingworth and other collieries and gained a measure of fame by inventing a mine-safety lamp. In 1821 he heard of a project for a railroad, employing draft horses, to be built from Stockton to Darlington to facilitate exploitation of a rich vein of coal. At Darlington he interviewed the promoter, Edward Pease, and so impressed him that Pease commissioned him to build a steam locomotive for the line. On Sept. 27, 1825, railroad transportation was born when the first public passenger train, pulled by Stephenson's *Active* (later renamed *Locomotion*), ran from Darlington to Stockton, carrying 450 persons at 15 miles (24 km) per hour. Liverpool and Manchester interests called him in to build a 40-mile (64-kilometre) railroad line to connect the two cities. To survey and construct the line, Stephenson had to outwit the violent hostility of farmers and landlords who feared, among other things, that the railroad would supplant horse-drawn transportation and shut off the market for oats.

When the Liverpool-Manchester line was nearing completion in 1829, a competition was held for locomotives; Stephenson's new engine, the *Rocket*, which he built with his son, Robert, won with a speed of 36 miles (58 km) per hour. Eight locomotives were used when the Liverpool-Manchester line opened on Sept. 15, 1830, and all of them had been built in Stephenson's Newcastle works. From this time on, railroad building spread rapidly throughout Britain, Europe, and North America, and George Stephenson continued as the chief guide of the revolutionary transportation medium, solving problems of roadway construction, bridge design, and locomotive and rolling-stock manufacture. He built many other railways in the Midlands, and he acted as consultant on many railroad projects at home and abroad.

LOUIS DAGUERRE

(b. Nov. 18, 1787, Cormeilles, near Paris, France—d. July 10, 1851, Brysur-Marne)

Louis-Jacques-Mandé Daguerre, a French painter and physicist, invented the first practical process of photography, known as the daguerreotype. Though the first permanent photograph from nature was made in 1826/27 by Nicéphore Niépce of France, it was of poor quality and required about eight hours' exposure time. The process that Daguerre developed required only 20 to 30 minutes.

Daguerre was at first an inland revenue officer and then a scene painter for the opera. Between 1822 and 1839 he was coproprietor of the Diorama in Paris, an auditorium in which he and his partner Charles-Marie Bouton displayed immense paintings, 45.5 by 71.5 feet (14 by 22 metres) in size, of famous places and historical events. A similar establishment that he opened in Regent's Park, London,

Louis-Jacques-Mandé Daguerre, lithograph. Library of Congress, Washington, D.C.

was destroyed by fire in 1839. The partners painted the scenes on translucent paper or muslin and, by the careful use of changing lighting effects, were able to present vividly realistic tableaux. The views provided grand, illusionistic entertainment, and the amazing trompe l'oeil effect was purposely heightened by the accompaniment of appropriate music and the positioning of real objects, animals, or people in front of the painted scenery.

Like many other artists of his time, Daguerre made preliminary sketches by tracing the images produced by both the camera obscura and the camera lucida, a prism-fitted instrument that was invented in 1807. His attempt to retain the duplication of nature he perceived in the camera obscura's ground glass led in 1829 to a partnership with Niépce, with whom he worked in person and by correspondence for the next four years (Niépce died in 1833). However, Daguerre's interest was in shortening the exposure time necessary to obtain an image of the real world, while Niépce remained interested in producing reproducible plates. It appears that by 1835 Daguerre had discovered that a latent image forms on a plate of iodized silver and that it can be "developed" and made visible by exposure to mercury vapour, which settles on the exposed parts of the image. Exposure times could thus be reduced from eight hours to 30 minutes. The results were not permanent, however; when the developed picture was exposed to light, the unexposed areas of silver darkened until the image was no longer visible. By 1837 Daguerre was able to fix the image permanently by using a solution of table salt to dissolve the unexposed silver iodide. That year he produced a photograph of his studio on a silvered copper plate, a photograph that was remarkable for its fidelity and detail. Also that year, Niépce's son Isidore signed an agreement with Daguerre affirming Daguerre as the inventor of a new process, "the daguerreotype."

On Jan. 9, 1839, a full description of Daguerre's process was announced at a meeting of the Academy of Sciences by the eminent astronomer and physicist François Arago. On August 19 full working details were published. Daguerre wrote a booklet describing the process, *An Historical and Descriptive Account of the Various Processes of the Daguerreotype and the Diorama*, which at once became a best seller; 29 editions and translations appeared before the end of 1839. Also in 1839 Daguerre and the heir of Niépce were assigned annuities of 6,000 francs and 4,000 francs, respectively, in return for their photographic process. Daguerre was appointed an officer of the Legion of Honour.

SAMUEL F.B. MORSE

(b. April 27, 1791, Charlestown, Mass., U.S.—d. April 2, 1872, New York, N.Y.)

Samuel Finley Breese Morse was an American painter and inventor who, independent of similar efforts in Europe, developed an electric telegraph (1832–35). In 1838 he developed the Morse code.

Morse was the son of Jedidiah Morse, the distinguished geographer and Congregational clergyman. From Phillips Academy in Andover, where he had been an unsteady and eccentric student, his parents sent him to Yale College. Although an indifferent scholar, his interest was aroused by lectures on the then little-understood subject of electricity. To the distress of his austere parents, he also enjoyed painting miniature portraits.

After graduating from Yale in 1810, Morse became a clerk for a Boston book publisher. But painting continued to be his main interest, and in 1811 his parents helped him

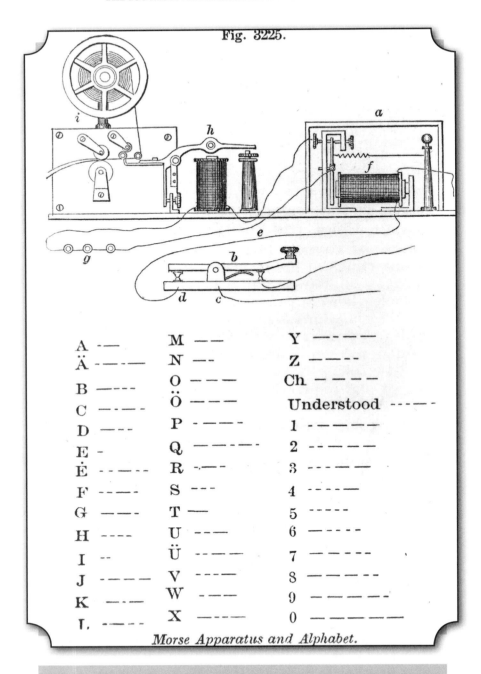

Fig. 3225.

A	·—	M	——	Y	—·———
Ä	·—·—	N	—·	Z	——··
B	—···	O	———	Ch	————
C	—·—·	Ö	———·	Understood	···—·
D	—··	P	·——·	1	·————
E	·	Q	——·—	2	··———
Ė	··—··	R	·—·	3	···——
F	··—·	S	···	4	····—
G	——·	T	—	5	·····
H	····	U	··—	6	—····
I	··	Ü	··——	7	——···
J	·———	V	···—	8	———··
K	—·—	W	·——	9	————·
L	·—··	X	—··—	0	—————

Morse Apparatus and Alphabet.

This print shows the machines used for sending and receiving coded telegraph messages, as well as the alphabet for Morse code. Library of Congress

to go to England in order to study that art. During the War of 1812, between Great Britain and the United States, Morse reacted to the English contempt for Americans by becoming passionately pro-American. Like the majority of Americans of his time, however, he accepted English artistic standards, including the "historical" style of painting—the romantic portrayal of legends and historical events with personalities gracing the foreground in grand poses and brilliant colours.

But when, on his return home in 1815, Morse found that Americans did not appreciate his historical canvases, he reluctantly took up portraiture again to earn a living. He began as an itinerant painter in New England, New York, and South Carolina; after 1825, on settling in New York City, he painted some of the finest portraits ever done by an American artist. He combined technical competence and a bold rendering of his subjects' character with a touch of the Romanticism he had imbibed in England.

Although often poor during those early years, Morse was sociable and at home with intellectuals, the wealthy, the religiously orthodox, and the politically conservative. In addition, he possessed the gift of friendship. Among his friends in his middle years were the French hero of the American Revolution, the marquis de Lafayette, whose attempts to promote liberal reform in Europe Morse ardently endorsed, and the novelist James Fenimore Cooper. Morse and Cooper shared several traits: both were ardent U.S. republicans, though both had aristocratic social tastes, and both suffered from the American preference for European art.

Morse also had the gift of leadership. As part of a campaign against the licentiousness of the theatre, he helped launch, in 1827, the New York *Journal of Commerce*, which refused theatre advertisements. He also was a founder of the National Academy of Design, organized to increase U.S. respect for painters, and was its first president from 1826 to 1845.

In 1832, while returning by ship from studying art in Europe, Morse conceived the idea of an electric telegraph as the result of hearing a conversation about the newly discovered electromagnet. Although the idea of an electric telegraph had been put forward before 1800, Morse believed that his was the first proposal. He probably made his first working model by 1835. Meanwhile, he was still devoting most of his time to painting, teaching art at the University of the City of New York (later New York University), and to politics. But, by 1837, he turned his full attention to the new invention. A colleague at the university showed him a detailed description of an alternative model proposed in 1831, and a friend offered to provide materials and labour to build models in his family's ironworks. These two became partners in Morse's telegraph rights. By 1838 he had developed the system of dots and dashes that became known throughout the world as the Morse code. In 1838, while unsuccessfully attempting to interest Congress in building a telegraph line, he acquired a congressman as an additional partner. After failing to organize the construction of a Morse line in Europe, Morse was finally able to obtain, without his partners' cooperation, financial support from Congress for the first telegraph line in the United States, from Baltimore to Washington. In 1844 the line was completed, and he sent the first message, "What hath God wrought!"

Morse was immediately involved in legal claims by his partners and by rival inventors. He fought vigorously in this dispute, and a series of legal battles culminating in a U.S. Supreme Court decision established his patent rights in 1854. As telegraph lines lengthened on both sides of the Atlantic, his wealth and fame increased. By 1847 Morse had bought Locust Grove, an estate overlooking the

Hudson River near Poughkeepsie, New York, where, early in the 1850s, he built an Italian villa-style mansion. He spent his summers there with his large family of children and grandchildren, returning each winter season to his brownstone home in New York City.

In his old age, Morse, a patriarch with a flowing beard, became a philanthropist. He gave generously to Vassar College, of which he was a founder and trustee; to his alma mater, Yale College; and to churches, theological seminaries, Bible societies, mission societies, and temperance societies, as well as to poor artists.

Even during Morse's own lifetime, the world was much changed by the telegraph. After his death in 1872, his fame as the inventor of the telegraph was obscured by the invention of the telephone, radio, and television, while his reputation as an artist has grown. At one time he did not wish to be remembered as a portrait painter, but his powerful and sensitive portraits, among them those of Lafayette, the American writer William Cullen Bryant, and other prominent men, have been exhibited throughout the United States. His 1837 telegraph instrument is preserved by the Smithsonian Institution's National Museum of American History in Washington, D.C., while his estate, Locust Grove, is now designated a historic landmark.

CHARLES BABBAGE
(b. Dec. 26, 1791, London, Eng.—d. Oct. 18, 1871, London)

Charles Babbage, an English mathematician and inventor, is credited with having conceived the first automatic digital computer.

In 1812 Babbage helped found the Analytical Society, whose object was to introduce developments from the European continent into English mathematics. In 1816 he was elected a fellow of the Royal Society of London. He was instrumental in founding the Royal Astronomical (1820) and Statistical (1834) societies. In the meantime (1828–39) he served as Lucasian Professor of Mathematics at the University of Cambridge.

As a founding member of the Royal Astronomical Society, Babbage had seen a clear need to design and build a mechanical device that could automate long, tedious astronomical calculations. He began by writing a letter in 1822 to Sir Humphry Davy, president of the Royal Society, about the possibility of automating the construction of mathematical tables—specifically, logarithm tables for use in navigation. He then wrote a paper, "On the Theoretical Principles of the Machinery for Calculating Tables," which he read to the society later that year. (It won the Royal Society's first Gold Medal in 1823.) Tables then in use often contained errors, which could be a life-and-death matter for sailors at sea, and Babbage argued that, by automating the production of the tables, he could assure their accuracy. Having gained support in the society for his Difference Engine, as he called it, Babbage next turned to the British government to fund development, obtaining one of the world's first government grants for research and technological development.

Babbage approached the project very seriously: he hired a master machinist, set up a fireproof workshop, and built a dustproof environment for testing the device. Up until then calculations were rarely carried out to more than six digits; Babbage planned to produce 20- or 30-digit results routinely. The Difference Engine was a digital device: it operated on discrete digits rather than smooth quantities, and the digits were decimal (0–9), represented by positions on toothed wheels, rather than binary digits, or "bits." When one of the toothed wheels turned from 9 to 0, it caused the next wheel to advance one position, carrying the digit.

The Difference Engine was more than a simple calculator, however. It mechanized not just a single calculation but a whole series of calculations on a number of variables to solve a complex problem. It went far beyond calculators in other ways as well. Like modern computers, the Difference Engine had storage—that is, a place where data could be held temporarily for later processing—and it was designed to stamp its output into soft metal, which could later be used to produce a printing plate.

Nevertheless, the Difference Engine performed only one operation. The operator would set up all of its data registers with the original data, and then the single operation would be repeatedly applied to all of the registers, ultimately producing a solution. Still, in complexity and audacity of design, it dwarfed any calculating device then in existence.

The full engine, designed to be room-sized, was never built, at least not by Babbage. Although he received several government grants, they were sporadic—governments changed, funding often ran out, and he had to personally bear some of the financial costs—and he was working at or near the tolerances of the construction methods of the day and ran into numerous construction difficulties. All design and construction ceased in 1833, when Joseph Clement, the machinist responsible for actually building the machine, refused to continue unless he was prepaid. (Between 1985 and 2002 British computer scientists built Difference Engine No. 2, a replica faithful to Babbage's original specifications. The completed engine is on permanent exhibit at the Science Museum in London.)

THE ANALYTICAL ENGINE

While working on the Difference Engine, a simpler calculating machine commissioned by the British government, Babbage began to imagine ways to improve it. Chiefly he thought about generalizing its operation so that it could perform other kinds of calculations. By the time funding ran out for his Difference Engine in 1833, he had conceived of something far more revolutionary: a general-purpose computing machine called the Analytical Engine.

The Analytical Engine was to be a general-purpose, fully program-controlled, automatic mechanical digital computer. It would be able to perform any calculation set before it. There is no evidence that anyone before Babbage had ever conceived of such a device, let alone attempted to build one. The machine was designed to consist of four components: the mill, the store, the reader, and the printer. These components are the essential components of every computer today. The mill was the calculating unit, analogous to the central processing unit (CPU) in a modern computer; the store was where data were held prior to processing, exactly analogous to memory and storage in today's computers; and the reader and printer were the input and output devices.

As with the Difference Engine, the project was far more complex than anything theretofore built. The store was to be large enough to hold 1,000 50-digit numbers; this was larger than the storage capacity of any computer built before 1960. The machine was to be steam-driven and run by one attendant. The printing capability was also ambitious, as it had been for the Difference Engine: Babbage wanted to automate the process as much as possible, right up to producing printed tables of numbers.

The reader was another new feature of the Analytical Engine. Data (numbers) were to be entered on punched cards, using the card-reading technology of the Jacquard loom. Instructions were also to be entered on cards, another idea taken directly from Joseph-Marie Jacquard. The use of instruction cards would make it a programmable device and far more flexible than any machine then in existence. Another element of programmability was to be its ability to execute instructions in other than sequential order. It was to have a kind of decision-making ability in its conditional control transfer, also known as conditional branching, whereby it would be able to jump to a different instruction depending on the value of some data. This extremely powerful feature was missing in many of the early computers of the 20th century.

By most definitions, the Analytical Engine was a real computer as understood today—or would have been, had Babbage not run into implementation problems again. Actually building his ambitious design was judged infeasible given the current technology, and Babbage's failure to generate the promised mathematical tables with his Difference Engine had dampened enthusiasm for further government funding. Indeed, it was apparent to the British government that Babbage was more interested in innovation than in constructing tables.

All the same, Babbage's Analytical Engine was something new under the sun. Its most revolutionary feature was the ability to change its operation by changing the instructions on punched cards. Until this breakthrough, all the mechanical aids to calculation were merely calculators or, like the Difference Engine, glorified calculators. The Analytical Engine, although not actually completed, was the first machine that deserved to be called a computer. Babbage worked on the machine until his death. His design was forgotten until his unpublished notebooks were discovered in 1937.

Babbage made notable contributions in other areas as well. He assisted in establishing the modern postal system in England and compiled the first reliable actuarial tables. He also invented a type of speedometer and the locomotive cowcatcher. It was Babbage who first suggested that the weather of years past could be read from tree rings. He also had a lifelong fascination with keys, ciphers, and mechanical dolls.

SIR ROWLAND HILL

(b. Dec. 3, 1795, Kidderminster, Worcestershire, Eng.—d. Aug. 27, 1879, Hampstead, London)

Rowland Hill, knighted Sir Rowland in 1860, was an English administrator and educator and the originator of the penny postage system. He is principally known for his development of the modern postal service, which was subsequently adopted throughout the world.

The son of an English schoolmaster, Hill was interested in problems of teaching; for about 15 years he operated schools in which he emphasized student democracy, rigid self-discipline, and intensive teaching. His wide-ranging interests included printing, astronomy, mathematics, and transportation.

Hill's proposals for postal reform were formulated between 1835 and 1837 and were based on the notion that revenue derived from taxes should increase with the growth of the population and national prosperity. In 1837 he published *Post Office Reform: Its Importance and Practicability*, which is justly regarded as one of the most important milestones in postal progress. Based on an exhaustive study of the cost structure of postal operations, it demonstrated conclusively that conveyance charges were an insignificant factor in the total cost of handling a letter. The then current intricate charging scales based on distance were shown to be irrelevant: they inflated operating costs by requiring a host of clerks to apply them and to prepare complicated interoffice accounts. He also realized that another major item in the current cost structure—the collection of money payments on delivery—was easily avoidable. Hill's solution was a uniform rate of postage, regardless of distance, and prepayment of postage by means of adhesive stamps sold by the post office. Hill proposed a basic rate of one penny for each half ounce, calculating the "natural cost of distribution" to be slightly less than this. The cheapest current rate of postage was fourpence, and the average charge 6 1/4 pence (11.56 cents).

Not surprisingly, Hill's proposals rapidly gained strong support: popular agitation for the "penny post" overcame initial political disinterest—and bureaucratic hostility— and the uniform rate and a system of prepayment by stamps were introduced in 1840. The originality of Hill's proposal for an adhesive postage stamp has been questioned but is irrelevant in considering the overall merits of his work. The significance of his reforms lies not only in the fact that they brought the post within the means of the mass of the people but also in the less obvious way in which they gave the postal system the technical capacity to deal with the vastly increased demand for postal service that ensued. The radical simplification of postal organization and methods characterizing Hill's reforms are the key to the speed and economy with which modern postal systems in many countries handle tens of millions of letters daily.

The chief features of Hill's system were gradually adopted in varying degrees by other countries throughout the world, first among which were Switzerland and Brazil in 1843.

CHARLES GOODYEAR

(b. Dec. 29, 1800, New Haven, Conn., U.S.—d. July 1, 1860, New York City)

Charles Goodyear was an American inventor whose vulcanization process made possible the commercial use of rubber. Though subsequent discoveries have refined Goodyear's original techniques, the vulcanization process remains fundamentally the same as it was in his day.

Goodyear began his career as a partner in his father's hardware business, which went bankrupt in 1830. He then became interested in discovering a method of treating india rubber so that it would lose its adhesiveness and susceptibility to extremes of heat and cold. He developed a nitric acid treatment and in 1837 contracted for the manufacture by this process of mailbags for the U.S. government, but the rubber fabric proved useless at high temperatures.

For the next few years he worked with Nathaniel M. Hayward (1808–65), a former employee of a rubber factory in Roxbury, Mass., who had discovered that rubber treated with sulfur was not sticky. Goodyear bought Hayward's process. In 1839 he accidentally dropped some India rubber mixed with sulfur on a hot stove and so discovered vulcanization (after Vulcan, the Roman god of fire). Goodyear found that a mixture of rubber with about 8 percent by weight of sulfur and some white lead as an accelerant was transformed, on heating, to an elastic solid that remained elastic and resilient at high temperatures and yet stayed soft at low temperatures. It is now known that sulfur atoms react to form interlinks between the long, chainlike rubber molecules, making a loose molecular network. The original rubber liquid is thus converted into a solid that will not flow even when warm because the molecules are now permanently tied together. Moreover, the addition of a small amount of sulfur in various forms makes the rubber molecules sufficiently irregular that crystallization (and, hence, hardening at low temperatures) is greatly impeded.

Goodyear was granted his first patent in 1844 but had to fight numerous infringements in court; the decisive victory did not come until 1852. That year he went to England, where articles made under his patents had been displayed at the International Exhibition of 1851; while there he unsuccessfully attempted to establish factories. He also lost his patent rights there and in France because of technical and legal problems. In France a company that manufactured vulcanized rubber by his process failed, and in December 1855 Goodyear was imprisoned for debt in Paris. Meanwhile, in the United States, his patents continued to be infringed upon. Although his invention made millions for others, at his death he left debts of some $200,000. He wrote an account of his discovery entitled *Gum-Elastic and Its Varieties* (2 vol.; 1853–55).

JOHN DEERE

(b. Feb. 7, 1804, Rutland, Vt., U.S.—d. May 17, 1886, Moline, Ill.)

John Deere was a pioneer American inventor and manufacturer of agricultural implements.

Apprenticed to a blacksmith at age 17, Deere set up his own smithy trade four years later and, for 12 years, did work in various towns of his native Vermont. In 1837, when 33 years old, he headed west and eventually settled in Grand Detour, Ill., where he set up a blacksmith's shop, and sent for his wife and children the following year. He joined in a partnership with Major Leonard Andrus.

In his work, Deere found, through the frequent repairs that he had to make, that the wood and cast-iron plow, used in the sandy soils of the eastern United States from the 1820s, was not suited to the heavy, sticky soils of the prairies. Calculating that an answer lay in an all-steel one-piece share and moldboard, he began experimenting, and by 1838 he and his partner had sold three newly fashioned plows. He kept experimenting, producing 10 improved plows in 1839 and 40 new plows in 1840. By 1846 the annual output was about a thousand plows. Deciding that Grand Detour was not well situated in regard to transportation and resources, Deere sold his interest in the shop to Andrus in 1847 and moved to Moline, Ill. There he began using imported English steel with great success and soon negotiated with Pittsburgh manufacturers for the development of comparable steel plate. By 1857 Deere's annual output of plows had risen to 10,000.

In 1858 Deere took his son Charles into partnership and in 1863 his son-in-law, Stephen H. Velie; in 1868 the firm was incorporated as Deere & Company. Deere remained president of the company for the rest of his life. Gradually Deere & Company began manufacturing cultivators and other agricultural implements. It is still a major American manufacturer of farm machinery and industrial equipment. Still headquartered in Moline, Ill., it witnessed five generations of Deere family leadership from its inception until 1982.

CLAUDE-ÉTIENNE MINIÉ

(b. Feb. 13, 1804, Paris, France—d. Dec. 14, 1879, Paris)

Claude-Étienne Minié was a French army officer who solved the problem of designing a bullet for the muzzle-loading rifle. The bullet became known as the Minié ball.

After serving in several African campaigns in the Chasseurs, Minié rose to the rank of captain. In the 1840s he applied himself to the problem of rifled weapons. As killing machines, the old smoothbore infantry muskets were relatively inefficient. Their heavy, round lead balls delivered lethal blows when they hit a human body, but beyond 75 yards (68 metres) even trained infantrymen found it difficult to hit an individual adversary, and at 300 yards (274 metres) balls from muzzle-loaders lost most of their lethality. These ballistic shortcomings were a product of the requirement that the projectile, in order to be quickly rammed from muzzle to breech, had to fit loosely in the barrel. When discharged, it wobbled down the barrel, contributing to erratic flight after it left the muzzle. Rifled barrels, in which spiral grooves were cut into the bore, were known to improve accuracy by imparting a gyroscopic spin to the projectile, but reloading rifled weapons was slowed because the lead ball had to be driven into the barrel's rifling. In 1826 Henri-Gustave Delvigne of France, seeking a means of expanding the projectile without making it difficult to ram home, created a narrow powder chamber at the breech end of the barrel against which a loosely fitting lead ball came to rest. Ramrod blows expanded the soft lead at the mouth of the chamber so that, when fired, the bullet fit the rifling tightly. In 1844 another French officer, Louis-Étienne de Thouvenin, introduced yet a better method for expanding bullets. His carabine à tige embodied a post or pillar (tige) at the breech against which the bullet was expanded.

These rifles worked better than earlier types, but their deformed balls flew with reduced accuracy. Minié, inspired by Delvigne's later work with cylindrical bullets, designed longer, smaller-diameter projectiles, which, having the same weight as larger round balls, possessed greater cross-sectional density and therefore retained their velocity better. In order to combat the tendency of muzzle-loading rifles to become difficult to load as gunpowder residue collected in the barrels, Minié suggested a major simplification—eliminating the pillar of Thouvenin's weapons and employing in its place a hollow-based bullet with an iron expander plug that caused the projectile to engage the rifling when the weapon was fired.

This new projectile could be loaded into dirty rifles with ease, and, because it was not deformed while loading, it had greater accuracy.

Officials in several countries, notably Britain and the United States, saw the significance of Minié's invention. In the Crimean War (1854–56), Russian troops armed with smoothbore muskets were no match for Britons shooting Minié balls from rifled muskets. Massed formations were easy prey, as were cavalry and artillery units. A correspondent for the *Times* of London wrote: "The Minié is king of weapons . . . the volleys of the Minié cleft [Russian soldiers] like the hand of the Destroying Angel." The American Civil War, in which both sides fielded Minié-type infantry weapons, clearly demonstrated the deadly effect of rifled muskets, although many battlefield commanders only slowly appreciated the changing nature of warfare. Individual soldiers could hit their opposing numbers with accurate fire out to 250 yards (223 metres), so that frontal assaults, in which soldiers advanced in neat ranks across open fields, had to be abandoned. By 1862 both sides were building field entrenchments and barricades to provide protection from rifle and artillery fire.

Minié was rewarded by the French government with 20,000 francs and an appointment to the staff of the military school at Vincennes. After retiring in 1858 with the rank of colonel, he served as a military instructor for the khedive of Egypt and as a manager at the Remington Arms Company in the United States.

LOUIS BRAILLE

(b. Jan. 4, 1809, Coupvray, near Paris, France—d. Jan. 6, 1852, Paris)

Louis Braille was a French educator who developed a system of printing and writing that is extensively used by the blind and that was named for him.

Braille was himself blinded at the age of three in an accident that occurred while he was playing with tools in his father's harness shop. A tool slipped and plunged into his right eye. Sympathetic ophthalmia and total blindness followed. Nevertheless, he became a notable musician and excelled as an organist. Upon receiving a scholarship, he went to Paris in 1819 to attend the National Institute for Blind Children, and from 1826 he taught there.

Braille became interested in a system of writing, exhibited at the school by Charles Barbier, in which a message coded in dots symbolizing phonetic sounds was embossed on cardboard. It was called night writing and was intended for nighttime battlefield communications. In 1824, when he was only 15 years old, Braille worked out an adaptation,

Louis Braille's language system enables blind people to read; they memorize the meaning of patterns of raised dots and interpret them with their fingers. Getty/Raymond Kleboe

written with a simple instrument, that met the needs of the sightless. He later took this system, which consists of a six-dot code in various combinations, and adapted it to musical notation. He published a treatise on his type system in 1829, and in 1837 he published a three-volume Braille edition of a popular history schoolbook.

During the last years of his life Braille was ill with tuberculosis. His system had been immediately accepted and used by his fellow students, but wider acceptance was slow in coming. The system was not officially adopted by the school in Paris until 1854, two years after Braille's death. A universal Braille code for the English-speaking world was not adopted until 1932, when representatives from agencies for the blind in Great Britain and the United States met in London and agreed upon a system known as Standard English Braille, grade 2. In 1957 Anglo-American experts again met in London to further improve the system. A century after his death, Braille's remains (minus his hands, which were kept in his birthplace of Coupvray) were moved to Paris for burial in the Panthéon.

CYRUS McCORMICK

(b. Feb. 15, 1809, Rockbridge county, Va., U.S.—d. May 13, 1884, Chicago, Ill.)

Cyrus Hall McCormick, an American industrialist and inventor, is generally credited with the development (from 1831) of the mechanical reaper.

McCormick was the eldest son of Robert McCormick, a farmer, blacksmith, and inventor. McCormick's education, in local schools, was limited. Reserved, determined, and serious-minded, he spent all of his time in his father's workshop.

The elder McCormick had invented several practical farm implements but, like other inventors in the United

States and England, had failed in his attempt to build a successful reaping machine. In 1831 Cyrus, aged 22, tried his hand at building a reaper. Resembling a two-wheeled, horse-drawn chariot, the machine consisted of a vibrating cutting blade, a reel to bring the grain within its reach, and a platform to receive the falling grain. The reaper embodied the principles essential to all subsequent grain-cutting machines.

For farmers in the early 19th century, harvesting required a large number of labourers, and, if they could be found, the cost of hiring them was high. When McCormick's reaper was tested on a neighbour's farm in 1831, it offered the hope that the yield of the farmer's fields would soon not be limited to the amount of labour available. The machine had defects, not the least of which was a clatter so loud that slaves were required to walk alongside to calm the frightened horses.

McCormick took out a patent in 1834, but his chief interest at that time was the family's iron foundry. When the foundry failed in the wake of the Bank Panic of 1837, leaving the family deeply in debt, McCormick turned to his still-unexploited reaper and improved it. He sold two reapers in 1841, seven in 1842, 29 in 1843, and 50 the following year.

An 1844 visit to the prairie states in the Midwest convinced McCormick that the future of his reaper and of the world's wheat production lay in this vast fertile land rather than in the rocky, hilly East. In 1847, with further patented improvements, he opened a factory in the then small, swampy, lakeside town of Chicago in partnership with the mayor, William Ogden, who capitalized the venture with $50,000 of his own money. The first year, 800 machines were sold. More were sold the next year, and McCormick was able to buy out Ogden.

McCormick's main rival was Obed Hussey, whose machine proved to be inferior as a reaper but superior as a mower. When McCormick's basic patent expired in 1848, competing manufacturers—Hussey among them—tried to block renewal. The ensuing legal battle was but one of many in McCormick's career. He was involved in endless litigation not only with rival manufacturers and infringers but also with the New York Central Railroad, which he sued for $20,000 damages following an altercation over an $8.75 overcharge on his wife's baggage. He fought this particular case up to the Supreme Court three times— and won, even though it took 20 years. He did not win his 1848 patent renewal battle, however. Except for improvements on the reaper patented after 1831, the basic machine passed into the public domain. McCormick then set out to beat his manufacturing competitors another way: by outselling them.

Pockets stuffed with order blanks, McCormick rode over the plains selling his reaper to farmers and would-be farmers. To increase sales, he used innovations such as mass production, advertising, public demonstration, warranty of product, and extension of credit to his customers. Soon the factory expanded, and the company had a traveling sales force. By 1850 the McCormick reaper was known in every part of the United States, and at the Great Exhibition of 1851 in London it was introduced to European farmers. Although mocked by the *Times* of London as "a cross between an Astley Chariot, a wheelbarrow, and a flying machine," the reaper took the Grand Prize. In 1855 it won the Grand Medal of Honour at the Paris International Exposition. There followed a long series of prize honours and awards that made the McCormick reaper known to farmers throughout the world.

By 1856 McCormick was selling more than 4,000 machines a year. In the 1858 account of his marriage to Nancy (Nettie) Fowler, the *Chicago Daily Press* referred to him as the "massive Thor of industry." Business did not absorb all of his energy, however. He became active in the Democratic Party and in the Presbyterian Church, establishing the McCormick Theological Seminary in Chicago.

In 1871 the Chicago Fire gutted his factory. Then—more than 60 years old, his fortune long since made—he rebuilt. When he died, his business was still growing. In 1902 the McCormick Harvesting Company joined with other companies to form International Harvester Company, with McCormick's son, Cyrus, Jr., as its first president.

ELISHA GRAVES OTIS

(b. Aug. 3, 1811, Halifax, Vt., U.S.—d. April 8, 1861, Yonkers, N.Y.)

Elisha Graves Otis was the American inventor of the safety elevator.

A descendant of a James Otis who emigrated from England to New England in 1631, the young Otis grew up in Vermont and, at age 19, moved to Troy, N.Y., and later to Brattleboro, Vt., working at various jobs. From 1838 to 1845, in Brattleboro, he manufactured wagons and carriages and then moved his family to Albany, N.Y., where, while employed as a master mechanic in a bedstead factory, he invented several labour-saving machines. In 1851 he was in Bergen, N.J., again as master mechanic in a bedstead factory. The Bergen firm sent him to Yonkers, N.Y., in 1852 to operate a new factory and to install its machinery. There he designed and installed what he called the "safety hoist," the first elevator equipped with an automatic safety device to prevent it from falling if the lifting chain or rope broke. Prior to this invention, the poor reliability of the ropes (generally hemp) used at that time made lifting platforms unsatisfactory for passenger use. Otis's device incorporated a clamping arrangement that gripped the guide rails on which the car moved when tension was released from the hoist rope. The next year Otis resigned from his job and set up a small elevator shop in Yonkers, selling his first elevator machine on Sept. 20, 1853. It hauled freight. Orders were few until May 1854, when, at the Crystal Palace in New York City, he demonstrated his elevator by riding the platform high in the air and ordering the rope cut. On March 23, 1857, he installed the first safety elevator for passenger service in the store of E.V. Haughwout & Co. in New York City; driven by steam power, it climbed five stories in less than a minute and was a pronounced success. On Jan. 15, 1861, Otis patented an independently controlled steam engine for elevator use (installed in 1862). This invention laid the foundation for the business that his two sons, Charles and Norton, carried on after his death as owners of what eventually became the Otis Elevator Company.

Otis also devised a number of other mechanical contrivances. In 1852 he patented some railroad-car trucks and brakes. In 1857 he patented a steam plow, and in 1858 he patented a bake oven.

SIR HENRY BESSEMER

(b. Jan. 19, 1813, Charlton, Hertfordshire, Eng. — d. March 15, 1898, London)

Sir Henry Bessemer was an English inventor and engineer who developed the first process for manufacturing steel inexpensively (1856), leading to the development of the Bessemer converter. He was knighted in 1879.

Bessemer was the son of an engineer and typefounder. He early showed considerable mechanical skill and inventive powers. After the invention of movable stamps for dating deeds and other government documents and the improvement of a typesetting machine, he went to the manufacture of "gold" powder from brass for use in paints. The florid decoration of the time demanded great quantities of such material, and Bessemer's secret process soon brought him great wealth.

He developed other inventions, notably sugarcane-crushing machinery of advanced design, but he was soon devoted to metallurgy. In his time there were but two iron-based construction materials: cast iron made by the treatment of iron ore with coke in the blast furnace and wrought iron made from cast iron in primitive furnaces by the laborious manual process of "puddling" (stirring the melted iron to remove carbon and raking off the slag). Cast iron was excellent for load-bearing purposes, such as columns or bridge piers, and for engine parts, but for girders and other spans, and particularly for rails, only wrought iron was suitable. Puddling removed carbon, which makes cast iron brittle, and produced a material that could be rolled or forged, but only in "blooms," or large lumps of 100–200 pounds (45–90 kg), and that was full of slag. The blooms had to be laboriously forged together by steam hammers before they could be rolled to any useful length or shape. The only material known as steel was made by adding carbon to pure forms of wrought iron, also by slow and discontinuous methods; the material was hard, would take an edge, and was used almost entirely for cutting tools.

During the Crimean War, Bessemer invented an elongated artillery shell that was rotated by the powder gases. The French authorities with whom he was negotiating, however, pointed out that their cast-iron cannon would not be strong enough for this kind of shell. He thereupon attempted to produce a stronger cast iron. In his experiments he discovered that the excess oxygen in the hot gases of his furnace appeared to have removed the carbon from the iron pigs that were being preheated—much as the carbon is removed in a puddling furnace—leaving a skin of pure iron. Bessemer then found that blowing air through melted cast iron not only purified the iron but also heated it further, allowing the purified iron to be easily poured. This heating effect is caused by the reaction of oxygen with the carbon and silicon in the iron. Utilizing these new techniques, which later became known as the Bessemer process, he was soon able to produce large, slag-free ingots as workable as any wrought-iron bloom, and far larger; he invented the tilting converter into which molten pig iron could be poured before air was blown in from below. Eventually, with the aid of an iron-manganese alloy, which was developed at that time by Robert Forester Mushet, Bessemer also found how to remove excess oxygen from the decarburized iron.

His announcement of the process in 1856 before the British Association for the Advancement of Science in Cheltenham, Gloucestershire, brought many ironmasters to his door, and many licenses were granted. Very soon, however, it became clear that two elements harmful to iron, phosphorus and sulfur, were not removed by the process—or at least not by the fireclay lining of Bessemer's converter. It was not until about 1877 that the British metallurgist Sidney Gilchrist Thomas developed a lining that removed phosphorus and made possible the use of phosphoric ores of the Continent.

Bessemer had, unknown to himself, been using phosphorus-free iron, but the ironmasters were not so lucky. Their iron was perfectly satisfactory for the puddling process, in which phosphorus is removed because the temperatures are lower, but it could not be used in the Bessemer process. Bessemer was forced to call in his licenses and find a phosphorus-free source of iron in northwestern England; thus he was able to enter the steel market on his own. Once the phosphorus problem was recognized and solved, he became a licensor once again, and vast profits flowed in. It became clear that "mild steel"—as it was known to distinguish it from the hard tool steels—could more clearly and reliably be used in place of wrought iron for ship plate, girders, sheet, rods, wire, rivets, and other items. The invention of the open-hearth (Siemens-Martin) process in the late 1860s eventually outstripped that of the Bessemer process. This has now yielded place, in great measure, to oxygen steel-making, which is a further development and refinement of the Bessemer process.

In his later years—the process had not become a clear success until he was nearing 70—Bessemer continued to invent and make discoveries. The solar furnace he built was more than a successful toy; he designed and built an astronomical telescope for his own amusement; and he developed a set of machines for polishing diamonds that helped to reestablish that trade in London.

Apart from his knighthood, he received many honours, such as the Fellowship of the Royal Society. Bessemer's *An Autobiography* (1905), with a concluding chapter by his son, Henry Bessemer, is the only comprehensive biography and the source of most material written about him since.

SAMUEL COLT

(b. July 19, 1814, Hartford, Conn., U.S.—d. Jan. 10, 1862, Hartford)

Samuel Colt was an American firearms manufacturer who popularized the revolver.

Until the mid-1840s most pistols were single-shot muzzle-loaders fired by wheel lock, flintlock, and percussion ignition systems. Some early pistols, known as "pepper-boxes," had several barrels, and as early as the 17th century pistols were manufactured with a revolving chamber to load cartridges successively into a single barrel. However, the principle of the revolving chamber was not used successfully to produce a practical weapon until Colt patented his version.

When Colt was a young seaman, he carved a wooden model of a revolver, and years later he perfected a working version that was patented in England and France in 1835 and in the United States the following year. In the frame of this weapon was a revolving cylinder drilled with several chambers (usually five or six), into which powder and ball (or combustible paper cartridges containing powder and ball) were loaded from the front. In the rear of each chamber a percussion cap was placed over a hollow nipple that directed the jet of flame to the powder when the cap was struck by the hammer. This type of revolver was eventually called "cap-and-ball." Where earlier revolvers required the shooter to line up a chamber with the barrel and cock the hammer in separate steps, Colt devised a single-action mechanical linkage that rotated the cylinder as the hammer was cocked with the thumb.

Colt's single-barreled pistols and rifles were slow to gain acceptance, and a company that formed to manufacture them in Paterson, N.J., failed in 1842. The following year he devised an electrically discharged naval mine, the first device using a remotely controlled explosive, and he also conducted a telegraph business that utilized the first underwater cable.

Word from military units that Colt's multi-shot weapons had been effective against Indians in Florida and Texas prompted a government order for 1,000 pistols during the Mexican War, and Colt resumed firearms manufacture in 1847. In 1855 he opened the world's largest private armoury, the Colt's Patent Fire Arms Manufacturing Company, on the banks of the Connecticut River in Hartford. Assisted by Eli Whitney, Jr., he developed beyond any industrialist before him the manufacture of interchangeable parts and the production line, and he also applied progressive ideas concerning employee welfare. Colt dominated the manufacture of revolvers until the expiration of his U.S. patent in 1857; his invention made him a wealthy man. His firm produced the pistols most widely used during the American Civil War. Its six-shot, single-action .45-calibre Single Action Army Model 1873, a breech-loading revolver using metallic cartridges, became the most famous sidearm of the West.

RICHARD J. GATLING

(b. Sept. 12, 1818, Maney's Neck, N.C., U.S.—d. Feb. 26, 1903, New York, N.Y.)

American inventor Richard Jordan Gatling is best known for his invention of the Gatling gun, a crank-operated, multibarrel machine gun, which he patented in 1862.

Gatling's career as an inventor began when he assisted his father in the construction and perfecting of machines for sowing cotton seeds and for thinning cotton plants. In 1839 he perfected a practical screw propeller for steamboats, only to find that a patent had been granted to John Ericsson for a similar invention a few months earlier. He established himself in St. Louis, Mo., in 1844, and, taking the cotton-sowing machine as a basis, he adapted it for sowing rice, wheat, and other grains. The introduction of these machines did much to revolutionize the agricultural system in the country.

Becoming interested in the study of medicine during an attack of smallpox, Gatling completed a course at the Ohio Medical College in 1850. In the same year, he invented a hemp-breaking machine, and in 1857 a steam plow. At the outbreak of the American Civil War he devoted himself at once to the perfecting of firearms. In 1861 he conceived the idea of the rapid-fire machine gun that is associated with his name. After early experiments with a single barrel using paper cartridges (which had to have a separate percussion cap), he saw in the newly invented brass cartridge (which had its own percussion cap) an opportunity to fashion a truly rapid-fire weapon. Gatling contrived a cluster of 10 barrels, each of which, when rotated by a crank, was loaded and fired once during a complete rotation. The barrels were loaded by gravity and the camming action of the cartridge container, located directly above the gun. Each barrel was loaded and fired during a half-rotation around the central shaft, and the spent cases were ejected during the second half-rotation. By 1862 Gatling had succeeded in perfecting his weapon; but the war was practically over before the federal authorities consented to its official adoption. A few were used by U.S. forces in Cuba in 1898 and in minor military operations around the world. It and all other hand-operated machine guns were made obsolete by truly automatic machine guns, which operated under the energy generated by a fired round. These became militarily effective following the invention of smokeless gunpowder.

JAMES STARLEY

(b. April 21, 1830, Albourne, Sussex, Eng.—d. June 17, 1881, Coventry, Warwickshire)

James Starley was an English inventor whose prolific improvements for bicycles and tricycles earned him the title "Father of the Cycle Trade."

In 1855 Starley moved to London, where he was employed in the manufacture of sewing machines, and two years later he moved to Coventry, where he became managing foreman at the Coventry Sewing Machine Company (later the Coventry Machinists' Company Ltd.).

There he invented and patented new models, and many of his features are used in modern sewing machines.

In 1868 Starley became interested in bicycle improvement. At that time the bicycle trade was dominated by French-made velocipedes (*vélocipèdes de pedale*), iron-framed and wooden-wheeled vehicles whose hard ride earned them the sobriquet of "boneshaker"—though innovations such as solid rubber tires and wire-spoked wheels helped to soften the ride. Starley's first bicycle, the Coventry, was quickly followed by the Ariel (1871), notable for its use of centre pivot steering. The Ariel had a 48-inch (122-cm) front wheel and a 30-inch (76-cm) rear wheel. Considered the first true bicycle by many historians, the Ariel was the immediate precursor of the high-wheel "ordinary" bicycle and was the standard of bicycle design for the next decade. Starley also invented and manufactured a tangentially spoked wheel, with the spokes connected to the hub at a tangent. His design was a great improvement over radially spoked wheels and is still in use. In 1876 he introduced the highly successful Coventry tricycle and the following year incorporated into it the patented use of the differential gear in conjunction with chain drive.

The ordinary's cranks were directly connected to the front wheel, so that its speed was limited by pedaling cadence and wheel diameter. Larger front wheels went faster and handled better on bad roads, but mounting and dismounting required skill, and the rider sat almost directly over the large front wheel. From that position he could be pitched forward onto his head by road hazards. By the 1890s the term "penny-farthing" had come into use as a pejorative for ordinaries, comparing the front wheel to the large British penny and the rear wheel to the much smaller farthing (quarter-penny). Yet even as the ordinary was developing, numerous designs offered safer alternatives.

In 1885 Starley's nephew, John Kemp Starley, designed and manufactured the Rover, regarded as the first successful "safety" bicycle and the prototype of all modern bicycles. The Rover provided all the essential features of the safety bicycle: spoked wheels roughly 30 inches (76 cm) in diameter, a chain-driven rear wheel with the front chainwheel roughly twice as large as the rear sprocket, a low centre of gravity, and direct front steering. The design had decisive advantages in stability, braking, and ease of mounting. Prior to 1885 many alternative designs were called safety bicycles, but, after the Rover pattern took over the market in the late 1880s, safety bicycles were simply called bicycles. The last catalog year for ordinaries in England was 1892.

ALFRED NOBEL

(b. Oct. 21, 1833, Stockholm, Swed.—d. Dec. 10, 1896, San Remo, Italy)

Alfred Bernhard Nobel, a Swedish chemist, engineer, and industrialist, invented dynamite and other, more powerful explosives, but he is also renowned for having founded the Nobel Prizes.

Nobel was the fourth son of Immanuel and Caroline Nobel. Immanuel was an inventor and engineer who had married Caroline Andrietta

The noted scientist Alfred Nobel, pictured here at around age 30, was a Swedish chemist and industrialist known both for inventing dynamite and for founding the Nobel Prize. Hulton Archive/Getty Images

Ahlsell in 1827. The couple had eight children, of whom only Alfred and three brothers reached adulthood. Alfred was prone to illness as a child, but he enjoyed a close relationship with his mother and displayed a lively intellectual curiosity from an early age. He was interested in explosives, and he learned the fundamentals of engineering from his father. Immanuel, meanwhile, had failed at various business ventures until moving in 1837 to St. Petersburg in Russia, where he prospered as a manufacturer of explosive mines and machine tools. The Nobel family left Stockholm in 1842 to join the father in St. Petersburg. Alfred's newly prosperous parents were now able to send him to private tutors, and he proved to be an eager pupil. He was a competent chemist by age 16 and was fluent in English, French, German, and Russian, as well as Swedish.

Alfred Nobel left Russia in 1850 to spend a year in Paris studying chemistry and then spent four years in the United States working under the direction of John Ericsson, the builder of the ironclad warship *Monitor*. Upon his return to St. Petersburg, Nobel worked in his father's factory, which made military equipment during the Crimean War. After the war ended in 1856, the company had difficulty switching to the peacetime production of steamboat machinery, and it went bankrupt in 1859.

Alfred and his parents returned to Sweden, while his brothers Robert and Ludvig stayed behind in Russia to salvage what was left of the family business. Alfred soon began experimenting with explosives in a small laboratory on his father's estate. At the time, the only dependable explosive for use in mines was black powder, a form of gunpowder. A recently discovered liquid compound, nitroglycerin, was a much more powerful explosive, but it was so volatile that it could not be handled with any degree of safety. Nevertheless, Nobel in 1862 built a small factory to manufacture nitroglycerin, and at the same time he undertook research in the hope of finding a safe way to control the explosive's detonation. In 1863 he invented a practical detonator consisting of a wooden plug inserted into a larger charge of nitroglycerin held in a metal container; the explosion of the plug's small charge of black powder serves to detonate the much more powerful charge of liquid nitroglycerin. This detonator marked the beginning of Nobel's reputation as an inventor as well as the fortune he was to acquire as a maker of explosives. In 1865 Nobel invented an improved detonator called a blasting cap; it consisted of a small metal cap containing a charge of mercury fulminate that can be exploded by either shock or moderate heat. The invention of the blasting cap inaugurated the modern use of high explosives.

Nitroglycerin itself, however, remained difficult to transport and extremely dangerous to handle. So dangerous, in fact, that Nobel's nitroglycerin factory blew up in 1864, killing his younger brother Emil and several other people. Undaunted by this tragic accident, Nobel built several factories to manufacture nitroglycerin for use in concert with his blasting caps. These factories were as safe as the knowledge of the time allowed, but accidental explosions still occasionally occurred. Nobel's second important invention was that of dynamite in 1867. By chance, he discovered that nitroglycerin was absorbed to dryness by kieselguhr, a porous siliceous earth, and the resulting mixture was much safer to use and easier to handle than nitroglycerin alone. Nobel named the new product dynamite (from Greek *dynamis*, "power") and was granted patents for it in Great Britain (1867) and the United States (1868). Dynamite established Nobel's fame worldwide and was soon put to use in blasting tunnels, cutting canals, and building railways and roads.

In the 1870s and '80s Nobel built a network of factories throughout Europe to manufacture dynamite, and he formed a web of corporations to produce and market his explosives. He also continued to experiment in search of better ones, and in 1875 he invented a more powerful form of dynamite, blasting gelatin, which he patented the following year. Again by chance, he had discovered that mixing a solution of nitroglycerin with a fluffy substance known as nitrocellulose results in a tough, plastic material that has a high water resistance and greater blasting power than ordinary dynamites. In 1887 Nobel introduced ballistite, one of the first nitroglycerin smokeless powders and a precursor of cordite. Although Nobel held the patents to dynamite and his other explosives, he was in constant conflict with competitors who stole his processes, a fact that forced him into protracted patent litigation on several occasions.

Nobel's brothers Ludvig and Robert, in the meantime, had developed newly discovered oilfields near Baku (now in Azerbaijan) along the Caspian Sea and had themselves become immensely wealthy. Alfred's worldwide interests in explosives, along with his own holdings in his brothers' companies in Russia, brought him a large fortune. In 1893 he became interested in Sweden's arms industry, and the following year he bought an ironworks at Bofors, near Varmland, that became the nucleus of the well-known Bofors arms factory. Besides explosives, Nobel made many other inventions, such as artificial silk and leather, and altogether he registered more than 350 patents in various countries.

A Paradoxical Figure

Nobel's complex personality puzzled his contemporaries. Although his business interests required him to travel almost constantly, he remained a lonely recluse who was prone to fits of depression. He led a retired and simple life and was a man of ascetic habits, yet he could be a courteous dinner host, a good listener, and a man of incisive wit.

He never married, and apparently preferred the joys of inventing to those of romantic attachment. He had an abiding interest in literature and wrote plays, novels, and poems, almost all of which remained unpublished. He had amazing energy and found it difficult to relax after intense bouts of work. Among his contemporaries, he had the reputation of a liberal or even a socialist, but he actually distrusted democracy, opposed suffrage for women, and maintained an attitude of benign paternalism toward his many employees. Though Nobel was essentially a pacifist and hoped that the destructive powers of his inventions would help bring an end to war, his view of mankind and nations was pessimistic.

By 1895 Nobel had developed angina pectoris, and he died of a cerebral hemorrhage at his villa in San Remo, Italy, in 1896. At his death his worldwide business empire consisted of more than 90 factories manufacturing explosives and ammunition. The opening of his will, which he had drawn up in Paris on Nov. 27, 1895, and had deposited in a bank in Stockholm, contained a great surprise for his family, friends, and the general public. He had always been generous in humanitarian and scientific philanthropies, and he left the bulk of his fortune in trust to establish what came to be the most highly regarded of international awards, the Nobel Prizes.

We can only speculate about the reasons for Nobel's establishment of the prizes that bear his name. He was reticent about himself, and he confided in no one about his decision in the months preceding his death. The most plausible assumption is that a bizarre incident in 1888 may have triggered the train of reflection that culminated in his bequest for the Nobel Prizes. That year Alfred's brother Ludvig had died while staying in Cannes, France. The French newspapers reported Ludvig's death but confused him with Alfred, and one paper sported the headline "Le marchand de la mort est mort" ("The merchant of death is dead.") Perhaps Alfred Nobel established the prizes to avoid precisely the sort of posthumous reputation suggested by this premature obituary. It is certain that the actual awards he instituted reflect his lifelong interest in the fields of physics, chemistry, physiology, and literature. There is also abundant evidence that his friendship with the prominent Austrian pacifist Bertha von Suttner inspired him to establish the prize for peace.

Nobel himself, however, remains a figure of paradoxes and contradictions: a brilliant, lonely man, part pessimist and part idealist, who invented the powerful explosives used in modern warfare but also established the world's most prestigious prizes for intellectual services rendered to humanity.

JOHN WESLEY HYATT

(b. Nov. 28, 1837, Starkey, N.Y., U.S.—d. May 10, 1920, Short Hills, N.J.)

John Wesley Hyatt, an American inventor and industrialist, discovered the process for making celluloid, the first practical artificial plastic.

As a young man, Hyatt trained as a printer in Illinois and then in Albany, N.Y. In 1863 he was attracted by a reward of $10,000 offered by a New York billiards company to anyone who could invent a satisfactory substitute for ivory billiard balls. Hyatt experimented with several compositions, none of which produced a successful billiard ball, but he was able to go into business with his brothers making one of the mixtures—a composite of wood pulp and shellac—into embossed checkers and dominoes. Continuing his experiments, Hyatt found that an attractive and practical plastic material could be made by mixing nitrocellulose (a flammable nitrate of common wood or cotton cellulose), camphor (a waxy resin obtained from Asian camphor trees), and alcohol and then pressing the mixture in a heated mold. The solid solution was kneaded into a doughlike mass to which colouring agents could be added either in the form of dyes for transparent colours or as pigments for opaque colours. The coloured mass was rolled, sheeted, and then pressed into blocks. After seasoning, the blocks were sliced; at this point they could be further fabricated, or the sheeting and pressing process could be repeated for various mottled and variegated effects. The plastic, which softened at the temperature of boiling water, could be heated and then pressed into innumerable shapes, and at room temperature it could be sawed, drilled, turned, planed, buffed, and polished.

Hyatt and his brother Isaiah first attempted to market the plastic, which they patented in 1870 as celluloid, as a substitute for hard rubber in denture plates. In 1872 they moved their Celluloid Manufacturing Company from Albany to Newark, N.J., where they put numerous patents to work in building up what became the premier celluloid company in the world. The Hyatts concentrated on forming celluloid into sheets, rods, and other unfinished shapes, usually leaving their fabrication into practical objects to licensed companies such as the Celluloid Brush Company, the Celluloid Waterproof Cuff and Collar Company, and the Celluloid Piano Key Company.

A tough, flexible, and moldable material, resistant to water, oils, and dilute acids, and capable of low-cost production in a variety of colours, celluloid was made into many other mass-produced goods. In all of these applications celluloid was marketed as an affordable and practical substitute for natural materials such as ivory, tortoise shell, and horn. Beginning in the 1880s celluloid acquired one of its most prominent uses as a substitute for linen in detachable collars and cuffs for men's clothing. Over the years a number of competing plastics were introduced under such fanciful names as Coralline, Ivoride, and Pyralin, and celluloid became a generic term. In 1882 John H. Stevens, a chemist at the Hyatts' company, discovered that amyl acetate was a suitable solvent for diluting celluloid. This allowed the material to be made into clear, flexible film, which other researchers such as Henry Reichenbach of the Eastman Kodak Company further processed into film for still photography and, later, motion pictures. Despite its flammability and tendency to discolour with age, celluloid was virtually unchallenged as the medium for motion pictures until the 1930s, when it began to be replaced by cellulose acetate "safety film." Other disadvantages of celluloid were its tendency to soften under heat and its unsuitability for new, efficient fabrication processes such as injection molding. In the 1920s and '30s celluloid began to be replaced in most of its applications by more versatile materials such as cellulose acetate, Bakelite, and the new vinyl polymers.

In the 1880s the Hyatts set up a company that employed a patented process for purifying water through the use of coagulants and filters. John Hyatt went on to invent a number of new or improved industrial devices, including roller bearings, sugarcane mills, and sewing machines.

FERDINAND VON ZEPPELIN

(b. July 8, 1838, Konstanz, Baden [now in Ger.]—d. March 8, 1917, Charlottenburg, near Berlin)

Ferdinand Adolf August Heinrich, Graf (count) von Zeppelin, was the first notable builder of rigid dirigible airships, for which his surname is still a popular generic term.

Zeppelin received a military commission in 1858. He made the first of several balloon ascensions at St. Paul,

Minn., while acting as a military observer (1863) for the Union Army during the American Civil War. He saw military action in 1866 during the Seven Weeks' War and in 1870–71 during the Franco-German War, serving successively in the armies of Württemberg, Prussia, and imperial Germany. He retired in 1890 and devoted the rest of his life to the creation of the rigid airship for which he is known.

Zeppelin struggled for 10 years to produce his lighter-than-air craft. In previous experimentation on dirigibles, hydrogen and illuminating gas were substituted for hot air to provide buoyancy, and a motor was mounted on a gas bag fitted with propellers and rudders. Small steam engines were tried, but as progress took place first electric motors

The airship Schwaben *landing at Potsdam, Ger., September 1911.* Encyclopædia Britannica, Inc.

and, in Germany after 1888, gasoline engines were used. The problem remained how to maintain the shape of the gas bags. Fully filled with gas under the right pressure, a cigar shape could be maintained and steered; but a partially deflated bag was almost impossible to direct. It was Zeppelin who first saw clearly that maintaining a steerable shape was essential, so he created a rigid but very light trussed and covered frame supported by internal gas cells. This solved many of the steering problems, but how to give the frame sufficient strength to deal with torque introduced by air currents in storms continued to be a severe challenge.

The initial flight (July 2, 1900) of the LZ-1 (for Luftschiff Zeppelin) from a floating hangar on Lake Constance, near Friedrichshafen, Ger., was not entirely successful. The LZ-1 flew for 17 minutes before sinking to the surface of the lake and impaling itself on a buoy that punctured the gas bag. Nevertheless, it had the effect of promoting the airship to the degree that public subscriptions and donations thereafter funded the count's work. After years of cautious changes in design Zeppelin was ready in 1908 with the LZ-4, 446 feet (134 metres) long and carrying more than half a million cubic feet (14,000 cubic metres) of hydrogen. On July 1 he achieved 12 hours of sustained flight at a speed of 40 miles (65 km) per hour over central Switzerland.

With the LZ-5, the dirigible became a potentially practical air transport. A passenger service known as Delag (Deutsche-Luftschiffahrts AG) was established in 1910, becoming the first well-financed air transportation company. In the five-year period up to the outbreak of World War I Delag made 1,588 flights, safely carrying 34,228 passengers, covering a total of some 170,000 miles (270,000 km). During the war 88 zeppelins (as they came to be known) were constructed for military purposes, among which was the introduction of the first sustained distant aerial warfare, which included the bombing of London and a flight from Yambol, Bulg., of 2,800 miles (4,500 km) toward German East Africa.

Zeppelin died before attaining his goal of transcontinental flight. However, when Germany was permitted to return to civilian flying in the mid-1920s, the Luftschiffsbau-Zeppelin (Zeppelin Company) began planning a transatlantic passenger voyage. In 1928 the company completed a new airship, the *Graf Zeppelin*, which inaugurated transatlantic flight service. By the time of its decommissioning in 1937 the *Graf Zeppelin* had made 590 flights, including 144 ocean crossings, and had flown more than 1 million miles (1.6 million km). In 1929 the craft covered about 21,500 miles (34,600 km) in a round-the-world flight that was completed in 21 days, 5 hours, and 54 minutes (of which only 47 hours had been spent on the ground), yielding an average speed of some 70 miles (112 km) per hour. On July 2, 1996, the 96th anniversary of the inaugural flight of the LZ-1, the Zeppelin Museum Friedrichshafen was opened in a restored railway station on the shore of Lake Constance.

GEORGES LECLANCHÉ

(b. 1839, Paris, France—d. Sept. 14, 1882, Paris)

Georges Leclanché was a French engineer who in about 1866 invented the battery that bears his name. In slightly modified form, the Leclanché cell is produced in great quantities and is widely used in devices such as flashlights and portable radios.

After completing a technical education in 1860, Leclanché began work as an engineer. Six years later he developed his battery, which contained a conducting solution (electrolyte) of ammonium chloride, a negative

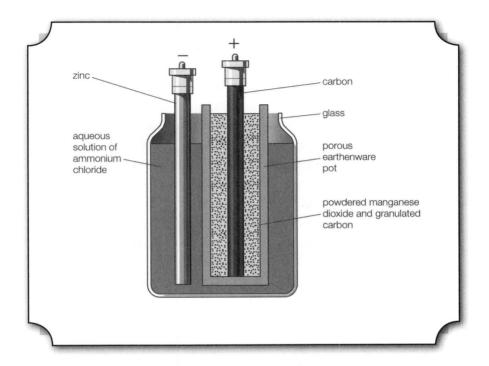

Georges Leclanché's cell. Invented in 1866, this dry cell and its later variations, the zinc chloride and alkaline cells, are batteries commonly used throughout the world. Encyclopædia Britannica, Inc.

terminal of zinc, and a positive terminal of manganese dioxide. The Leclanché cell immediately became a commercial success in large sizes because of its readily available low-cost constituent materials.

The original version of the Leclanché cell was actually "wet," as it had an electrolyte consisting of a solution of ammonium chloride. The idea of employing an immobilized electrolyte was finally introduced in the late 1880s and launched the dry-cell industry that continues to flourish today. The Leclanché cell remains the least expensive dry cell and is available nearly everywhere. The anode (negative terminal) of this battery is a zinc alloy sheet or "can," the alloy containing small amounts of lead, cadmium, and mercury. The electrolyte consists of a saturated aqueous solution of ammonium chloride containing roughly 20 percent zinc chloride. The cathode (positive terminal) is made of impure manganese dioxide. This compound is blended with carbon black and electrolyte to create a damp, active cathode mixture which is formed around a carbon collector rod, also called an electrode. All batteries of this type are provided with an overwrap structure with metal covers for electrical contact.

In 1867 Leclanché gave up his job to devote full time to his invention; a year later it was adopted by the telegraph service of Belgium. He subsequently opened a factory to produce the battery and other electric devices; the business was taken over by his brother Maurice upon Georges's death in 1882.

HIRAM MAXIM

(b. Feb. 5, 1840, Sangerville, Maine, U.S.—d. Nov. 24, 1916, London, Eng.)

Hiram Stevens Maxim was a prolific inventor best known for the Maxim machine gun.

The eldest son of a farmer who was a locally notable mechanic, Maxim was apprenticed at 14 to a carriage maker. Exhibiting an early genius for invention, he obtained his first patent in 1866, for a hair-curling iron. His iron was followed by a device for generating illuminating gas and a locomotive headlight; in 1878 he was hired as chief engineer of the United States Electric Lighting Company, the first such company in the United States. In that post he produced a basic invention, a method of manufacturing carbon filaments. In 1881 he exhibited an electric pressure regulator at the Paris Exposition.

Maxim's interest in the problem of automatic weapons led him to settle in London. In 1884 he produced the first satisfactory fully automatic machine gun, employing the recoil energy of the bullet to unlock the breechblock from the barrel, extract and eject the fired case from the gun, and store sufficient energy in a main spring to push the bolt forward, pick up a fresh round, load the chamber, and lock the piece. Both barrel and breechblock, locked together, recoiled a short distance to the rear; then the barrel was stopped and the block continued back alone. If the trigger was held in firing position, the weapon would continue to fire until it expended all of its ammunition. Rounds were fed to the gun on belts, which could be

German infantrymen operating a Maxim machine gun during World War I. Imperial War Museum

clipped together to provide continuous fire, and overheating was solved by surrounding the barrel in a metal jacket in which water was circulated from a separate container. To improve the efficiency of his gun, Maxim developed his own smokeless powder, cordite.

Maxim's salesmen provided armies with guns in any calibre, usually matching their current rifle cartridge, and within a few years every army was equipped with Maxim guns or adaptations. The light weight of the guns, made possible because the cartridge was the sole source of power, allowed them to be operated by special infantry units. In warfare, machine guns of the Maxim type had a destructive power never seen before. In the 1890s, British infantry units used Maxim guns, fabricated under contract by Vickers Sons, to cut down hordes of poorly armed rebels in Africa and Afghanistan. In World War I, a few of them could cause thousands of casualties. Their defensive fire so limited the offensive power of infantry that the entire Western Front, from the Swiss border to the English Channel, became one vast siege operation.

In the 1890s Maxim experimented with airplanes, producing one powered by a light steam engine that successfully rose from the ground; he recognized that the real solution to flight was the internal-combustion engine but did not attempt to develop it. His hundreds of patents in the United States and Great Britain included a mousetrap, an automatic sprinkling system, an automatic steam-powered water pump, vacuum pumps, engine governors, and gas motors.

His Maxim Gun Company, founded in 1884, was later absorbed into Vickers, Ltd., of which he became a director. In 1900 he became a naturalized British subject, and in 1901 he was knighted by Queen Victoria.

JOHN P. HOLLAND

(b. Feb. 29, 1840, Liscannor, County Clare, Ire.—d. Aug. 12, 1914, Newark, N.J., U.S.)

John Philip Holland designed and built the first underwater vessel accepted by the U.S. Navy. He is considered to be the father of the modern submarine.

Educated at Limerick, Holland taught school until 1872 in Ireland and in 1873 emigrated to the United States. Settling in Paterson, N.J., he taught there until 1879, when, with financial support from the Irish Fenian Society (who hoped to use submarines against Britain), he built the *Fenian Ram*, a small sub that proved a limited success in a test run. Holland's early submarines were significant in combining water ballast with horizontal rudders for diving. In 1895 his J.P. Holland Torpedo Boat Company received a contract from the U.S. Navy to build a submarine. This was to be the *Plunger*, propelled by steam on the surface and by electricity when submerged. The craft underwent many design changes and finally was abandoned before completion. Holland returned the funds advanced by the navy and built his next submarine (his sixth) at his own expense. This was the *Holland*, a 53-foot (16-metre) craft launched in 1897 and accepted by the navy in 1900. For underwater propulsion the *Holland* had an electric motor, and it was propelled on the surface by a gasoline engine. The *Holland* had a surface speed of 7 knots (nautical miles per hour; 13 km per hour). The submarine's armament consisted of a bow torpedo tube, for which three torpedoes were carried, and two dynamite guns. With its nine-man crew the *Holland* was a successful boat; it was modified many times to test different arrangements of propellers, diving planes, rudders, and other equipment. The U.S. government ordered six more; similar orders came from Britain, Japan, and Russia.

Holland's final years were marked by litigation with his financial backers. One of his last inventions was an apparatus designed to enable sailors to escape from damaged submarines.

KARL BENZ AND GOTTLIEB DAIMLER

Most authorities are inclined to honour Karl Benz and Gottlieb Daimler of Germany as the most important pioneer contributors to the gasoline-engine automobile. Benz ran his first car in 1885, Daimler in 1886. Although there is no reason to believe that Benz had ever seen a motor vehicle before he made his own, he and Daimler had been preceded by Étienne Lenoir in France and Siegfried Marcus in Austria, in 1862 and 1864–65, respectively, but neither Lenoir nor Marcus had persisted. Benz and Daimler did persist—indeed, to such purpose that their successor firm of Daimler AG can trace its origins back to the 1890s and claim, with the Peugeot SA firm of France, to be one of the oldest automobile-manufacturing firms in the world. Oddly, Benz and Daimler never met.

KARL BENZ

(b. Nov. 25, 1844, Karlsruhe, Baden [now in Ger.]—d. April 4, 1929, Ladenburg, near Mannheim, Ger.)

Karl Friedrich Benz was a mechanical engineer who designed and built the world's first practical automobile to be powered by an internal-combustion engine. In 1883 he founded Benz & Co. in Mannheim to build stationary internal-combustion engines, but he was completely dedicated to the proposition that the internal-combustion engine would supersede the horse and revolutionize the world's transportation. He persisted in his efforts to build a gasoline-fueled vehicle in the face of many obstacles, including lack of money to the point of poverty and the bitter objections of his associates, who considered him unbalanced on the subject.

Benz ran his first car, a three-wheeler powered by a two-cycle, one-cylinder engine, on a happy and triumphant day early in 1885. He circled a cinder track beside his small factory, his workmen running beside the car, his wife running too, clapping her hands; the little machine made four circuits of the track, stalling only twice before a broken chain stopped it. Even Max Rose, Benz's skeptical partner, whose money had made the car possible, conceded that he was mildly impressed; but he remained convinced to the end of his association with Benz that there was no future in the horseless carriage. The original Benz three-wheeled vehicle, the *Motorwagen*, is now preserved in Munich. Although it first ran early in 1885, its design was not patented until Jan. 29, 1886.

In his way, Benz was dogmatic and reactionary; he objected to redesign of his original cars, and some authorities believe that he was never really convinced that his original concepts had been improved upon. Gradually, however, the soundness of his design and the quality and care that went into the material and the construction of his cars bore weight, and they sold well. He made his first sale to a Parisian named Émile Roger in 1888. That year he was employing some 50 workmen to build the tricycle car. The company completed its first four-wheeled automobile in 1893 and produced the first of a series of racing cars in 1899. In 1926 the Benz company merged with Daimler-Motoren-Gesellschaft to form Daimler-Benz, maker of Mercedes-Benz automobiles. Benz had left the firm about 1906 to organize C. Benz Söhne, Ladenburg, with his sons, Eugen and Richard.

GOTTLIEB DAIMLER

(b. March 17, 1834, Schorndorf, Württemberg [now in Ger.] — d. March 6, 1900, Cannstatt, near Stuttgart)

Mechanical engineer Gottlieb Wilhelm Daimler became a major figure in the early history of the automotive industry. Gunsmithing was his first vocation, and he showed marked talent, but he abandoned the trade to go to engineering school, studying in Germany, England, and France. In Germany he worked for various engineering and machining concerns, including the Karlsruhe Maschinenbaugesellschaft, a firm that much earlier had employed Benz.

In 1872 Daimler became technical director in the firm of Nikolaus A. Otto, the man who had invented the four-stroke internal-combustion engine. Otto's firm was then building stationary gasoline engines. During the next decade, important work was done on the four-stroke engine. Daimler brought in several brilliant researchers, among them Wilhelm Maybach, but in 1882 both Daimler and Maybach resigned because of Daimler's conviction that Otto did not understand the

Gottlieb Daimler. Encyclopædia Britannica, Inc.

potential of the internal-combustion engine. They set up a shop in Bad Cannstatt and built an air-cooled, one-cylinder engine in 1885. The first high-speed internal-combustion engine, it was designed to run at 900 revolutions per minute (rpm). For comparison, Benz's first tricycle engine had operated at only 250 rpm. Daimler and Maybach used one of their early gasoline engines on a wooden bicycle fitted with an outrigger, which first ran on Nov. 10, 1885. This may have been the first motorcycle in the world. The next year the first Daimler four-wheeled road vehicle was made: a horse-drawn carriage modified to be driven by a one-cylinder engine.

Daimler appears to have believed that the first phase of the automobile era would be a mass conversion of carriages to engine drive; Benz apparently thought of the motorcar as a separate device. Nevertheless, Daimler and Maybach's 1889 car was a departure from previous practice. Designed from the start as an automobile and not a carriage, it was based on a framework of light tubing; it had the engine in the rear; its wheels were driven by a belt; and it was steered by a tiller. Remarkably, it had four speeds. This car had obvious commercial value, and in the following year the Daimler Motoren-Gesellschaft was founded. The British Daimler automobile was started as a manufactory licensed by the German company but later became quite independent of it. (To distinguish machines made by the two firms in the early years, the German cars are usually referred to as Cannstatt-Daimlers.) In 1899 the firm built the first Mercedes car. The Daimler and Benz firms were merged in 1926, and products thereafter have been sold under the name Mercedes-Benz. This practice continued even during the 1998–2007 merger with the American firm Chrysler Corporation to form DaimlerChrysler AG.

WILHELM CONRAD RÖNTGEN

(b. March 27, 1845, Lennep, Prussia [now Remscheid, Ger.]—d. Feb. 10, 1923, Munich, Ger.)

Wilhelm Conrad Röntgen was a German physicist who was a recipient of the first Nobel Prize for Physics, in 1901, for his discovery of X-rays, which heralded the age of modern physics and revolutionized diagnostic medicine.

Röntgen studied at the Polytechnic in Zürich and then was professor of physics at the universities of Strasbourg (1876–79), Giessen (1879–88), Würzburg (1888–1900), and Munich (1900–20). His research also included work on elasticity, capillary action of fluids, specific heats of gases, conduction of heat in crystals, absorption of heat by gases, and piezoelectricity.

In 1895, while experimenting with electric current flow in a partially evacuated glass tube (cathode-ray tube), Röntgen observed that a nearby piece of barium platinocyanide gave off light when the tube was in operation. He theorized that when the cathode rays (electrons) struck the glass wall of the tube, some unknown radiation was formed that traveled across the room, struck the chemical, and caused the fluorescence. Further investigation revealed that paper, wood, and aluminum, among other materials, are transparent to this new form of radiation. He found that it affected photographic plates, and, since it did not noticeably exhibit any properties of light, such as reflection or refraction, he mistakenly thought the rays were unrelated to light. In view of its uncertain nature, he called the phenomenon X-radiation, though it also became known as Röntgen radiation. He took the first X-ray photographs, of the interiors of metal objects and of the bones in his wife's hand.

Röntgen's discovery of X-rays was met with worldwide scientific and popular excitement. Within months of the discovery there was extensive literature on the subject: a British surgeon had localized a bullet in a boy's wrist before operating; stones in the urinary bladder and gallbladder had been demonstrated; and fractures had been displayed. Along with the discoveries of radioactivity (1896) and the electron (1897), the discovery of X-rays ushered in the study of the atomic world and the era of modern physics.

THOMAS EDISON

Thomas Alva Edison demonstrating his tinfoil phonograph, photograph by Mathew Brady, 1878. Courtesy of the Edison National Historical Site, West Orange, N.J.

(b. Feb. 11, 1847, Milan, Ohio, U.S.—d. Oct. 18, 1931, West Orange, N.J.)

Thomas Alva Edison was an American inventor who, singly or jointly, held a world record 1,093 U.S. patents. In addition, he created the world's first industrial research laboratory.

Edison was the quintessential American inventor in the era of Yankee ingenuity. He began his career in 1863, in the adolescence of the telegraph industry, when virtually the only source of electricity was primitive batteries putting out a low-voltage current.

Before he died, in 1931, he had played a critical role in introducing the modern age of electricity. From his laboratories and workshops emanated the phonograph, the carbon-button transmitter for the telephone speaker and microphone, the incandescent lamp, a revolutionary generator of unprecedented efficiency, the first commercial electric light and power system, an experimental electric railroad, and key elements of motion-picture apparatus, as well as a host of other inventions.

Early Years

Edison was the seventh and last child—the fourth surviving—of Samuel Edison, Jr., and Nancy Elliot Edison. At an early age he developed hearing problems, which have been variously attributed but were most likely due to a familial tendency to mastoiditis. Whatever the cause, Edison's deafness strongly influenced his behaviour and career, providing the motivation for many of his inventions.

In 1854 Samuel Edison became the lighthouse keeper and carpenter on the Fort Gratiot military post near Port Huron, Mich., where the family lived in a substantial home. Alva, as the inventor was known until his second marriage, entered school there and attended sporadically for five years. He was imaginative and inquisitive, but because much instruction was by rote and he had difficulty hearing, he was bored and was labeled a misfit. To compensate, he became an avid and omnivorous reader. Edison's lack of formal schooling was not unusual. At the time of the Civil War the average American had attended school a total of 434 days—little more than two years' schooling by today's standards.

In 1859 Edison quit school and began working as a trainboy on the railroad between Detroit and Port Huron. Four years earlier, the Michigan Central had initiated the commercial application of the telegraph by using it to control the movement of its trains, and the Civil War brought a vast expansion of transportation and communication. Edison took advantage of the opportunity to learn telegraphy and in 1863 became an apprentice telegrapher.

Messages received on the initial Morse telegraph were inscribed as a series of dots and dashes on a strip of paper that was decoded and read, so Edison's partial deafness was no handicap. Receivers were increasingly being equipped with a sounding key, however, enabling telegraphers to "read" messages by the clicks. The transformation of telegraphy to an auditory art left Edison more and more disadvantaged during his six-year career as an itinerant telegrapher in the Midwest, the South, Canada, and New England. Amply supplied with ingenuity and insight, he devoted much of his energy toward improving the inchoate equipment and inventing devices to facilitate some of the tasks that his physical limitations made difficult. By January 1869 he had made enough progress with a duplex telegraph (a device capable of transmitting two messages simultaneously on one wire) and a printer, which converted electrical signals to letters, that he abandoned telegraphy for full-time invention and entrepreneurship.

Edison moved to New York City, where he initially went into partnership with Frank L. Pope, a noted electrical expert, to produce the Edison Universal Stock Printer and other printing telegraphs. Between 1870 and 1875 he worked out of Newark, N.J., and was involved in a variety of partnerships and complex transactions in the fiercely competitive and convoluted telegraph industry, which was dominated by the Western Union Telegraph Company. As an independent entrepreneur he was available to the highest bidder and played both sides against the middle. During this period he worked on improving an automatic telegraph system for Western Union's rivals.

The automatic telegraph, which recorded messages by means of a chemical reaction engendered by the electrical transmissions, proved of limited commercial success, but the work advanced Edison's knowledge of chemistry and laid the basis for his development of the electric pen and mimeograph, both important devices in the early office machine industry, and indirectly led to the discovery of the phonograph. Under the aegis of Western Union he devised the quadruplex, capable of transmitting four messages simultaneously over one wire, but railroad baron and Wall Street financier Jay Gould, Western Union's bitter rival, snatched the quadruplex from the telegraph company's grasp in December 1874 by paying Edison more than $100,000 in cash, bonds, and stock, one of the larger payments for any invention up to that time. Years of litigation followed.

MENLO PARK

Although Edison was a sharp bargainer, he was a poor financial manager, often spending and giving away money more rapidly than he earned it. In 1871 he married 16-year-old Mary Stilwell, who was as improvident in household matters as he was in business, and before the end of 1875 they were in financial difficulties. To reduce his costs and the temptation to spend money, Edison brought his now-widowed father from Port Huron to build a 2 1/2-story laboratory and machine shop in the rural environs of Menlo Park, N.J.—12 miles south of Newark—where he moved in March 1876. Accompanying him were two key associates, Charles Batchelor and John Kruesi. Batchelor, born in Manchester in 1845, was a master mechanic and draftsman who complemented Edison perfectly and served as his "ears" on such projects as the phonograph and telephone. He was also responsible for fashioning the drawings that Kruesi, a Swiss-born machinist, translated into models.

Edison experienced his finest hours at Menlo Park. While experimenting on an underwater cable for the automatic telegraph, he found that the electrical resistance and conductivity of carbon (then called plumbago) varied according to the pressure it was under. This was a major theoretical discovery, which enabled Edison to devise a "pressure relay" using carbon rather than the usual magnets to vary and balance electric currents. In February 1877 Edison began experiments designed to produce a pressure relay that would amplify and improve the audibility of the telephone, a device that Edison and others had studied but which Alexander Graham Bell was the first to patent, in 1876. By the end of 1877 Edison had developed the carbon-button transmitter that is still used in telephone speakers and microphones.

THE PHONOGRAPH

Edison invented many items, including the carbon transmitter, in response to specific demands for new products or improvements. But he also had the gift of serendipity: when some unexpected phenomenon was observed, he did not hesitate to halt work in progress and turn off course in a new direction. This was how, in 1877, he achieved his most original discovery, the phonograph. Because the telephone was considered a variation of acoustic telegraphy, Edison during the summer of 1877 was attempting to devise for it, as he had for the automatic telegraph, a machine that would transcribe signals as they were received, in this instance in the form of the human voice, so that they could then be delivered as telegraph messages. (The telephone was not yet conceived as a general, person-to-person means of communication.) Some earlier researchers, notably the French inventor

Léon Scott, had theorized that each sound, if it could be graphically recorded, would produce a distinct shape resembling shorthand, or phonography ("sound writing"), as it was then known. Edison hoped to reify this concept by employing a stylus-tipped carbon transmitter to make impressions on a strip of paraffined paper. To his astonishment, the scarcely visible indentations generated a vague reproduction of sound when the paper was pulled back beneath the stylus.

Edison unveiled the tinfoil phonograph, which replaced the strip of paper with a cylinder wrapped in tinfoil, in December 1877. It was greeted with incredulity. Indeed, a leading French scientist declared it to be the trick device of a clever ventriloquist. The public's amazement was quickly followed by universal acclaim. Edison was projected into worldwide prominence and was dubbed the Wizard of Menlo Park, although a decade passed before the phonograph was transformed from a laboratory curiosity into a commercial product.

THE ELECTRIC LIGHT

Another offshoot of the carbon experiments reached fruition sooner. Samuel Langley, Henry Draper, and other American scientists needed a highly sensitive instrument that could be used to measure minute temperature changes in heat emitted from the Sun's corona during a solar eclipse along the Rocky Mountains on July 29, 1878. To satisfy those needs Edison devised a "microtasimeter" employing a carbon button. This was a time when great advances were being made in electric arc lighting, and during the expedition, which Edison accompanied, the men discussed the practicality of "subdividing" the intense arc lights so that electricity could be used for lighting in the same fashion as with small, individual gas "burners." The basic problem seemed to be to keep the burner, or bulb, from being consumed by preventing it from overheating. Edison thought he would be able to solve this by fashioning a microtasimeter-like device to control the current. He boldly announced that he would invent a safe, mild, and inexpensive electric light that would replace the gaslight.

The incandescent electric light had been the despair of inventors for 50 years, but Edison's past achievements commanded respect for his boastful prophecy. Thus, a syndicate of leading financiers, including J.P. Morgan and the Vanderbilts, established the Edison Electric Light Company and advanced him $30,000 for research and development. Edison proposed to connect his lights in a parallel circuit by subdividing the current, so that, unlike arc lights, which were connected in a series circuit, the failure of one light bulb would not cause a whole circuit to fail. Some eminent scientists predicted that such a circuit could never be feasible, but their findings were based on systems of lamps with low resistance—the only successful type of electric light at the time. Edison, however, determined that a bulb with high resistance would serve his purpose, and he began searching for a suitable one.

He had the assistance of 26-year-old Francis Upton, a graduate of Princeton University with an M.A. in science. Upton, who joined the laboratory force in December 1878, provided the mathematical and theoretical expertise that Edison himself lacked. (Edison later revealed, "At the time I experimented on the incandescent lamp I did not understand Ohm's law." On another occasion he said, "I do not depend on figures at all. I try an experiment and reason out the result, somehow, by methods which I could not explain.")

By the summer of 1879 Edison and Upton had made enough progress on a generator—which, by reverse action, could be employed as a motor—that Edison, beset by failed incandescent lamp experiments, considered offering a system of electric distribution for power, not light. By October Edison and his staff had achieved encouraging results with a complex, regulator-controlled vacuum bulb with a platinum filament, but the cost of the platinum would have made the incandescent light impractical. While experimenting with an insulator for the platinum wire, they discovered that, in the greatly improved vacuum they were now obtaining through advances made in the vacuum pump, carbon could be maintained for some time without elaborate regulatory apparatus. Advancing on the work of Joseph Wilson Swan, an English physicist, Edison found that a carbon filament provided a good light with the concomitant high resistance required for subdivision. Steady progress ensued from the first breakthrough in mid-October until the initial demonstration for the backers of the Edison Electric Light Company on December 3.

It was, nevertheless, not until the summer of 1880 that Edison determined that carbonized bamboo fibre made a satisfactory material for the filament, although the world's first operative lighting system had been installed on the steamship *Columbia* in April. The first commercial land-based "isolated" (single-building) incandescent system was placed in the New York printing firm of Hinds and Ketcham in January 1881. In the fall a temporary, demonstration central power system was installed at the Holborn Viaduct in London, in conjunction with an exhibition at the Crystal Palace. Edison himself supervised the laying of the mains and installation of the world's first permanent, commercial central power system in lower Manhattan, which became operative in September 1882. Although the early systems were plagued by problems and many years passed before incandescent lighting powered by electricity from central stations made significant inroads into gas lighting, isolated lighting plants for such enterprises as hotels, theatres, and stores flourished—as did Edison's reputation as the world's greatest inventor.

One of the accidental discoveries made in the Menlo Park laboratory during the development of the incandescent light anticipated the British physicist J.J. Thomson's discovery of the electron 15 years later. In 1881–82 William J. Hammer, a young engineer in charge of testing the light globes, noted a blue glow around the positive pole in a vacuum bulb and a blackening of the wire and the bulb at the negative pole. This phenomenon was first called "Hammer's phantom shadow," but when Edison patented the bulb in 1883 it became known as the "Edison effect." Scientists later determined that this effect was explained by the thermionic emission of electrons from the hot to the cold electrode, and it became the basis of the electron tube and laid the foundation for the electronics industry.

Edison had moved his operations from Menlo Park to New York City when work commenced on the Manhattan power system. Increasingly, the Menlo Park property was used only as a summer home. In August 1884 Edison's wife, Mary, suffering from deteriorating health and subject to periods of mental derangement, died there of "congestion of the brain," apparently a tumour or hemorrhage. Her death and the move from Menlo Park roughly mark the halfway point of Edison's life.

THE EDISON LABORATORY

A widower with three young children, Edison, on Feb. 24, 1886, married 20-year-old Mina Miller, the daughter of a prosperous Ohio manufacturer. He purchased a hilltop estate in West Orange, N.J., for his new bride and constructed nearby a grand, new laboratory, which he intended to be the world's first true research facility. There, he produced the commercial phonograph, founded the motion-picture industry, and developed the alkaline storage battery. Nevertheless, Edison was past the peak of his productive period. A poor manager and organizer, he worked best in intimate, relatively unstructured surroundings with a handful of close associates and assistants; the West Orange laboratory was too sprawling and diversified for his talents. Furthermore, as a significant portion of the inventor's time was taken up by his new role of industrialist, which came with the commercialization of incandescent lighting and the phonograph, electrical developments were passing into the domain of university-trained mathematicians and scientists. Above all, for more than a decade Edison's energy was focused on a magnetic ore-mining venture that proved the unquestioned disaster of his career.

The first major endeavour at the new laboratory was the commercialization of the phonograph, a venture launched in 1887 after Alexander Graham Bell, his cousin Chichester, and Charles Tainter had developed the graphophone—an improved version of Edison's original device—which used waxed cardboard instead of tinfoil. Two years later, Edison announced that he had "perfected" the phonograph, although this was far from true. In fact, it was not until the late 1890s, after Edison had established production and recording facilities adjacent to the laboratory, that all the mechanical problems were overcome and the phonograph became a profitable proposition.

In the meantime, Edison conceived the idea of popularizing the phonograph by linking to it in synchronization a zoetrope, a device that gave the illusion of motion to photographs shot in sequence. He assigned the project to

William K.L. Dickson, an employee interested in photography, in 1888. After studying the work of various European photographers who also were trying to record motion, Edison and Dickson succeeded in constructing a working camera and a viewing instrument, which were called, respectively, the Kinetograph and the Kinetoscope. Synchronizing sound and motion proved of such insuperable difficulty, however, that the concept of linking the two was abandoned, and the silent movie was born. Edison constructed at the laboratory the world's first motion-picture stage, nicknamed the "Black Maria," in 1893, and the following year Kinetoscopes, which had peepholes that allowed one person at a time to view the moving pictures, were introduced with great success. Rival inventors soon developed screen-projection systems that hurt the Kinetoscope's business, however, so Edison acquired a projector developed by Thomas Armat and introduced it as "Edison's latest marvel, the Vitascope."

Another derivative of the phonograph was the alkaline storage battery, which Edison began developing as a power source for the phonograph at a time when most homes still lacked electricity. Although it was 20 years before all the difficulties with the battery were solved, by 1909 Edison was a principal supplier of batteries for submarines and electric vehicles and had even formed a company for the manufacture of electric automobiles. In 1912 Henry Ford, one of Edison's greatest admirers, asked him to design a battery for the self-starter, to be introduced on the Model T. Ford's request led to a continuing relationship between these two Americans, and in October 1929 he staged a 50th-anniversary celebration of the incandescent light that turned into a universal apotheosis for Edison.

Most of Edison's successes involved electricity or communication, but throughout the late 1880s and early

1890s the Edison Laboratory's top priority was the magnetic ore-separator. Edison had first worked on the separator when he was searching for platinum for use in the experimental incandescent lamp. The device was supposed to cull platinum from iron-bearing sand. During the 1880s iron ore prices rose to unprecedented heights, so that it appeared that, if the separator could extract the iron from unusable low-grade ores, then abandoned mines might profitably be placed back in production. Edison purchased or acquired rights to 145 old mines in the east and established a large pilot plant at the Ogden mine, near Ogdensburg, N.J. He was never able to surmount the engineering problems or work the bugs out of the system, however, and when ore prices plummeted in the mid-1890s he gave up on the idea. By then he had liquidated all but a small part of his holdings in the General Electric Company, sometimes at very low prices, and had become more and more separated from the electric lighting field.

Failure could not discourage Edison's passion for invention, however. Although none of his later projects were as successful as his earlier ones, he continued to work even in his 80s.

ASSESSMENT

The thrust of Edison's work may be seen in the clustering of his patents: 389 for electric light and power, 195 for the phonograph, 150 for the telegraph, 141 for storage batteries, and 34 for the telephone. His life and achievements epitomize the ideal of applied research. He always invented for necessity, with the object of devising something new that he could manufacture. The basic principles he discovered were derived from practical experiments, invariably by chance, thus reversing the orthodox concept of pure research leading to applied research.

Edison's role as a machine shop operator and small manufacturer was crucial to his success as an inventor. Unlike other scientists and inventors of the time, who had limited means and lacked a support organization, Edison ran an inventive establishment. He was the antithesis of the lone inventive genius, although his deafness enforced on him an isolation conducive to conception. His lack of managerial ability was, in an odd way, also a stimulant. As his own boss, he plunged ahead on projects more prudent men would have shunned, then tended to dissipate the fruits of his inventiveness, so that he was both free and forced to develop new ideas. Few men have matched him in the positiveness of his thinking. Edison never questioned whether something might be done, only how.

Edison's career, the fulfillment of the American dream of rags-to-riches through hard work and intelligence, made him a folk hero to his countrymen. In temperament he was an uninhibited egotist, at once a tyrant to his employees and their most entertaining companion, so that there was never a dull moment with him. He was charismatic and courted publicity, but he had difficulty socializing and neglected his family. His shafts at the expense of the "long-haired" fraternity of theorists sometimes led formally trained scientists to deprecate him as anti-intellectual; yet he employed as his aides, at various times, a number of eminent mathematical physicists, such as Nikola Tesla and A.E. Kennelly. The contradictory nature of his forceful personality, as well as such eccentricities as his ability to catnap anywhere, contributed to his legendary status. By the time he was in his middle 30s Edison was said to be the best-known American in the world. When he died he was venerated and mourned as the man who, more than any other, had laid the basis for the technological and social revolution of the modern electric world.

ALEXANDER GRAHAM BELL

(b. March 3, 1847, Edinburgh, Scot. — d. Aug. 2, 1922, Beinn Bhreagh, Cape Breton Island, Nova Scotia, Can.)

Alexander Graham Bell was a Scottish-born American audiologist best known as the inventor of the telephone (1876). For two generations his family had been recognized as leading authorities in elocution and speech correction, with Alexander Melville Bell's *Standard Elocutionist* passing through nearly 200 editions in English. Young Bell and his two brothers were trained to continue the family profession. His early achievements on behalf of the deaf and his invention of the telephone before his 30th birthday bear testimony to the thoroughness of his training.

Alexander ("Graham" was not added until he was 11) was the second of the three sons of Alexander Melville Bell and Eliza Grace Symonds Bell. Apart from one year at a private school, two years at Edinburgh's Royal High School (from which he was graduated at 14), and attendance at a few lectures at Edinburgh University and at University College in London, Bell was largely family trained and self-taught. His first professional post was at Mr. Skinner's school in Elgin, County Moray, where he instructed the children in both music and elocution. In 1864 he became a resident master in Elgin's Weston House Academy, where he conducted his first studies in sound. Appropriately, Bell had begun professionally as he would continue through life — as a teacher-scientist.

In 1868 he became his father's assistant in London and assumed full charge while the senior Bell lectured in America. The shock of the sudden death of his older brother from tuberculosis, which had also struck down his younger brother, and the strain of his professional duties soon took their toll on young Bell. Concern for their only surviving son prompted the family's move to Canada in August 1870, where, after settling near Brantford, Ont., Bell's health rapidly improved.

In 1871 Bell spent several weeks in Boston, lecturing and demonstrating the system of his father's *Visible Speech*, published in 1866, as a means of teaching speech to the deaf. Each phonetic symbol indicated a definite position of the organs of speech such as lips, tongue, and soft palate and could be used by the deaf to imitate the sounds of speech in the usual way. Young A. Graham Bell, as he now preferred to be known, showed, using his father's system, that speech could be taught to the deaf. His astounding results soon led to further invitations to lecture.

Even while vacationing at his parents' home Bell continued his experiments with sound. In 1872 he opened his own school in Boston for training teachers of the deaf, edited his pamphlet *Visible Speech Pioneer*, and continued to study and tutor; in 1873 he became professor of vocal physiology at Boston University.

Never adept with his hands, Bell had the good fortune to discover and inspire Thomas Watson, a young repair mechanic and model maker, who assisted him enthusiastically in devising an apparatus for transmitting sound by electricity. Their long nightly sessions began to produce tangible results. The fathers of George Sanders and Mabel Hubbard, two deaf students whom he helped, were sufficiently impressed with the young teacher to assist him financially in his scientific pursuits. Nevertheless, during normal working hours Bell and Watson were still obliged to fulfill a busy schedule of professional demands. It is scarcely surprising that Bell's health again suffered. On April 6, 1875, he was granted the patent for his multiple telegraph; but after another exhausting six months of long nightly sessions in the workshop, while maintaining his daily professional schedule, Bell had to return to his

Alexander Graham Bell, who patented the telephone in 1876, inaugurating the 944-mile (1,520-km) telephone link between New York City and Chicago on Oct. 18, 1892. © Photos.com/Jupiterimages

parents' home in Canada to recuperate. In September 1875 he began to write the specifications for the telephone. On March 7, 1876, the United States Patent Office granted to Bell Patent Number 174,465 covering "The method of, and apparatus for, transmitting vocal or other sounds telegraphically . . . by causing electrical undulations, similar in form to the vibrations of the air accompanying the said vocal or other sounds."

Within a year followed the commercial application and, a few months later, the first of hundreds of legal suits. Ironically, the telephone—until then all too often regarded as a joke and its creator-prophet as, at best, an eccentric— was the subject of the most involved patent litigation in history. The most noteworthy contemporaries of Bell were Antonio Meucci, who filed a caveat (rather than a full patent) in 1871 and let it lapse through lack of funds, and Elisha Gray, who filed a caveat on Feb. 14, 1876, just a few hours after Bell submitted a patent claim. In recognition of Meucci's earlier work, the U.S. House of Representatives passed a resolution on June 11, 2002, honouring his work. The two most celebrated of the early actions were the Dowd and Drawbaugh cases wherein the fledgling Bell Telephone Company successfully challenged two subsidiaries of the giant Western Union Telegraph Company for patent infringement. The charges and accusations were especially painful to Bell's Scottish integrity, but the outcome of all the litigation, which persisted throughout the life of his patents, was that Bell's claims were upheld as the first to conceive and apply the undulatory current. In 1877 Bell married Mabel Hubbard, 10 years his junior.

BEYOND THE TELEPHONE

The Bell story does not end with the invention of the telephone; indeed, in many ways it was a beginning. A resident of Washington, D.C., Bell continued his experiments in communication, which culminated in the invention of the photophone—transmission of sound on a beam of light; in medical research; and in techniques for teaching speech to the deaf.

In 1880 France honoured Bell with the Volta Prize; and the 50,000 francs (roughly equivalent to U.S. $10,000) financed the Volta Laboratory, where, in association with Charles Sumner Tainter and his cousin, Chichester A. Bell, Bell invented the graphophone. Employing an engraving stylus, controllable speeds, and wax cylinders and disks, the graphophone presented a practical approach to sound recording. Bell's share of the royalties financed the Volta Bureau and the American Association to Promote the Teaching of Speech to the Deaf (since 1956 the Alexander Graham Bell Association for the Deaf). May 8, 1893, was one of Bell's happiest days; his 13-year-old prodigy, Helen Keller, participated in the groundbreaking ceremonies for the new Volta Bureau building—today an international information centre relating to the oral education of the deaf.

In 1885 Bell acquired land on Cape Breton Island in Nova Scotia. There, in surroundings reminiscent of his early years in Scotland, he established a summer home, Beinn Bhreagh, complete with research laboratories.

In 1898 Bell succeeded his father-in-law as president of the National Geographic Society. Convinced that geography could be taught through pictures, he sought to promote an understanding of life in distant lands in an age when travel was limited to a privileged few. Again he found the proper hands, Gilbert Grosvenor, his future son-in-law, who transformed a modest pamphlet into a unique educational journal reaching millions throughout the world.

As interest in the possibility of flight increased after the turn of the century, he experimented with giant man-carrying kites. Characteristically, Bell again found a group of four willing young enthusiasts to execute his theories. Always an inspiration, Mabel Hubbard Bell, wishing to maintain the stimulating influence of the group, soon founded the Aerial Experiment Association, the first research organization established and endowed by a woman. Deafness was no handicap to the wife of Professor Bell. At Beinn Bhreagh, Bell entered new subjects of investigation, such as sonar detection, solar distillation, the tetrahedron as a structural unit, and hydrofoil craft, one of which weighed more than 10,000 pounds and attained a speed record of 70 miles per hour in 1919.

Apart from his lifelong association with the cause of the deaf, Bell never lingered on one project. His research interests centred on basic principles rather than on refinements. The most cursory examination of his many notebooks shows marginal memos and jottings, often totally unrelated to the subject at hand—reminders of questions and ideas he wanted to investigate. It was impossible for him to carry each of his creative ideas through to a practical end. Many of his conceptions are only today seeing fruition; indeed, some undoubtedly have yet to be developed. The range of his inventive genius is represented only in part by the 18 patents granted in his name alone and the 12 he shared with his collaborators. These included 14 for the telephone and telegraph, 4 for the photophone, 1 for the phonograph, 5 for aerial vehicles, 4 for hydroairplanes, and 2 for a selenium cell.

Until a few days before his death Bell continued to make entries in his journal. During his last dictation he was reassured with "Don't hurry," to which he replied, "I have to."

OTTO LILIENTHAL

(b. May 23, 1848, Ankl am, Prussia [now in Ger.] — d. Aug. 10, 1896, Berlin)

O tto Lilienthal was a German aviation pioneer, the most significant aeronautical pioneer in the years leading up to the debut of the American Wright brothers.

Trained as a mechanical engineer, Lilienthal established his own machine shop and flight factory following service in the Franco-German War. Lilienthal began to conduct studies of the forces operating on wings in a stream of air in the late 1870s. The results of that research appeared in 1889 in a book entitled *Der Vogelflug als*

German aviation pioneer Otto Lilienthal piloting one of his gliders, c. 1895. Library of Congress, Washington, D.C. (digital id. ppmsca 02545)

Grundlage der Fliegekunst ("Bird Flight as the Basis of Aviation") and in an important series of articles that provided a foundation for the final effort to achieve mechanical flight. As transmitted by Octave Chanute, Lilienthal's friend and American correspondent, the tables of data served as the starting point for the earliest aircraft designs of the Wright brothers.

Having explored the physical principles governing winged flight, Lilienthal began to design and build gliders on the basis of the information he had gathered. Between 1891 and 1896, he completed some 2,000 flights in at least 16 distinct glider types. The largest number of flights were made with his standard glider, a monoplane aircraft with a stabilizing tail at the rear and wings that resembled "the outspread pinions of a soaring bird." The wing ribs and other covered portions of the aircraft were usually constructed of split willow. The wing covering was cotton twill shirting, doped with a colloidal solution to make it more airtight. In the standard glider, the operator hung suspended between the two halves of the wing. The operator shifted his weight to move the centre of gravity and exercise some measure of control over the motion of the craft. Although Lilienthal recognized the danger and inadequacy of this method of flight control and gave some thought to alternative systems, he did not develop or test them. Lilienthal sold several standard gliders to other experimenters as far distant as Russia and the United States.

Lilienthal's career as a builder and pilot of gliders coincided with the development of high-speed and stroboscopic photography. Images of Lilienthal flying through the air aboard his standard glider appeared around the globe in newspapers and the great illustrated magazines of the period. Those pictures convinced millions of readers in Europe and the United States that the age of flight was at hand. Lilienthal broke his back in a glider crash on Aug. 9, 1896, and died in a Berlin hospital the next day.

EMIL BERLINER

(b. May 20, 1851, Hannover, Hanover [now in Ger.] — d. Aug. 3, 1929, Washington, D.C., U.S.)

Emil (or Emile) Berliner, a German-born American inventor, made important contributions to microphone technology and developed the gramophone, the first viable disc-type record player.

Berliner immigrated to the United States in 1870. In 1877, a year after Alexander Graham Bell invented the telephone, Berliner, while working as a clerk in Washington, D.C., developed a transmitter employing a loose metal contact separated by a layer of carbon. The device did not perform well as a telephone transmitter, as Berliner was later to admit. Nevertheless, the rights to the invention were purchased by the Bell Telephone Company, which used it to develop the carbon microphone — thus earning Berliner a dubious reputation as "inventor of the microphone."

In 1884, after several years' association with Bell Telephone, Berliner established his own independent laboratory in Washington. There he made another contribution of major significance: the flat recording disc, on which a spiral recording groove was inscribed by a stylus that moved laterally, rather than vertically, thus producing excellent sound on a surface that could be manufactured more efficiently than Edison-type cylinder recordings. Berliner patented his invention, which he called the Gramophone, in 1887. He then embarked on a series of efforts to establish gramophone businesses in North America and Europe, all the while working on methods to improve the recording and disc-replicating process. The machine itself would not be perfected until after 1896, the year that Eldridge Johnson began to make spring-driven players for the Berliner Gramophone Company. The Berliner Gramophone Company supplied machines and recorded discs to the independent National Gramophone Company, which in turn sold the products in the United States. In 1897 the Gramophone Company, Ltd., was started up in London and the Gram-o-Phone Company was established in Montreal. In 1898 Berliner, with his brothers Joseph and Jacob, founded the Deutsche Grammophon Gesellshaft manufacturing plant in Hannover.

In 1901 Berliner pooled his patent and trademark rights with those of Eldridge Johnson, who formed the Victor Talking Machine Company. Berliner subsequently became interested in aeronautics; in 1908 he designed a lightweight internal-combustion engine that became a widely imitated prototype power plant for aircraft. Under his general supervision, his son, Henry Berliner, designed a helicopter that flew successfully as early as 1919. Returning to problems of sound reproduction, the elder Berliner in 1925 invented an acoustic tile for use in auditoriums and concert halls.

NIKOLA TESLA

(b. July 9/10, 1856, Smiljan, Austria-Hungary [now in Croatia]—d. Jan. 7, 1943, New York City, N.Y., U.S.)

Nikola Tesla was a Serbian-American inventor and engineer who discovered and patented the rotating magnetic field, the basis of most alternating-current machinery. He also developed the three-phase system of electric power transmission. He immigrated to the United States in 1884 and sold the patent rights to his system of alternating-current dynamos, transformers, and motors to George Westinghouse. In 1891 he invented the Tesla coil, an induction coil widely used in radio technology.

Tesla was from a family of Serbian origin. His father was an Orthodox priest; his mother was unschooled but highly intelligent. As he matured, he displayed remarkable imagination and creativity as well as a poetic touch.

Training for an engineering career, he attended the Technical University at Graz, Austria, and the University of Prague. At Graz he first saw the Gramme dynamo, which operated as a generator and, when reversed, became an electric motor, and he conceived a way to use alternating current to advantage. Later, at Budapest, he visualized the principle of the rotating magnetic field and developed plans for an induction motor that would become his first step toward the successful utilization of alternating current. In 1882 Tesla went to work in Paris for the Continental Edison Company, and, while on assignment to Strassburg in 1883, he constructed, in after-work hours, his first induction motor. Tesla sailed for America in 1884 arriving in New York with four cents in his pocket, a few of his own poems, and calculations for a flying machine. He first found employment with Thomas Edison, but

Photo. Barra[

This photo of Nikola Tesla is from the fall of 1900, around the time he made what he considered his most important discovery: terrestrial stationary waves. Getty/Herbert Barraud

the two inventors were far apart in background and methods, and their separation was inevitable.

In May 1885, George Westinghouse, head of the West-inghouse Electric Company in Pittsburgh, bought the patent rights to Tesla's polyphase system of alternating-current dynamos, transformers, and motors. The transaction pre-cipitated a titanic power struggle between Edison's direct-current systems and the Tesla–Westinghouse alternating-current approach, which eventually won out.

Tesla soon established his own laboratory, where his inventive mind could be given free rein. He experimented with shadowgraphs similar to those that later were to be used by Wilhelm Röntgen when he discovered X-rays in 1895. Tesla's countless experiments included work on a carbon button lamp, on the power of electrical resonance, and on various types of lighting.

In order to allay fears of alternating currents, Tesla gave exhibitions in his laboratory in which he lit lamps by allowing electricity to flow through his body. He was often invited to lecture at home and abroad. The Tesla coil, which he invented in 1891, is widely used today in radio and television sets and other electronic equipment. That year also marked the date of Tesla's U.S. citizenship.

Westinghouse used Tesla's alternating current system to light the World's Columbian Exposition at Chicago in 1893. This success was a factor in their winning the con-tract to install the first power machinery at Niagara Falls, which bore Tesla's name and patent numbers. The project carried power to Buffalo by 1896.

In 1898 Tesla announced his invention of a teleautomatic boat guided by remote control. When skepticism was voiced, Tesla proved his claims for it before a crowd in Madison Square Garden.

In Colorado Springs, Colo., where he stayed from May 1899 until early 1900, Tesla made what he regarded as his most important discovery—terrestrial stationary waves. By this discovery he proved that the Earth could be used as a conductor and made to resonate at a certain electrical frequency. He also lit 200 lamps without wires from a distance of 25 miles (40 km) and created man-made lightning, producing flashes measuring 135 feet (41 metres). At one time he was certain he had received signals from another planet in his Colorado laboratory, a claim that was met with derision in some scientific journals.

Returning to New York in 1900, Tesla began construction on Long Island of a wireless world broadcasting tower, with $150,000 capital from the American financier J. Pierpont Morgan. Tesla claimed he secured the loan by assigning 51 percent of his patent rights of telephony and telegraphy to Morgan. He expected to provide worldwide communication and to furnish facilities for sending pictures, messages, weather warnings, and stock reports. The project was abandoned because of a financial panic, labour troubles, and Morgan's withdrawal of support. It was Tesla's greatest defeat.

Tesla's work then shifted to turbines and other projects. Because of a lack of funds, his ideas remained in his notebooks, which are still examined by enthusiasts for unexploited clues. In 1915 he was severely disappointed when a report that he and Edison were to share the Nobel Prize proved erroneous. Tesla was the recipient of the Edison Medal in 1917, the highest honour that the American Institute of Electrical Engineers could bestow.

Tesla allowed himself only a few close friends. Among them were the writers Robert Underwood Johnson, Mark Twain, and Francis Marion Crawford. He was quite impractical in financial matters and an eccentric, driven by compulsions and a progressive germ phobia. But he had a way of intuitively sensing hidden scientific secrets and employing his inventive talent to prove his hypotheses.

Tesla was a godsend to reporters who sought sensational copy but a problem to editors who were uncertain how seriously his futuristic prophecies should be regarded. Caustic criticism greeted his speculations concerning communication with other planets, his assertions that he could split the Earth like an apple, and his claim of having invented a death ray capable of destroying 10,000 airplanes at a distance of 250 miles (400 km).

After Tesla's death the custodian of alien property impounded his trunks, which held his papers, his diplomas and other honours, his letters, and his laboratory notes. These were eventually inherited by Tesla's nephew, Sava Kosanovich, and later housed in the Nikola Tesla Museum in Belgrade. Hundreds filed into New York City's Cathedral of St. John the Divine for his funeral services, and a flood of messages acknowledged the loss of a great genius. Three Nobel Prize recipients addressed their tribute to "one of the outstanding intellects of the world who paved the way for many of the technological developments of modern times."

RUDOLF DIESEL

(b. March 18, 1858, Paris, France—d. Sept. 29, 1913, at sea in the English Channel)

Rudolf Christian Karl Diesel was a German thermal engineer who invented the internal-combustion engine that bears his name. He was also a distinguished connoisseur of the arts, a linguist, and a social theorist.

Diesel, the son of German-born parents, grew up in Paris until the family was deported to England in 1870 following the outbreak of the Franco-German War. From London Diesel was sent to Augsburg, his father's native town, to continue his schooling. There and later at the Technische Hochschule (Technical High School) in

Munich he established a brilliant scholastic record in fields of engineering. At Munich he was a protégé of the refrigeration engineer Carl von Linde, whose Paris firm he joined in 1880.

Diesel devoted much of his time to the self-imposed task of developing an internal combustion engine that would approach the theoretical efficiency of the Carnot cycle. For a time he experimented with an expansion engine using ammonia. About 1890, in which year he moved to a new post with the Linde firm in Berlin, he conceived the idea for the diesel engine. He obtained a German development patent in 1892 and the following year published a description of his engine under the title *Theorie und Konstruktion eines rationellen Wäremotors* (*Theory and Construction of a Rational Heat Motor*). With support from the Maschinenfabrik Augsburg and the Krupp firms, he produced a series of increasingly successful models, culminating in his demonstration in 1897 of a 25-horsepower, four-stroke, single vertical cylinder compression engine. The high efficiency of Diesel's engine, together with its comparative simplicity of design, made it an immediate commercial success, and royalty fees brought great wealth to its inventor.

Diesel disappeared from the deck of the mail steamer *Dresden* en route to London and was assumed to have drowned.

GEORGE WASHINGTON CARVER

(b. 1861?, near Diamond Grove, Mo., U.S.—d. Jan. 5, 1943, Tuskegee, Ala.)

George Washington Carver was an American agricultural chemist, agronomist, and experimenter whose development of new products derived from peanuts (groundnuts), sweet potatoes, and soybeans helped revolutionize the agricultural economy of the South. For most of his career he taught and conducted research at the Tuskegee Normal and Industrial Institute (now Tuskegee University) in Tuskegee, Ala.

Carver was the son of a slave woman owned by Moses Carver. During the Civil War, slave owners found it difficult to hold slaves in the border state of Missouri, and Moses Carver therefore sent his slaves, including the young child and his mother, to Arkansas. After the war, Moses Carver learned that all his former slaves had disappeared except for a child named George. Frail and sick, the motherless child was returned to his former master's home and nursed back to health. The boy had a delicate sense of colour and form and learned to draw; later in life he devoted considerable time to painting flowers, plants, and landscapes. Though the Carvers told him he was no longer a slave, he remained on their plantation until he was about 10 or 12 years old, when he left to acquire an education. He spent some time wandering about, working with his hands and developing his keen interest in plants and animals.

By both books and experience, George acquired a fragmentary education while doing whatever work came to hand in order to subsist. He supported himself by varied occupations that included general household worker, hotel cook, laundryman, farm labourer, and homesteader. In his late 20s he managed to obtain a high school education in Minneapolis, Kan., while working as a farmhand. After a university in Kansas refused to admit him because he was black, Carver matriculated at Simpson College, Indianola, Iowa, where he studied piano and art, subsequently transferring to Iowa State Agricultural College (Ames, Iowa), where he received a bachelor's degree in agricultural science in 1894 and a master of science degree in 1896.

Carver left Iowa for Alabama in the fall of 1896 to direct the newly organized department of agriculture at the Tuskegee Normal and Industrial Institute, a school headed by the noted black American educator Booker T. Washington. At Tuskegee, Washington was trying to improve the lot of black Americans through education and the acquisition of useful skills rather than through political agitation; he stressed conciliation, compromise, and economic development as the paths for black advancement in American society. Despite many offers elsewhere, Carver would remain at Tuskegee for the rest of his life.

After becoming the institute's director of agricultural research in 1896, Carver devoted his time to research projects aimed at helping Southern agriculture, demonstrating ways in which farmers could improve their economic situation. He conducted experiments in soil management and crop production and directed an experimental farm. At this time agriculture in the Deep South was in serious trouble because the unremitting single-crop cultivation of cotton had left the soil of many fields exhausted and worthless, and erosion had then taken its toll on areas that could no longer sustain any plant cover. As a remedy, Carver urged Southern farmers to plant peanuts and soybeans, which, since they belong to the legume family, could restore nitrogen to the soil while also providing the protein so badly needed in the diet of many Southerners. Carver found that Alabama's soils were particularly well-suited to growing peanuts and sweet potatoes, but when the state's farmers began cultivating these crops instead of cotton, they found little demand for them on the market. In response to this problem, Carver set about enlarging the commercial possibilities of the peanut and sweet potato through a long and ingenious program of laboratory research. He ultimately developed 300 derivative products from peanuts—among them cheese, milk, coffee, flour, ink, dyes, plastics, wood stains, soap, linoleum, medicinal oils, and cosmetics — and 118 from sweet potatoes, including flour, vinegar, molasses, rubber, ink, a synthetic rubber, and postage stamp glue.

In 1914, at a time when the boll weevil had almost ruined cotton growers, Carver revealed his experiments to the public, and increasing numbers of the South's farmers began to turn to peanuts, sweet potatoes, and their derivatives for income. Much exhausted land was renewed, and the South became a major new supplier of agricultural products. When Carver arrived at Tuskegee in 1896, the peanut had not even been recognized as a crop, but within the next half century it became one of the six leading crops throughout the United States and, in the South, the second cash crop (after cotton) by 1940. In 1942 the U.S. government allotted 5,000,000 acres of peanuts to farmers. Carver's efforts had finally helped liberate the South from its excessive dependence on cotton.

Among Carver's many honours were his election to Britain's Society for the Encouragement of Arts, Manufactures, and Commerce (London) in 1916 and his receipt of the Spingarn Medal in 1923. Late in his career he declined an invitation to work for Thomas A. Edison at a salary of more than $100,000 a year. Presidents Calvin Coolidge and Franklin D. Roosevelt visited him, and his friends included Henry Ford and Mohandas K. Gandhi. Foreign governments requested his counsel on agricultural matters: Joseph Stalin, for example, in 1931 invited him to superintend cotton plantations in southern Russia and to make a tour of the Soviet Union, but Carver refused.

In 1940 Carver donated his life savings to the establishment of the Carver Research Foundation at Tuskegee for continuing research in agriculture. During World War II he worked to replace the textile dyes formerly imported from Europe, and in all he produced dyes of 500 different shades.

Many scientists thought of Carver more as a concoction-ist than as a contributor to scientific knowledge. Many of his fellow blacks were critical of what they regarded as his subservience. Certainly, this small, mild, soft-spoken, innately modest man, eccentric in dress and mannerism, seemed unbelievably heedless of the conventional pleasures and rewards of this life. But these qualities endeared Carver to many whites, who were almost invariably charmed by his humble demeanour and his quiet work in self-imposed segregation at Tuskegee. As a result of his accommodation to the mores of the South, whites came to regard him with a sort of patronizing adulation.

Carver thus increasingly came to stand for much of white America as a kind of saintly and comfortable symbol of the intellectual achievements of black Americans. Carver was evidently uninterested in the role his image played in the racial politics of the time. His great desire in later life was simply to serve humanity; and his work, which began for the sake of the poorest of the black sharecroppers, paved the way for a better life for the entire South. His efforts brought about a significant advance in agricultural training in an era when agriculture was the largest single occupation of Americans, and he extended Tuskegee's influence throughout the South by encouraging improved farm methods, crop diversification, and soil conservation.

JAMES A. NAISMITH

(b. Nov. 6, 1861, Almonte, Ont., Can.—d. Nov. 28, 1939, Lawrence, Kan., U.S.)

James A. Naismith was a Canadian-American physical-education director who, in December 1891, at the International Young Men's Christian Association Training

School, afterward Springfield (Mass.) College, invented the game of basketball.

As a young man, Naismith (who had no middle name but adopted the initial "A.") studied theology and excelled in various sports. In the autumn of 1891 he was appointed an instructor by Luther Halsey Gulick, Jr., head of the Physical Education Department at Springfield. Gulick asked Naismith and other instructors to devise indoor games that could replace the boring or dangerous exercises used at the school during the winter. For his new game Naismith selected features of soccer, American football, field hockey, and other outdoor sports but (in theory) eliminated body contact between players. Because his physical education class at that time was composed of 18 men, basketball originally was played by nine on each side (eventually reduced to five).

For that first game of basketball in 1891, Naismith used as goals two half-bushel peach baskets, which gave the sport its name. The students were enthusiastic. After much running and shooting, William R. Chase made a midcourt shot—the only score in that historic contest. Word spread about the newly invented game, and numerous associations wrote Naismith for a copy of the rules, which were published in the Jan. 15, 1892, issue of the *Triangle*, the YMCA Training School's campus paper. Naismith's original rules, prohibiting walking or running with the ball and limiting physical contact, are still the basis of a game that spread throughout the world.

In 1898 Naismith received an M.D. from Gross Medical College, Denver, Colo., afterward the University of Colorado School of Medicine. From that year until 1937 he was chairman of the physical education department at the University of Kansas, Lawrence, where he also coached basketball until 1908. In addition to basketball, he is credited with inventing the protective helmet for football players. The Naismith Memorial Basketball Hall of Fame, in Springfield, Mass., was incorporated in 1959.

AUGUSTE AND LOUIS LUMIÈRE

respectively, (b. Oct. 19, 1862, Besançon, France—d. April 10, 1954, Lyon); (b. Oct. 5, 1864, Besançon, France—d. June 6, 1948, Bandol)

The Lumière brothers, Auguste and Louis, were French inventors and pioneer manufacturers of photographic equipment who devised an early motion-picture camera and projector called the Cinématographe (*cinema* is derived from this name). The two brothers created the film *La Sortie des ouvriers de l'usine Lumière* (1895; "Workers Leaving the Lumière Factory"), which is considered the first motion picture.

Sons of a painter turned photographer, the Lumière brothers displayed brilliance in science at school in Lyon, where their father had settled. Louis worked on the problem of commercially satisfactory development of film; at 18 he had succeeded so well that with his father's financial aid he opened a factory for producing photographic plates, which gained immediate success. By 1894 the Lumières were producing some 15,000,000 plates a year. That year the father, Antoine, was invited to a showing of Thomas Edison's Kinetoscope in Paris; his description of the peephole machine on his return to Lyon set Louis and Auguste to work on the problem of combining animation with projection. Louis found the solution, which was patented in 1895. At that time they attached less importance to this invention than to improvements they had made simultaneously in colour photography. But on Dec. 28, 1895, a showing at the Grand Café on the boulevard des Capucines in Paris brought wide public acclaim and the beginning of cinema history.

The Lumière apparatus consisted of a single camera used for both photographing and projecting at 16 frames per second. Their first films (they made more than 40 during 1896) recorded everyday French life—e.g., the arrival of a train, a game of cards, a toiling blacksmith, the feeding of a baby, soldiers marching, the activity of a city street. Others were early comedy shorts. The Lumières presented the first newsreel, a film of the French Photographic Society Conference, and the first documentaries, four films about the Lyon fire department. Beginning in 1896 they sent a trained crew of innovative cameraman-projectionists to cities throughout the world to show films and shoot new material.

HENRY FORD

(b. July 30, 1863, Wayne county, Mich., U.S.—d. April 7, 1947, Dearborn, Mich.)

Henry Ford was an American industrialist who revolutionized factory production with his assembly-line methods, which he applied in particular to his car for the common man, the Model T.

Ford spent most of his life making headlines, good, bad, but never indifferent. Celebrated as both a technological genius and a folk hero, Ford was the creative force behind an industry of unprecedented size and wealth that in only a few decades permanently changed the economic and social character of the United States. When young Ford left his father's farm in 1879 for Detroit, only two out of eight Americans lived in cities; when he died at age 83, the proportion was five out of eight. Once Ford realized the tremendous part he and his Model T

The 1909 Model T. Courtesy of the Ford Motor Company

automobile had played in bringing about this change, he wanted nothing more than to reverse it, or at least to recapture the rural values of his boyhood. Henry Ford, then, is an apt symbol of the transition from an agricultural to an industrial America.

EARLY LIFE

Henry Ford was one of eight children of William and Mary Ford. He was born on the family farm near Dearborn, Mich., then a town eight miles west of Detroit. Abraham Lincoln was president of the 24 states of the Union, and Jefferson Davis was president of the 11 states of the

Confederacy. Ford attended a one-room school for eight years when he was not helping his father with the harvest. At age 16 he walked to Detroit to find work in its machine shops. After three years, during which he came in contact with the internal-combustion engine for the first time, he returned to the farm, where he worked part-time for the Westinghouse Engine Company and in spare moments tinkered in a little machine shop he set up. Eventually he built a small "farm locomotive," a tractor that used an old mowing machine for its chassis and a homemade steam engine for power.

GOING INTO BUSINESS

Ford moved back to Detroit nine years later as a married man. His wife, Clara Bryant, had grown up on a farm not far from Ford's. They were married in 1888, and on Nov. 6, 1893, she gave birth to their only child, Edsel Bryant. A month later Ford was made chief engineer at the main Detroit Edison Company plant with responsibility for maintaining electric service in the city 24 hours a day. Because he was on call at all times, he had no regular hours and could experiment to his heart's content. He had determined several years before to build a gasoline-powered vehicle, and his first working gasoline engine was completed at the end of 1893. By 1896 he had completed his first horseless carriage, the "Quadricycle," so called because the chassis of the four-horsepower vehicle was a buggy frame mounted on four bicycle wheels. Unlike many other automotive inventors, including Charles Edgar and J. Frank Duryea, Elwood Haynes, Hiram Percy Maxim, and his Detroit acquaintance Charles Brady King, all of whom had built self-powered vehicles before Ford but who held onto their creations, Ford sold his to finance work on a second vehicle, and a third, and so on.

During the next seven years he had various backers, some of whom, in 1899, formed the Detroit Automobile Company (later the Henry Ford Company), but all eventually abandoned him in exasperation because they wanted a passenger car to put on the market while Ford insisted always on improving whatever model he was working on, saying that it was not ready yet for customers. He built several racing cars during these years, including the "999" racer driven by Barney Oldfield, and set several new speed records. In 1902 he left the Henry Ford Company, which subsequently reorganized as the Cadillac Motor Car Company. Finally, in 1903, Ford was ready to market an automobile. The Ford Motor Company was incorporated, this time with a mere $28,000 in cash put up by ordinary citizens, for Ford had, in his previous dealings with backers, antagonized the wealthiest men in Detroit.

The company was a success from the beginning, but just five weeks after its incorporation the Association of Licensed Automobile Manufacturers threatened to put it out of business because Ford was not a licensed manufacturer. He had been denied a license by this group, which aimed at reserving for its members the profits of what was fast becoming a major industry. The basis of their power was control of a patent granted in 1895 to George Baldwin Selden, a patent lawyer of Rochester, N.Y. The association claimed that the patent applied to all gasoline-powered automobiles. Along with many rural Midwesterners of his generation, Ford hated industrial combinations and Eastern financial power. Moreover, Ford thought the Selden patent preposterous. All invention was a matter of evolution, he said, yet Selden claimed genesis. He was glad to fight, even though the fight pitted the puny Ford Motor Company against an industry worth millions of dollars. The gathering of evidence and actual court hearings took six years. Ford lost the original case in 1909;

he appealed and won in 1911. His victory had wide implications for the industry, and the fight made Ford a popular hero.

The Model T and the Assembly Line

"I will build a motor car for the great multitude," Ford proclaimed in announcing the birth of the Model T in October 1908. In the 19 years of the Model T's existence, he sold 15,500,000 of the cars in the United States, almost 1,000,000 more in Canada, and 250,000 in Great Britain, a production total amounting to half the auto output of the world. The motor age arrived owing mostly to Ford's vision of the car as the ordinary man's utility rather than as the rich man's luxury. Once only the rich had travelled freely around the country; now millions could go wherever they pleased. The Model T was the chief instrument of one of the greatest and most rapid changes in the lives of the common people in history, and it effected this change in less than two decades. Farmers were no longer isolated on remote farms. The horse disappeared so rapidly that the transfer of acreage from hay to other crops caused an agricultural revolution. The automobile became the main prop of the American economy and a stimulant to urbanization—cities spread outward, creating suburbs and housing developments—and to the building of the finest highway system in the world.

The remarkable birthrate of Model T's was made possible by the most advanced production technology yet conceived. After much experimentation by Ford and his engineers, the system that had evolved by 1913–14 in Ford's new plant in Highland Park, Mich., was able to deliver parts, subassemblies, and assemblies (themselves built on subsidiary assembly lines) with precise timing to a constantly moving main assembly line, where a complete chassis was turned out every 93 minutes, an enormous improvement over the 728 minutes formerly required. The minute subdivision of labour and the coordination of a multitude of operations produced huge gains in productivity.

In 1914 the Ford Motor Company announced that it would henceforth pay eligible workers a minimum wage of $5 a day (compared to an average of $2.34 for the industry) and would reduce the workday from nine hours to eight, thereby converting the factory to a three-shift day. Overnight Ford became a worldwide celebrity. People either praised him as a great humanitarian or excoriated him as a mad socialist. Ford said humanitarianism had nothing to do with it. Previously profit had been based on paying wages as low as workers would take and pricing cars as high as the traffic would bear. Ford, on the other hand, stressed low pricing (the Model T cost $950 in 1908 and $290 in 1927) in order to capture the widest possible market and then met the price by volume and efficiency. Ford's success in making the automobile a basic necessity turned out to be but a prelude to a more widespread revolution. The development of mass-production techniques, which enabled the company eventually to turn out a Model T every 24 seconds; the frequent reductions in the price of the car made possible by economies of scale; and the payment of a living wage that raised workers above subsistence and made them potential customers for, among other things, automobiles — these innovations changed the very structure of society.

REGINALD FESSENDEN

(b. Oct. 6, 1866, Milton, Que., Can. — d. July 22, 1932, Hamilton, Bermuda)

Reginald Aubrey Fessenden was a Canadian-American radio pioneer who broadcast the first program of music and voice ever transmitted over long distances.

After study at Trinity College School, in Port Hope, Ont., and Bishop's College in Lennoxville, Que., Fessenden went to Bermuda as principal of the Whitney Institute, where he developed an interest in science that led him to resign and go to New York. Working as a tester at the Thomas Edison Machine Works, he met Thomas Edison and in 1887 became chief chemist of the Edison Laboratory at Orange, N.J. In 1890 he became chief electrician at the Westinghouse works at Pittsfield, Mass., and in 1892 turned to an academic career, as professor of electrical engineering first at Purdue University, West Lafayette, Ind., then at the Western University of Pennsylvania (now the University of Pittsburgh), where he worked on the problem of wireless communication.

In 1900 Fessenden left the university to conduct experiments in wireless telegraphy for the U.S. Weather Bureau, which wanted to adapt radiotelegraphy to weather forecasting. He then became interested in voice transmission and developed the idea of superimposing electric waves, vibrating at the frequencies of sound waves, upon a constant radio frequency, so as to modulate the amplitude of the radio wave into the shape of the sound wave. (This is the principle of amplitude modulation, or AM.) Fessenden also invented an electrolytic radio detector sensitive enough for use in radiotelephony.

In 1902 Fessenden joined two financiers in organizing the National Electric Signalling Company to manufacture his inventions. He directed Ernst Alexanderson of the General Electric Company in building a 50,000-hertz alternator that made possible the realization of radiotelephony, and Fessenden at once built a transmitting station at Brant Rock, Mass. On Dec. 24, 1906, wireless operators as far away as Norfolk, Va., were startled to hear speech and music from Brant Rock through their own receivers. That same year, Fessenden established two-way transatlantic wireless telegraphic communication between Brant Rock and Scotland.

Fessenden further contributed in 1902 to the development of radio by demonstrating the heterodyne principle of converting high-frequency wireless signals to a lower frequency that is more easily controlled and amplified. This was the forerunner of the superheterodyne principle, which made easy tuning of radio signals possible and was a critical factor for the growth of commercial broadcasting.

Fessenden has also been credited with inventing the radio compass, the sonic depth finder, submarine signalling devices, and the turboelectric drive for battleships.

WILBUR AND ORVILLE WRIGHT

respectively, (b. April 16, 1867, near Millville, Ind., U.S.—d. May 30, 1912, Dayton, Ohio), ; (b. Aug. 19, 1871, Dayton—d. Jan. 30, 1948, Dayton)

The Wright brothers, Wilbur and Orville, were American inventors and aviation pioneers who achieved the first powered, sustained, and controlled airplane flight (1903) and built and flew the first fully practical airplane (1905).

EARLY FAMILY LIFE

Wilbur and Orville were the sons of Milton Wright, an ordained minister of the Church of the United Brethren in Christ, and Susan Catherine Koerner Wright, whom Milton had met while he was training for the ministry and while Susan was a student at a United Brethren college in Hartsville, Ind. Two boys, Reuchlin (1861–1920) and Lorin (1862–1939), were born to the couple before Wilbur was born on a farm near Millville, Ind. The young family then moved to Dayton, Ohio, so that Milton could take up duties as the editor of a church newspaper. In that city a pair of twins, Otis and Ida, were born and died in 1870. Orville arrived a year later, followed by Katharine (1874–1929).

Elected a bishop of the church in 1877, Milton spent long periods of time away from home visiting the Brethren congregations for which he was responsible. The family moved often: to Cedar Rapids, Iowa, in 1878; to a farm near Richmond, Ind., in 1881; and back to Dayton in 1884. The Wright children were educated in public schools and grew up, as Orville later explained, in a home where "there was always much encouragement to children to pursue intellectual interests; to investigate whatever aroused curiosity." In a less-nourishing environment, Orville believed, "our curiosity might have been nipped long before it could have borne fruit."

These were not tranquil years for Bishop Wright. As the leader of a conservative faction opposed to modernization in the church, he was involved in a 20-year struggle that led to a national schism in 1889 and was followed by multiple lawsuits for possession of church property. Even as these decades of crisis were approaching a conclusion, an entirely new conflict developed, this time within the small schismatic branch that Bishop Wright had led away from the original church. The resulting church disciplinary hearings and civil court cases continued up to the time of the bishop's retirement in 1905.

Bishop Wright exercised an extraordinary influence on the lives of his children. Wilbur and Orville, like their father, were independent thinkers with a deep confidence in their own talents, an unshakable faith in the soundness of their judgment, and a determination to persevere in the face of disappointment and adversity. Those qualities, when combined with their unique technical gifts, help to explain the success of the Wright brothers as inventors. At the same time, the bishop's rigid adherence to principle and disinclination to negotiate disputes may have had some influence on the manner in which the brothers, later in life, conducted the marketing of their invention.

PRINTERS AND BICYCLE MAKERS

Wilbur and Orville were the only members of the Wright family who did not attend college or marry. Wilbur's plans to enter college came to an end when he was injured in a hockey accident in the winter of 1885–86. He spent the following three years recovering his health, reading extensively in his father's library, assisting the bishop with his legal and church problems, and caring for his invalid mother, who died of tuberculosis in 1889.

Following their mother's death, Orville, who had spent several summers learning the printing trade, persuaded Wilbur to join him in establishing a print shop. In addition to normal printing services, the brothers edited and published two short-lived local newspapers, and they also developed a local reputation for the quality of the presses that they designed, built, and sold to other printers. These printing presses were one of the first indications of the Wright brothers' extraordinary technical ability and their unique approach to the solution of problems in mechanical design.

In 1892 the brothers opened a bicycle sales and repair shop, and they began to build bicycles on a small scale in 1896. They developed their own self-oiling bicycle wheel hub and installed a number of light machine tools in the shop. Profits from the print shop and the bicycle operation eventually were to fund the Wright brothers' aeronautical experiments from 1899 to 1905. In addition, the experience of designing and building lightweight, precision machines of wood, wire, and metal tubing was ideal preparation for the construction of flying machines.

In later years the Wrights dated their fascination with flight to a small helicopter toy that their father had brought home from his travels when the family was living in Iowa. A decade later, they had read accounts of the work of the German glider pioneer Otto Lilienthal. But it was news reports of Lilienthal's death in a glider crash in August 1896 that marked the beginning of their serious interest in flight. By 1899 the brothers had exhausted the resources of the local library and had written to the Smithsonian Institution for suggestions as to further reading in aeronautics. The following year they wrote to introduce themselves to Octave Chanute, a leading civil engineer and an authority on aviation who would remain a confidant of the brothers during the critical years from 1900 to 1905.

EARLY GLIDER EXPERIMENTS

The ability of the Wright brothers to analyze a mechanical problem and move toward a solution was apparent from the outset of their work in aeronautics. The brothers realized that a successful airplane would require wings to generate lift, a propulsion system to move it through the air, and a system to control the craft in flight. Lilienthal, they reasoned, had built wings capable of carrying him in flight, while the builders of self-propelled vehicles were developing lighter and more powerful internal-combustion engines. The final problem to be solved, they concluded, was that of control.

Most aeronautical experimenters up to that time had sought to develop flying machines incorporating a measure of inherent stability, so that the aircraft would tend to fly a straight and level course unless the pilot

intervened to change altitude or direction. As experienced
cyclists, the Wrights preferred to place complete control of their machine in the hands of the operator.
Moreover, aware of the dangers of weight-shifting control
(a means of controlling the aircraft by shifting the position of the pilot), the brothers were determined to
control their machine through a precise manipulation
of the centre of pressure on the wings. After considering various mechanical schemes for obtaining such
control, they decided to try to induce a helical twist
across the wings in either direction. The resulting
increase in lift on one side and decrease on the other
would enable the pilot to raise or lower either wing tip
at will.

*This 1902 photo depicts Wilbur Wright flying the glider biplane he designed
with the help of his brother Orville.* Getty/Hulton Archive

Their first experiments with "wing warping," as the system would be called, were made with a small biplane kite flown in Dayton in the summer of 1899. Discovering that they could cause the kite to climb, dive, and bank to the right or left at will, the brothers began to design their first full-scale glider using Lilienthal's data to calculate the amount of wing surface area required to lift the estimated weight of the machine and pilot in a wind of given velocity.

Realizing that Dayton, with its relatively low winds and flat terrain, was not the ideal place to conduct aeronautical experiments, the Wrights requested of the U.S. Weather Bureau a list of more suitable areas. They selected Kitty Hawk, an isolated village on the Outer Banks of North Carolina, which offered high average winds, tall dunes from which to glide, and soft sand for landings.

Tested in October 1900, the first Wright glider was a biplane featuring 165 square feet (15 square metres) of wing area and a forward elevator for pitch control. The glider developed less lift than expected, however, and very few free flights were made with a pilot on board. The brothers flew the glider as a kite, gathering information on the performance of the machine that would be critically important in the design of future aircraft.

Eager to improve on the disappointing performance of their 1900 glider, the Wrights increased the wing area of their next machine to 290 square feet (26 square metres). Establishing their camp at the foot of the Kill Devil Hills, 4 miles (6.5 km) south of Kitty Hawk, the brothers completed 50 to 100 glides in July and August of 1901. As in 1900, Wilbur made all the glides, the best of which covered nearly 400 feet (120 metres). The 1901 Wright aircraft was an improvement over its predecessor, but it still did not perform as well as their calculations had predicted. Moreover, the experience of 1901 suggested that the problems of control were not fully resolved.

Discouraged, but determined to preserve a record of their aeronautical work to date, Wilbur accepted Chanute's invitation to address the prestigious Western Society of Engineers. Wilbur's talk was delivered in Chicago on Sept. 18, 1901, and was published as "Some Aeronautical Experiments" in the journal of the society. It indicated the extent to which the Wright brothers, in spite of their disappointments, had already moved beyond other flying machine experimenters.

SOLVING THE PROBLEMS OF LIFT AND CONTROL

Realizing that the failure of their gliders to match calculated performance was the result of errors in the experimental data published by their predecessors, the Wrights constructed a small wind tunnel with which to gather their own information on the behaviour in an airstream of model wings of various shapes and sizes. The brilliance of the Wright brothers, their ability to visualize the behaviour of a machine that had yet to be constructed, was seldom more apparent than in the design of their wind-tunnel balances, the instruments mounted inside the tunnel that actually measured the forces operating on the model wings. During the fall and early winter of 1901 the Wrights tested between 100 and 200 wing designs in their wind tunnel, gathering information on the relative efficiencies of various airfoils and determining the effect of different wing shapes, tip designs, and gap sizes between the two wings of a biplane.

With the results of the wind-tunnel tests in hand, the brothers began work on their third full-scale glider. They tested the machine at the Kill Devil Hills camp in September and October of 1902. It performed exactly as the design calculations predicted. For the first time, the brothers shared the flying duties, completing 700–1,000 flights, covering distances up to 622.5 feet (189.75 metres), and remaining in the air for as long as 26 seconds. In addition to gaining significant experience in the air, the Wrights were able to complete their control system by adding a movable rudder linked to the wing-warping system.

Powered, Sustained Flight

With the major aerodynamic and control problems behind them, the brothers pressed forward with the design and construction of their first powered machine. They designed and built a four-cylinder internal-combustion engine with the assistance of Charles Taylor, a machinist whom they employed in the bicycle shop. Recognizing that propeller blades could be understood as rotary wings, the Wrights were able to design twin pusher propellers on the basis of their wind-tunnel data.

The brothers returned to their camp near the Kill Devil Hills in September 1903. They spent the next seven weeks assembling, testing, and repairing their powered machine and conducting new flight tests with the 1902 glider. Wilbur made the first attempt at powered flight on December 14, but he stalled the aircraft on takeoff and damaged the forward section of the machine. Three days were spent making repairs and waiting for the return of good weather. Then, at about 10:35 on the morning of Dec. 17, 1903, Orville made the first successful flight, covering 120 feet (36 metres) through the air in 12 seconds. Wilbur flew 175 feet (53 metres) in 12 seconds on his first attempt, followed by Orville's second effort of 200 feet (60 metres) in 15 seconds. During the fourth and final flight of the day, Wilbur flew 852 feet (259 metres) over the sand in 59 seconds. The four flights were witnessed by five local citizens. For the first time in history, a heavier-than-air machine had demonstrated powered and sustained flight under the complete control of the pilot.

Determined to move from the marginal success of 1903 to a practical airplane, the Wrights in 1904 and 1905 built and flew two more aircraft from Huffman Prairie, a pasture near Dayton. They continued to improve the design of their machine during these years, gaining skill and confidence in the air. By October 1905 the brothers could remain aloft for up to 39 minutes at a time, performing circles and other maneuvers. Then, no longer able to hide the extent of their success from the press, and concerned that the essential features of their machine would be understood and copied by knowledgeable observers, the Wrights decided to cease flying and remain on the ground until their invention was protected by patents and they had negotiated a contract for its sale.

Making the Invention Public

The claim of the Wright brothers to have flown was widely doubted during the years 1906–07. During that period a handful of European and American pioneers struggled into the air in machines designed on the basis of an incomplete understanding of Wright technology. Meanwhile the brothers, confident that they retained a commanding lead over their rivals, continued to negotiate with financiers and government purchasing agents on two continents.

In February 1908 the Wrights signed a contract for the sale of an airplane to the U.S. Army. They would receive $25,000 for delivering a machine capable of flying for at least one hour with a pilot and passenger at an average speed of 40 miles (65 km) per hour. The following month, they signed a second agreement with a group of French investors interested in building and selling Wright machines under license.

With the new aircraft that they would fly in America and France ready for assembly, the Wright brothers returned to the Kill Devil Hills in May 1908, where they made 22 flights with their old 1905 machine, modified with upright seating and hand controls. On May 14, Wilbur carried aloft the first airplane passenger—mechanic Charles Furnas.

Wilbur then sailed to France, where he captured the European imagination with his first public flight; this took place over the Hunaudières Race Course near Le Mans on Aug. 8, 1908. During the months that followed, the elite of the continent traveled to watch Wilbur fly at Le Mans and Pau in France and at Centocelle near Rome.

Orville began the U.S. Army trials at Fort Myer, Va., with a flight on Sept. 3, 1908. Fourteen days later a split propeller precipitated a crash that killed his passenger, Lt. Thomas E. Selfridge, and badly injured the pilot. During the course of his recovery, Orville and his sister Katharine visited Wilbur in Europe. Together, the brothers returned to Fort Myer to complete the Army trials in 1909. Having exceeded the required speed of 40 miles (65 km) per hour, the Wrights earned a bonus of $5,000 beyond the $25,000 contract price.

Following the successful Fort Myer trials, Orville traveled to Germany, where he flew at Berlin and Potsdam. Wilbur made several important flights as part of New York City's Hudson-Fulton Celebration, then went to College Park, Md., where he taught the first three U.S. Army officers to fly.

GOING INTO BUSINESS

In November 1909 the Wright Company was incorporated with Wilbur as president, Orville as one of two vice presidents, and a board of trustees that included some of the leaders of American business. The Wright Company established a factory in Dayton and a flying field and flight school at Huffman Prairie. Among the pilots trained at the facility was Henry H. "Hap" Arnold, who would rise to command of the U.S. Army Air Forces during World War II.

The brothers also formed the Wright Exhibition Company in March 1910, with A. Roy Knabenshue, an experienced balloon and airship pilot, as manager. Although the Wrights were not eager to enter what they regarded as a "mountebank business," they recognized that an exhibition team would generate steady revenues to supplement funds received from the sale of aircraft, flight instruction, and license fees. Orville began training pilots for the exhibition team at Montgomery, Ala., and continued instruction at Huffman Prairie. The exhibition company made its first appearance at Indianapolis, Ind., in June 1910 and remained in business until November 1911, by which time the deaths of several team members convinced the Wright brothers to discontinue operations.

After the summer of 1909, Wilbur focused his energies on business and legal activities. He took the lead in bringing a series of lawsuits against rival aircraft builders in the United States and Europe who the brothers believed had infringed upon their patent rights. In Germany, the Wright claims were disallowed on the basis of prior disclosure. Even in France and America, where the position of the Wright brothers was upheld in virtually every court judgment, the defendants were able to manipulate the legal process in such a manner as to avoid substantial payments. Moreover, the Wrights' spirited pursuit of their international patent rights significantly complicated their public image. Once inaccurately regarded as a pair of naive mechanical geniuses, they were now unfairly blamed for having retarded the advance of flight technology by bringing suit against other talented experimenters. The era of the lawsuits came to an effective end in 1917, when the Wright patents expired in France and the U.S. government created a patent pool in the interest of national defense.

ORVILLE CARRIES ON THE LEGACY

Exhausted by business and legal concerns and suffering from typhoid fever, Wilbur died in his bed early on the morning of May 30, 1912. Wilbur had drawn Orville into aeronautics and had taken the lead in business matters since 1905. Upon Wilbur's decease, Orville assumed leadership of the Wright Company, remaining with the firm until 1915, when he sold his interest in the company to a group of financiers. He won the 1913 Collier Trophy for his work on an automatic stabilizer for aircraft, and he worked as a consulting engineer during World War I, helping the Dayton-Wright Company plan for the production of foreign aircraft designs and assisting in the development of a pilotless aircraft bomb.

One of the most celebrated Americans of his time, Orville received honorary degrees and awards from universities and organizations across America and Europe. He remained active in aeronautics as a member of the National Advisory Committee for Aeronautics (1920–48) and as a leader of other organizations, notably the advisory board of the Daniel and Florence Guggenheim Fund for the Promotion of Aeronautics. Orville disliked public speaking, however, and enjoyed nothing more than spending time with friends and family in the privacy of his home and laboratory in Dayton or his vacation retreat on Georgian Bay, off of Lake Huron in Ontario, Can. During the last four decades of his life he devoted considerable energy to defending the priority of the Wright brothers as the inventors of the airplane. A long-running feud with the leadership of the Smithsonian Institution was particularly noteworthy. During the years prior to World War I, Smithsonian officials claimed that the third secretary of the institution, S.P. Langley, had constructed a machine "capable" of flight prior to the Wrights' success of December 1903. Unable to obtain a retraction of this claim by 1928, Orville lent the restored 1903 airplane to the Science Museum in London and did not consent to bringing the machine to Washington, D.C., until after the Smithsonian offered an apology in 1942.

On Jan. 27, 1948, Orville suffered a heart attack; he died three days later in a Dayton hospital. There is perhaps no better epitaph for both of the Wright brothers than the words crafted by a group of their friends to appear as a label identifying the 1903 Wright airplane on display at the Smithsonian: "By original scientific research, the Wright brothers discovered the principles of human flight. As inventors, builders and flyers, they further developed the aeroplane, taught man to fly, and opened the era of aviation."

LEE DE FOREST

(b. Aug. 26, 1873, Council Bluffs, Iowa, U.S.—d. June 30, 1961, Hollywood, Calif.)

Lee De Forest was an American inventor of the Audion vacuum tube, which made possible live radio broadcasting and became the key component of all radio, telephone, radar, television, and computer systems before the invention of the transistor in 1947. Although bitter over the financial exploitation of his inventions by others, he was widely honoured as the "father of radio" and the "grandfather of television." He was supported strongly but unsuccessfully for the Nobel Prize for Physics.

LIFE

De Forest was the son of a Congregational minister. His father moved the family to Alabama and there assumed the presidency of the nearly bankrupt Talladega College for Negroes. Ostracized by citizens of the white community who resented his father's efforts to educate blacks, Lee made his friends from among the black children of the town and, together with his brother and sister, spent a happy although sternly disciplined childhood in this rural community.

As a child, he was fascinated with machinery and was often excited when hearing of the many technological advances during the late 19th century. By age 13 he was an enthusiastic inventor of mechanical gadgets, such as a miniature blast furnace and locomotive and a working silver-plating apparatus.

His father had planned for him a career in the clergy, but Lee insisted on science and, in 1893, enrolled at the Sheffield Scientific School of Yale University, one of the few institutions in the United States then offering a first-class scientific education. Frugal and hardworking, he supplemented his scholarship and the slim allowance provided by his parents by working at menial jobs during his college years, and, despite a not-too-distinguished undergraduate career, he went on to earn the Ph.D. in physics in 1899.

By this time he had become interested in electricity, particularly the study of electromagnetic-wave propagation, then being pioneered chiefly by the German Heinrich Rudolf Hertz and the Italian Guglielmo Marconi. De

Forest's doctoral dissertation on the "Reflection of Hertzian Waves from the Ends of Parallel Wires" was possibly the first doctoral thesis in the United States on the subject that was later to become known as radio.

His first job was with the Western Electric Company in Chicago, where, beginning in the dynamo department, he worked his way up to the telephone section and then to the experimental laboratory. While working after hours on his own, he developed an electrolytic detector of Hertzian waves. The device was modestly successful, as was an alternating-current transmitter that he designed. In 1902 he and his financial backers founded the De Forest Wireless Telegraph Company. In order to dramatize the potential of this new medium of communication, he began, as early as 1902, to give public demonstrations of wireless telegraphy for businessmen, the press, and the military.

INVENTION OF THE AUDION TUBE

A poor businessman and a poorer judge of men, De Forest was defrauded twice by his own business partners. By 1906 his first company was insolvent, and he had been squeezed out of its operation. But in 1907 he patented a much more promising detector (developed in 1906), which he called the Audion; it was capable of more sensitive reception of wireless signals than were the electrolytic and Carborundum types then in use. It was a thermionic grid-triode vacuum tube—a three-element electronic "valve" similar to a two-element device patented by the Englishman Sir John Ambrose Fleming in 1905. In 1907 De Forest was able to broadcast experimentally both speech and music to the general public in the New York City area.

A second company, the De Forest Radio Telephone Company, began to collapse in 1909, again because of some of his partners. In the succeeding legal confusion,

De Forest was indicted in 1912 but later acquitted of federal charges of using the mails to defraud by seeking to promote a "worthless device"—the Audion tube.

In 1910 he broadcast a live performance by Enrico Caruso at the Metropolitan Opera in order to popularize the new medium further. In 1912 De Forest conceived the idea of "cascading" a series of Audion tubes so as to amplify high-frequency radio signals far beyond what could be accomplished by merely increasing the voltage on a single tube. He fed the output from the plate of one tube through a transformer to the grid of a second, the output of the second tube's plate to the grid of a third, and so forth, which thereby allowed for an enormous amplification of a signal that was originally very weak. This was an essential development for both radio and telephonic long-distance communication. He also discovered in 1912 that by feeding part of the output of his triode vacuum tube back into its grid, he could cause a self-regenerating oscillation in the circuit. The signal from this circuit, when fed to an antenna system, was far more powerful and effective than that of the crude transmitters then generally employed and, when properly modulated, was capable of transmitting speech and music. When appropriately modified, this single invention was capable of either transmitting, receiving, or amplifying radio signals.

Throughout De Forest's lifetime, the originality of his more important inventions was hotly contested, by both scientists and patent attorneys. In time, realizing that he could not succeed in business or manufacturing, he reluctantly sold his patents to major communications firms for commercial development. Some of the most important of these sales were made at very low prices to the American Telephone & Telegraph Company, which used the Audion as an essential amplification component for long-distance repeater circuits.

OTHER INVENTIONS

In 1920 De Forest began to work on a practical system for recording and reproducing sound motion pictures. He developed a sound-on-film optical recording system called Phonofilm and demonstrated it in theatres between 1923 and 1927. Although it was basically correct in principle, its operating quality was poor, and he found himself unable to interest film producers in its possibilities. Ironically, within a few years' time the motion-picture industry converted to talking pictures by using a sound-on-film process similar to De Forest's. During the 1930s De Forest developed Audion-diathermy machines for medical applications, and during World War II he conducted military research for Bell Laboratories.

GUGLIELMO MARCONI

(b. April 25, 1874, Bologna, Italy—d. July 20, 1937, Rome

Italian physicist Guglielmo Marconi was the inventor of a successful wireless telegraph (1896). In 1909 he received the Nobel Prize for Physics, which he shared with German physicist Ferdinand Braun. He later worked on the development of

Guglielmo Marconi, c.1908. Library of Congress, Washington, D.C.

shortwave wireless communication, which constitutes the basis of nearly all modern long-distance radio.

EDUCATION AND EARLY WORK

Marconi's father was Italian and his mother Irish. Educated first in Bologna and later in Florence, Marconi then went to the technical school in Leghorn, where, in studying physics, he had every opportunity for investigating electromagnetic wave technique, following the earlier mathematical work of James Clerk Maxwell and the experiments of Heinrich Hertz, who first produced and transmitted radio waves, and Sir Oliver Lodge, who conducted research on lightning and electricity.

In 1894 Marconi began experimenting at his father's estate near Bologna, using comparatively crude apparatuses: an induction coil for increasing voltages, with a spark discharger controlled by a Morse key at the sending end and a simple coherer (a device designed to detect radio waves) at the receiver. After preliminary experiments over a short distance, he first improved the coherer; then, by systematic tests, he showed that the range of signaling was increased by using a vertical aerial with a metal plate or cylinder at the top of a pole connected to a similar plate on the ground. The range of signaling was thus increased to about 1.5 miles (2.4 km), enough to convince Marconi of the potentialities of this new system of communication. During this period he also conducted simple experiments with reflectors around the aerial to concentrate the radiated electrical energy into a beam instead of spreading it in all directions.

Receiving little encouragement to continue his experiments in Italy, he went, in 1896, to London, where he was soon assisted by Sir William Preece, the chief engineer of the post office. Marconi filed his first patent in England in June 1896 and, during that and the following year, gave a series of successful demonstrations, in some of which he used balloons and kites to obtain greater height for his aerials. He was able to send signals over distances of up to 4 miles (6.4 km) on the Salisbury Plain and to nearly 9 miles (14.5 km) across the Bristol Channel. These tests, together with Preece's lectures on them, attracted considerable publicity both in England and abroad, and in June 1897 Marconi went to La Spezia, where a land station was erected and communication was established with Italian warships at distances of up to 11.8 miles (19 km).

There remained much skepticism about the useful application of this means of communication and a lack of interest in its exploitation. But Marconi's cousin Jameson Davis, a practicing engineer, financed his patent and helped in the formation of the Wireless Telegraph and Signal Company, Ltd. (changed in 1900 to Marconi's Wireless Telegraph Company, Ltd.). During the first years, the company's efforts were devoted chiefly to showing the full possibilities of radiotelegraphy. A further step was taken in 1899 when a wireless station was established at South Foreland, Eng., for communicating with Wimereux in France, a distance of 30 miles (50 km); in the same year, British battleships exchanged messages at 75 miles (120 km).

In September 1899 Marconi equipped two American ships to report to newspapers in New York City the progress of the yacht race for the America's Cup. The success of this demonstration aroused worldwide excitement and led to the formation of the American Marconi Company. The following year the Marconi International Marine Communication Company, Ltd., was established for the purpose of installing and operating services between ships and land stations. In 1900 also, Marconi filed his now-famous patent No. 7777 for Improvements in Apparatus for Wireless Telegraphy. The patent, based in part on earlier work in wireless telegraphy by Sir Oliver Lodge, enabled several stations to operate on different wavelengths without interference. (In 1943 the U.S. Supreme Court overturned patent No. 7777, indicating that Lodge, Nikola Tesla, and John Stone appeared to have priority in the development of radio-tuning apparatus.)

MAJOR DISCOVERIES AND INNOVATIONS

Marconi's great triumph was, however, yet to come. In spite of the opinion expressed by some distinguished mathematicians that the curvature of the Earth would limit practical communication by means of electric waves to a distance of 100–200 miles (160–320 km), Marconi succeeded in December 1901 in receiving at St. John's, Newfoundland, signals transmitted across the Atlantic Ocean from Poldhu in Cornwall, Eng. This achievement created an immense sensation in every part of the civilized world, and, though much remained to be learned about the laws of propagation of radio waves around the Earth and through the atmosphere, it was the starting point of the vast development of radio communications, broad-casting, and navigation services that took place in the next 50 years, in much of which Marconi himself continued to play an important part.

During a voyage on the U.S. liner *Philadelphia* in 1902, Marconi received messages from distances of 700 miles (1,125 km) by day and 2,000 miles (3,200 km) by night. He thus was the first to discover that, because some radio waves travel by reflection from the upper regions of the atmosphere, transmission conditions are sometimes more favourable at night than during the day. This circumstance is due to the fact that the upward travel of the waves is limited in the daytime by absorption in the lower atmosphere, which becomes ionized—and so electrically conducting—under the influence of sunlight. In 1902 also, Marconi patented the magnetic detector in which the magnetization in a moving band of iron wires is changed by the arrival of a signal causing a click in the telephone receiver connected to it. During the ensuing three years, he also developed and patented the horizontal directional aerial. Both of these devices improved the efficiency of the communication system. In 1910 he received messages at Buenos Aires from Clifden in Ireland over a distance of approximately 6,000 miles (10,000 km), using a wavelength of about 5 miles (8,000 metres). Two years later Marconi introduced further innovations that so improved transmission and reception that important long-distance stations could be established. This increased efficiency allowed Marconi to send the first radio message from England to Australia in September 1918.

In spite of the rapid and widespread developments then taking place in radio and its applications to maritime use, Marconi's intuition and urge to experiment were by no means exhausted. In 1916, during World War I, he saw the possible advantages of shorter wavelengths that would permit the use of reflectors around the aerial, thus minimizing the interception of transmitted signals by the enemy and also effecting an increase in signal strength. After tests in Italy (20 years after his original experiments with reflectors), Marconi continued the work in Great Britain and, on a wavelength of 50 feet (15 metres), received signals over a range of 20–100 miles (30–160 km). In 1923 the experiments were continued on board his steam yacht *Elettra*, which had been specially equipped. From a transmitter of 1 kilowatt at Poldhu, Cornwall, signals were received at a distance of 1,400 miles (2,250 km). These signals were much louder than those from Caernarfon, Wales, on a wavelength several hundred times as great and with 100 times the power at the transmitter. Thus began the development of shortwave wireless communication that, with the use of the beam aerial system for concentrating the energy in the desired direction, is the basis of most modern long-distance radio communication. In 1924 the Marconi company obtained a contract from the post office to establish shortwave communication between England and the countries of the British Commonwealth.

A few years later Marconi returned to the study of still shorter waves of about 20 inches (50 cm). At these very short wavelengths, a parabolic reflector of moderate size gives a considerable increase in power in the desired direction. Experiments conducted off the coast of Italy on the yacht *Elettra* soon showed that useful ranges of communication could be achieved with low-powered transmitters. In 1932, using very short wavelengths, Marconi installed a radiotelephone system between Vatican City and the pope's palace at Castel Gandolfo. In later work Marconi once more demonstrated that even radio waves as short as 22 inches (55 cm) are not limited in range to the horizon or to optical distance between transmitter and receiver.

Marconi received many honours and several honorary degrees. He was awarded the Nobel Prize for Physics (1909) for the development of wireless telegraphy; sent as plenipotentiary delegate to the peace conference in Paris (1919), in which capacity he signed the peace treaties with Austria and with Bulgaria; created marchese and nominated to the Italian senate (1929); and chosen president of the Royal Italian Academy (1930).

ROBERT GODDARD

(b. Oct. 5, 1882, Worcester, Mass., U.S.—d. Aug. 10, 1945, Baltimore, Md.)

Robert Hutchings Goddard was an American professor and inventor generally acknowledged to be the father of modern rocketry. He published his classic treatise, *A Method of Reaching Extreme Altitudes*, in 1919.

EARLY LIFE AND TRAINING

Goddard was the only child of a bookkeeper, salesman, and machine-shop owner of modest means. The boy had a genteel upbringing and in early youth felt the excitement of the post-Civil War Industrial Revolution when Worcester factories were producing machinery and goods for the burgeoning country. From childhood on he displayed great curiosity about physical phenomena and a bent toward inventiveness. He read in physics and mechanics and dreamed of great inventions.

In 1898 young Goddard's imagination was fired by the H.G. Wells space-fiction novel *War of the Worlds*, then serialized in the *Boston Post*. Shortly thereafter, as he recounted, he actually dreamed of constructing a workable space-flight machine. On Oct. 19, 1899, a day that became his "Anniversary Day," he climbed a cherry tree in his backyard and ". . . imagined how wonderful it would be to make some device which had even the *possibility* of ascending to Mars . . . when I descended the tree . . . ," he wrote in his diary, "existence at last seemed very purposive."

Goddard's fascination with space flight and the means of attaining it continued into his college years at the Worcester Polytechnic Institute. In an assigned theme, "Travelling in 1950," he was also intrigued with the notion of "the fastest possible travel for living bodies on the earth's surface" and projected a plan for travel inside a steel

Robert Goddard, the father of modern rocketry, poses in this 1928 photo with one of his creations—a rocket set in a frame with a combustion chamber. Getty/Hulton Archive

vacuum tube in which cars were suspended and driven by the attraction and repulsion of electromagnets. Patents on a vacuum-tube system of transport were later granted the inventor, with thrust—acceleration and deceleration— the chief principle.

RESEARCH IN MASSACHUSETTS

In 1908 Goddard began a long association with Clark University, Worcester, where he earned his doctorate, taught physics, and carried out rocket experiments. In his small laboratory there, he was the first to prove that thrust and consequent propulsion can take place in a vacuum, needing no air to push against. He was the first to explore mathematically the ratios of energy and thrust per weight of various fuels, including liquid oxygen and liquid hydrogen. He was also the first to develop a rocket motor using liquid fuels (liquid oxygen and gasoline), as used in the German V-2 rocket weapon 15 years later. In a small structure adjoining his laboratory, a liquid-propelled rocket in a static test in 1925 "operated satisfactorily and lifted its own weight," he wrote. On March 16, 1926, the world's first flight of a liquid-propelled rocket engine took place on his Aunt Effie's farm in Auburn, Mass., achieving a brief liftoff.

As is frequently the case with scientific theory and invention, developments proceeded in various parts of the world. In achieving liftoff of his small but sophisticated rocket engine, Goddard carried his experiments further than did the Russian and German space pioneers of the day. While Goddard was engaged in building models of a space-bound vehicle, he was unaware that an obscure schoolteacher in a remote village of Russia was equally fascinated by the potential for space flight. In 1903 Konstantin E. Tsiolkovsky wrote "Investigations of Space by Means of Rockets," which many years later was hailed by the Soviet Union as the forerunner of space flight. The other member of the pioneer space trio—Hermann Oberth of Germany—published his space-flight treatise, *Die Rakete zu den Planetenräumen*, in 1923, four years after the appearance of Goddard's early monograph.

Goddard's early tests and others were modestly financed over a period of several years by the Smithsonian Institution, whose secretary, Charles G. Abbot, had responded to Goddard's appeal for financial support. In 1929, following an aborted and noisy flight test that brought unwanted press notice to the publicity-shy inventor, Charles A. Lindbergh was instrumental in procuring greater financial assistance for Goddard's experiments. From 1930 to the mid-1940s, the Guggenheim Fund for the Promotion of Aeronautics financed the work on a scale that made possible a small shop and crew and experimental flights in the open spaces of the American southwest, at Roswell, N.M. There, Goddard spent most of his remaining days in the unending trial-and-error reach for high altitudes.

EXPERIMENTS AT ROSWELL

In the course of his experiments there he became the first to shoot a liquid-fuel rocket faster than the speed of sound (1935). He obtained the first patents of a steering apparatus for the rocket machine and of the use of "step rockets" to gain great altitudes. He also developed the first pumps suitable for rocket fuels, self-cooling rocket motors, and other components of an engine designed to carry man to outer space. Furthermore, his experiments and calculations took place at a time when any news of his work drew from the press and the public high amusement that "Moony" Goddard could take seriously the possibility of travel beyond Earth. His small rockets, early prototypes of the modern Moon thrusters, achieved altitudes of up to 1 mile (1.6 km) above the prairie.

During World War II, Goddard offered his work to the military, but lack of interest in rocket development led to his closing down the Roswell establishment and participating in the war effort through a small Navy contract for work at Annapolis, Md., on the development of a jet-thrust booster for seaplane takeoff. Lindbergh and the industrialist and philanthropist Harry F. Guggenheim remained staunch advocates of the Worcester inventor and the feasibility of space exploration.

Goddard died of throat cancer in 1945, at the threshold of the age of jet and rocket. Years later, his work was acknowledged by the United States government when a $1,000,000 settlement was made for the use of his patents. The Goddard Memorial Library at Clark University was named in his honour.

CLARENCE BIRDSEYE
(b. Dec. 9, 1886, New York, N.Y., U.S.—d. Oct. 7, 1956, New York)

Clarence Birdseye was an American businessman and inventor best known for developing a process for freezing foods in small packages suitable for retailing.

After working as a government naturalist, Birdseye went to Labrador as a fur trader in 1912 and again in 1916. There the people often froze food in the winter because of the difficulty of obtaining fresh food; this solution to their problem spurred Birdseye's imagination.

After returning to the United States, he began to experiment. In 1924 he helped found General Seafoods Company, having developed two processes for freezing fish based on a theory of quick freezing. His first patent, describing a method for preserving piscatorial products, involved placing food between two metal plates that were chilled by a calcium chloride solution to approximately -40 °F (-40 °C). The second process utilized two hollow metal plates that were cooled to -13 °F (-25 °C) by vaporization of ammonia. In 1929 Birdseye began selling his quick-frozen foods, a successful line of products that made him wealthy. Though his were not the first frozen foods, Birdseye's freezing processes were highly efficient ones that preserved the original flavour of a variety of foods, including fish, fruits, and vegetables. In 1929 Birdseye's company was bought by Postum, Inc., which changed its own name to the General Foods Corporation, retaining Birdseye as a consultant. From 1930 to 1934 Birdseye was president of Birds Eye Frosted Foods and from 1935 to 1938, of Birdseye Electric Company.

Birdseye held nearly 300 patents. Besides his frozen food process, he developed infrared heat lamps, a recoilless harpoon gun for taking whales, and a method of removing water from foods. A few years before his death he perfected a method of converting bagasse (crushed sugarcane residue) into paper pulp.

IGOR SIKORSKY

(b. May 25, 1889, Kiev, Russia—d. Oct. 26, 1972, Easton, Conn., U.S.)

Igor Ivan Sikorsky was a Russian-born U.S. pioneer in aircraft design who is best known for his successful development of the helicopter.

EDUCATION AND EARLY CAREER

Sikorsky's father was a physician and professor of psychology. His mother also was a physician but never practiced professionally. Her great interest in art and in the life and work of Leonardo da Vinci undoubtedly stimulated her son's early interest in experimenting with model flying machines; when he was 12 years old he made a small rubber-powered helicopter that could rise in the air.

In 1903 Sikorsky entered the Naval Academy in St. Petersburg, with the intention of becoming a career officer, but his interest in engineering led to his resignation from the service in 1906. After a brief period of engineering study in Paris, he entered the Kiev Polytechnic Institute. Following a reasonably successful academic year, however, he concluded that the abstract sciences and the higher mathematics as then taught had little relationship to the solution of practical problems, and he left the school, preferring to spend his time in his own shop and laboratory.

A trip through Europe in the summer of 1908 brought him into contact with the accomplishments of the Wright brothers and the group of European inventors who were trying to match their progress in flight. Returning to Kiev, Sikorsky came to the conclusion that the way to fly was "straight up," as Leonardo had proposed, a concept that called for a horizontal rotor. Assisted financially by his sister Olga, he returned to Paris in January 1909 for further study and to purchase a lightweight engine.

Back in Kiev in May of 1909 he began construction of a helicopter. Its failure revealed some of the practical obstacles. A second machine with a larger engine was tested in 1910, but it also failed to fly. He then made a major decision: "I had learned enough to recognize that with the existing state of the art, engines, materials, and—most of all—the shortage of money and lack of experience . . . I would not be able to produce a successful helicopter at that time." In fact, he had to wait 30 years before all conditions could be met.

For the time being Sikorsky decided to enter the field of fixed-wing design and began construction of his first airplane. Sikorsky's S-1 biplane was tested early in 1910, and, although its 15-horsepower engine proved inadequate, a redesigned airframe with a larger engine (S-2) carried him on his first short flight. The S-3, S-4, and S-5 followed in quick succession, each a refinement of its predecessor, and each adding to his piloting experience. Finally, by the summer of 1911, in an S-5 with a 50-horsepower engine, he was able to remain in the air for more than an hour, attain altitudes of 1,500 feet (450 metres), and make short cross-country flights. This success earned him International Pilot's License Number 64.

The subsequent S-6 series established Sikorsky as a serious competitor for supplying aircraft to the Russian Army. Characteristically, he soon took a giant step: the first four-engined airplane, called "Le Grand," the precursor of many modern bombers and commercial transports, which he built and flew successfully by 1913. Among its innovative features, not adopted elsewhere until the middle 1920s, was a completely enclosed cabin for pilots and passengers.

In the period of disruption following the Russian Revolution and the collapse of Germany, Sikorsky saw little opportunity for further aircraft development in Europe. He decided to start over again in the United States and in March 1919 landed in New York as an immigrant.

WORK IN THE UNITED STATES

After several lean years as a lecturer and schoolteacher, while trying to find a place for himself in the contracting postwar aircraft industry, he and a few associates, some of them former Russian officers, formed their own company, the Sikorsky Aero Engineering Corporation. They set up shop in an old barn on a farm near Roosevelt Field on Long Island. Sikorsky became a U.S. citizen in 1928. By 1929 the company, having become a division of United Aircraft

Corporation, occupied a large modern plant at Bridgeport, Conn., and was producing S-38 twin-engined amphibians in considerable numbers. In 1931 the first S-40, the "American Clipper," pioneered Pan American World Airways mail and passenger routes around the Caribbean and to South America. By the summer of 1937 Pan American began transpacific and transatlantic service with the first four-engined S-42 "Clipper," the last of the Sikorsky series, the ancestor of which had been "Le Grand" of 1913.

By the late 1930s changing requirements for military and commercial air transport forecast the termination of the large flying boat, and Sikorsky returned to his first love, the helicopter. Once again he was involved in "advanced pioneering work . . . where extremely little reliable information and no piloting experience whatever were available." The essential aerodynamic theory and construction techniques that had been lacking in 1910, however, were now available. Early in 1939, with a well-trained engineering group at his disposal, he started the construction of the VS-300 helicopter. As he said later, "There was a great satisfaction in knowing that, within a short period of time, good engineering along a novel line produced encouraging results." On Sept. 14, 1939, the VS-300 lifted off the ground on its first flight. Its designer was at the controls; during his entire career Sikorsky always insisted on making the first trial flight of any new design himself. On May 6, 1941, in an improved machine, he established an international endurance record of one hour 32.4 seconds.

It is doubtful that Sikorsky at that time fully envisioned the remarkable development of the vertical-lift machine in the next 30 years. Certainly he did not anticipate widespread use of the helicopter as an offensive military weapon. He regarded it as a useful tool for industry and air commerce but primarily as an effective device for rescue and relief of human beings caught in natural disasters, such as fire, flood, or famine. He estimated that more than 50,000 lives had been saved by helicopters.

Igor Sikorsky's active professional life covered virtually the entire span of practical flight by man, from the Wright brothers to space exploration. Few in aviation can claim such a span of personal participation, or personal contribution with such a wide range of innovative ideas. He only complained that, of all his past predictions, those that he lived to regret were on the "too conservative" side.

Sikorsky retired as engineering manager for his company in 1957 but remained active as a consultant until his death. In addition to his wife (married in 1924), he left one daughter and four sons. Sikorsky received many honorary doctorates in science and engineering, honorary fellowships in leading scientific and technical societies in the United States and Europe, and the highest medals and awards in aviation, including the Cross of St. Vladimir from Russia; the Sylvanus Albert Reed Award for 1942 from the Institute of Aeronautical Sciences in New York; the United States Presidential Certificate of Merit in 1948; the Daniel Guggenheim Medal and Certificate for 1951; the Elmer A. Sperry Award for 1964; and the National Defense Award in 1971.

Sikorsky's *Recollections and Thoughts of a Pioneer* (1964) reviews his own career and accomplishments and includes his views on the future trends of aviation development. *The Story of the Winged-S: Late Developments and Recent Photographs of the Helicopter*, rev. ed. (1967), an autobiography, includes a detailed account of his life and work through 1938, with supplementary chapters on his first helicopter experiments of 1939–40 and later work.

VLADIMIR ZWORYKIN

(b. July 30, 1889, Murom, Russia—d. July 29, 1982, Princeton, N.J., U.S.)

Vladimir Kosma Zworykin, a Russian-born American electronic engineer and inventor, is considered to be the father of modern television.

After education at the St. Petersburg Institute of Technology and the Collegè de France, in Paris, Zworykin served during World War I in the Russian Signal Corps. He emigrated to the United States in 1919 and became a naturalized citizen in 1924. In 1920 he joined the Westinghouse Electric Corporation in Pittsburgh, and in 1923 he filed a patent application for an all-electronic television system, although he was as yet unable to build and demonstrate it. In 1929 he convinced David Sarnoff, vice president and general manager of Westinghouse's parent company, the Radio Corporation of America (RCA), to support his research by predicting that in two years, with $100,000 of funding, he could produce a workable electronic television system. Meanwhile, the first demonstration of a primitive electronic system had been made in San Francisco in 1927 by Philo Taylor Farnsworth, a young man with only a high-school education. Farnsworth had garnered research funds by convincing his investors that he could market an economically viable television system in six months for an investment of only $5,000. In the event, it took the efforts of both men and more than $50 million before anyone made a profit.

With his first $100,000 of RCA research money, Zworykin developed a workable cathode-ray receiver that he called the Kinescope. At the same time, Farnsworth was perfecting his Image Dissector camera tube. In 1930 Zworykin visited Farnsworth's laboratory and was given a demonstration of the Image Dissector. At that point a healthy cooperation might have arisen between the two pioneers, but competition, spurred by the vision of corporate profits, kept them apart. Sarnoff offered Farnsworth $100,000 for his patents but was summarily turned down. Farnsworth instead accepted an offer to join RCA's rival Philco, but he soon left to set up his own firm. Then in 1931 Zworykin's RCA team, after learning much from the study of Farnsworth's Image Dissector, came up with the Iconoscope camera tube, and with it they finally had a working electronic system.

Zworykin's television system provided the impetus for the development of modern television as an entertainment and education medium. Although ultimately replaced by the orthicon and image orthicon tubes, the Iconoscope was the basis for further important developments in television cameras. The modern television picture tube is basically Zworykin's Kinescope. He also developed a colour-television system, for which he received a patent in 1928. His other developments in electronics include an early form of the electric eye and innovations in the electron microscope. His electron image tube, sensitive to infrared light, was the basis for the sniperscope and the snooperscope, devices first used in World War II for seeing in the dark. His secondary-emission multiplier was used in the scintillation counter, one of the most sensitive of radiation detectors.

In later life Zworykin lamented the way television had been abused to titillate and trivialize subjects rather than for the educational and cultural enrichment of audiences.

Named an honorary vice president of RCA in 1954, from then until 1962 Zworykin also served as director of the medical electronics centre of the Rockefeller Institute for Medical Research (now Rockefeller University) in New York City. In 1967 the National Academy of Sciences awarded him the National Medal of Science for his contributions to the instruments of science, engineering, and television and for his stimulation of the application of engineering to medicine. He was also founder-president of the International Federation for Medical Electronics and Biological Engineering, a recipient of the Faraday Medal from Great Britain (1965) and the U.S. Presidential Medal of Science (1966), and a member of the U.S. National Hall of Fame from 1977.

Zworykin wrote *Photocells and Their Applications* (1932), *Television* (1940; rev. ed., 1954), *Electron Optics and the Electron Microscope* (1946), *Photoelectricity and Its Application* (1949), and *Television in Science and Industry* (1958).

EDWIN H. ARMSTRONG

(b. Dec. 18, 1890, New York, N.Y., U.S.—d. Jan. 31/Feb. 1, 1954, New York City)

American inventor Edwin Howard Armstrong laid the foundation for much of modern radio and electronic circuitry, including the regenerative and superheterodyne circuits and the frequency modulation (FM) system.

EARLY LIFE

Armstrong was from a genteel, devoutly Presbyterian family of Manhattan. His father was a publisher and his mother a former schoolteacher. Armstrong was a shy boy interested from childhood in engines, railway trains, and all mechanical contraptions.

At age 14, fired by reading of the exploits of Guglielmo Marconi in sending the first wireless message across the Atlantic Ocean, Armstrong decided to become an inventor. He built a maze of wireless apparatus in his family's attic and began the solitary, secretive work that absorbed his life. Except for a passion for tennis and, later, for fast motor cars, he developed no other significant interests. Wireless was then in the stage of crude spark-gap transmitters and iron-filing receivers, producing faint Morse-code signals, barely audible through tight earphones. Armstrong joined in the hunt for improved instruments. On graduating from high school, he commuted to Columbia University's School of Engineering.

In his junior year at Columbia, Armstrong made his first, most seminal invention. Among the devices investigated for better wireless reception was the then little understood, largely unused Audion, or three-element vacuum tube, invented in 1906 by Lee De Forest, a pioneer in the development of wireless telegraphy and television. Armstrong made exhaustive measurements to find out how the tube worked and devised a circuit, called the regenerative, or feedback, circuit, that suddenly, in the autumn of 1912, brought in signals with a thousandfold amplification, loud enough to be heard across a room. At its highest amplification, he also discovered, the tube's circuit shifted from being a receiver to being an oscillator, or primary generator, of wireless waves. As a radio wave generator, this circuit is still at the heart of all radio-television broadcasting.

Armstrong's priority was later challenged by De Forest in a monumental series of corporate patent suits, extending more than 14 years, argued twice before the U.S. Supreme Court, and finally ending—in a judicial misunderstanding of the nature of the invention—in favour of De Forest. But the scientific community never accepted this verdict. The Institute of Radio Engineers refused to revoke an earlier gold-medal award to Armstrong for the discovery of the feedback circuit. Later he received the Franklin Medal, highest of the United States' scientific honours, reaffirming his invention of the regenerative circuit.

This youthful invention that opened the age of electronics had profound effects on Armstrong's life. It led him, after a stint as an instructor at Columbia University, into the U.S. Army Signal Corps laboratories in World War I in Paris, where he invented the superheterodyne circuit, a highly selective means of receiving, converting, and greatly amplifying very weak, high-frequency electromagnetic waves, which today underlies 98 percent of all radio, radar, and television reception over the airways. It brought him into early association with the man destined to lead the postwar Radio Corporation of America (RCA), David Sarnoff, whose young secretary Armstrong later married. Armstrong himself returned after the war to Columbia University to become assistant to Michael Pupin, the notable physicist and inventor and his revered teacher. In this period he sold patent rights on his circuits to the major corporations, including RCA, for large sums in cash and stock. Suddenly, in the radio boom of the 1920s, he found himself a millionaire. But he continued to teach at Columbia, financing his own research, working along with Pupin, whose professorship he inherited, on the long-unsolved problem of eliminating static from radio.

INVENTION OF FM BROADCASTING

In 1933 Armstrong secured four patents on advanced circuits that were to solve this last basic problem. They revealed an entirely new radio system, from transmitter to receiver. Instead of varying the amplitude, or power, of radio waves to carry voice or music, as in all radio before then, the new system varied, or modulated, the waves' frequency (number of waves per second) over a wide band of frequencies. This created a carrier wave that natural static—an amplitude phenomenon created by electrical storms—could not break into. As a result, FM's wide frequency range made possible the first clear, practical method of high-fidelity broadcasting.

Because the new system required a basic change in transmitters and receivers, it was not embraced with any alacrity by the established radio industry. Armstrong had to build the first full-scale FM station himself in 1939 at a cost of more than $300,000 to prove its worth. He then had to develop and promote the system, sustain it through World War II (while he again turned to military research), and fight off postwar regulatory attempts to hobble FM's growth. When FM slowly established itself, Armstrong again found himself entrapped in another interminable patent suit to retain his invention. Ill and aging in 1954, with most of his wealth gone in the battle for FM, he took his own life.

The years have brought increasing recognition of Armstrong's place in science and invention. FM is now the preferred system in radio, the required sound channel in all television, and the dominant medium in mobile radio, microwave relay, and space-satellite communications. Posthumously, Armstrong was elected to the pantheon of electrical greats by the International Telecommunications Union, to join such figures as André-Marie Ampère, Alexander Graham Bell, Michael Faraday, and Guglielmo Marconi.

R. BUCKMINSTER FULLER

(b. July 12, 1895, Milton, Mass., U.S.—d. July 1, 1983, Los Angeles, Calif.)

Richard Buckminster Fuller was a U.S. engineer and architect who developed the geodesic dome, the only large dome that can be set directly on the ground as a complete structure, and the only practical kind of building that has no limiting dimensions (i.e., beyond which the structural strength must be insufficient). Among the most noteworthy geodesic domes is the United States pavilion for Expo 67 in Montreal. Also a poet and a philosopher, he was noted for unorthodox ideas on global issues.

LIFE

Fuller was descended from a long line of New England Nonconformists, the most famous of whom was his great-aunt, Margaret Fuller, the critic, teacher, woman of letters and cofounder of *The Dial*, organ of the Transcendentalist movement. Fuller was twice expelled from Harvard University and never completed his formal education. He saw service in the U.S. Navy during World War I as commander of a crash-boat flotilla. In 1917 he married Anne Hewlett, daughter of James Monroe Hewlett, a well-known architect and muralist. Hewlett had invented a modular construction system using a compressed fibre block, and after the war Fuller and Hewlett formed a construction company that used this material (later known as Soundex, a Celotex product) in modules for house construction. In this operation Fuller himself supervised the erection of several hundred houses.

The construction company encountered financial difficulties in 1927, and Fuller, a minority stockholder, was forced out. He found himself stranded in Chicago, without income, alienated, dismayed, confused. At this point in his life, Fuller resolved to devote his remaining years to a nonprofit search for design patterns that could maximize the social uses of the world's energy resources and evolving industrial complex. The inventions, discoveries, and economic strategies that followed were interim factors related to that end.

In 1927, in the course of the development of his comprehensive strategy, he invented and demonstrated a factory-assembled, air-deliverable house, later called the

Dymaxion house, which had its own utilities. He designed in 1928, and manufactured in 1933, the first prototype of his three-wheeled omnidirectional vehicle, the Dymaxion car. This automobile, the first streamlined car, could cross open fields like a jeep, accelerate to 120 miles (190 km) per hour, make a 180-degree turn in its own length, carry 12 passengers, and average 28 miles per gallon (12 km per litre) of gasoline. In 1943, at the request of the industrialist Henry Kaiser, Fuller developed a new version of the Dymaxion car that was planned to be powered by three separate air-cooled engines, each coupled to its own wheel by a variable fluid drive. The projected 1943 Dymaxion, like its predecessor, was never commercially produced.

American architect Richard Buckminster Fuller is seen here with his most iconic design—the geodesic dome, a kind of structure that has no limiting dimensions. Getty/Hulton Archive

Assuming that there is in nature a vectorial, or directionally oriented, system of forces that provides maximum strength with minimum structures, as is the case in the nested tetrahedron lattices of organic compounds and of metals, Fuller developed a vectorial system of geometry that he called "Energetic-Synergetic geometry." The basic unit of this system is the tetrahedron (a pyramid shape with four sides, including the base), which, in combination with octahedrons (eight-sided shapes), forms the most economic space-filling structures. The architectural consequence of the use of this geometry by Fuller was the geodesic dome, a frame the total strength of which increases in logarithmic ratio to its size. Many thousands of geodesic domes have been erected in various parts of the world, the most publicized of which was the U.S. exhibition dome at Expo 67 in Montreal. One houses the tropical exhibit area of a St. Louis botanical garden; another, the Union Tank Car Company's dome, was built in 1958 in Baton Rouge, La., and was demolished in 2007. This dome, at the time of its construction the largest clear-span structure in existence, was 384 feet (117 metres) in diameter and 116 feet (35 metres) in height.

Other inventions and developments by Fuller included a system of cartography that presents all the land areas of the world without significant distortion; die-stamped prefabricated bathrooms; tetrahedronal floating cities; underwater geodesic-domed farms; and expendable paper domes. Fuller did not regard himself as an inventor or an architect, however. All of his developments, in his view, were accidental or interim incidents in a strategy that aimed at a radical solution of world problems by finding the means to do more with less.

Comprehensive and anticipatory design initiative alone, he held — exclusive of politics and political theory — can solve the problems of human shelter, nutrition, transportation, and pollution; and it can solve these with a fraction of the materials now inefficiently used. Moreover, energy, ever more available, directed by cumulative information stored in computers, is capable of synthesizing raw materials, of machining and packaging commodities, and of supplying the physical needs of the total global population.

Fuller was a research professor at Southern Illinois University (Carbondale) from 1959 to 1968. In 1968 he was named university professor, in 1972 distinguished university professor, and in 1975 university professor emeritus. Queen Elizabeth II awarded Fuller the Royal Gold Medal for Architecture. He also received the 1968 Gold Medal Award of the National Institute of Arts and Letters.

ASSESSMENT

Fuller—architect, engineer, inventor, philosopher, author, cartographer, geometrician, futurist, teacher, and poet—established a reputation as one of the most original thinkers of the second half of the 20th century. He conceived of man as a passenger in a cosmic spaceship—a passenger whose only wealth consists in energy and information. Energy has two phases—associative (as atomic and molecule structures) and dissociative (as radiation)—and, according to the first law of thermodynamics, the energy of the universe cannot be decreased. Information, on the other hand, is negatively entropic; as knowledge, technology, "know-how," it constantly increases. Research engenders research, and each technological advance multiplies the productive wealth of the world community. Consequently, "Spaceship Earth" is a regenerative system whose energy is progressively turned to human advantage and whose wealth increases by geometric increments.

Fuller's book *Nine Chains to the Moon* (1938) is an outline of his general technological strategy for maximizing the social applications of energy resources. He further developed this and other themes in such works as *No More Secondhand God* (1962), *Utopia or Oblivion* (1969), *Operating Manual for Spaceship Earth* (1969), *Earth, Inc.* (1973), and *Critical Path* (1981).

PAUL MÜLLER

(b. Jan. 12, 1899, Olten, Switz. — d. Oct. 12, 1965, Basel)

Paul Hermann Müller was a Swiss chemist who received the Nobel Prize for Physiology or Medicine in 1948 for discovering the potent toxic effects on insects of DDT. With its chemical derivatives, DDT became the most widely used insecticide for more than 20 years and was a major factor in increased world food production and the suppression of insect-borne diseases.

A research chemist at the J.R. Geigy Company, Basel (1925–65), Müller began his career with investigations of dyes and tanning agents. In 1935 he began his search for an "ideal" insecticide, one that would show

Paul Müller. Encyclopædia Britannica, Inc.

rapid, potent toxicity for the greatest number of insect species but would cause little or no damage to plants and warm-blooded animals. He also required that it have a high degree of chemical stability, so that its effect would persist for long periods of time and its manufacture would be economical. Four years later Müller tested a substance known as dichlorodiphenyltrichloroethane (DDT) and found that it satisfied these requirements. The German chemist Othmar Zeidler had first synthesized the compound in 1874 but had failed to realize its value as an insecticide.

In 1939 DDT was tested successfully against the Colorado potato beetle by the Swiss government and by the U.S. Department of Agriculture in 1943. In January 1944 DDT was used to quash an outbreak of typhus carried by lice in Naples, the first time a winter typhus epidemic had been stopped.

Although Müller had required his ideal insecticide to be relatively nontoxic to warm-blooded animals, the widespread use and persistence of DDT (in 1968 it was estimated that 1,000,000,000 pounds [453,000,000 kg] of the substance remained in the environment) made it a hazard to animal life, and it showed signs of disrupting ecological food chains. By 1970 DDT was rapidly being supplanted by more quickly degraded, less toxic agents; its use was banned in a number of countries.

ERNEST O. LAWRENCE

(b. Aug. 8, 1901, Canton, S.D., U.S. — d. Aug. 27, 1958, Palo Alto, Calif.)

Ernest Orlando Lawrence, an American physicist, was awarded the 1939 Nobel Prize for Physics for his invention of the cyclotron, the first particle accelerator to achieve high energies.

Lawrence earned his Ph.D. at Yale University in 1925. An assistant professor of physics at Yale (1927–28), he went to the University of California, Berkeley, as an associate professor and became full professor there in 1930.

Lawrence first conceived the idea for the cyclotron in 1929. One of his students, M. Stanley Livingston, undertook the project and succeeded in building a device that accelerated hydrogen ions (protons) to an energy of 13,000 electron volts (eV). Lawrence then set out to build a second cyclotron; when completed, it accelerated protons to 1,200,000 eV, enough energy to cause nuclear disintegration. To continue the program, Lawrence built the Radiation Laboratory at Berkeley in 1936 and was made its director.

One of Lawrence's cyclotrons produced technetium, the first element that does not occur in nature to be made artificially. His basic design was utilized in developing other particle accelerators, which have been largely responsible for the great advances made in the field of particle physics. With the cyclotron, he produced radioactive phosphorus and other isotopes for medical use, including radioactive iodine for the first therapeutic treatment of hyperthyroidism. In addition, he instituted the use of neutron beams in treating cancer.

During World War II he worked with the Manhattan Project as a program chief in charge of the development of the electromagnetic process of separating uranium-235 for the atomic bomb. In 1957 he received the Fermi Award from the U.S. Atomic Energy Commission. Besides his work in nuclear physics, Lawrence invented and patented a colour-television picture tube. In his honour were named Lawrence Berkeley Laboratory at Berkeley; Lawrence Livermore National Laboratory at Livermore, Calif.; and element 103, lawrencium.

CHARLES STARK DRAPER

(b. Oct. 2, 1901, Windsor, Mo., U.S.—d. July 25, 1987, Cambridge, Mass.)

C harles Stark Draper was an American aeronautical engineer, educator, and science administrator whose laboratory at the Massachusetts Institute of Technology (MIT) was a centre for the design of navigational and guidance systems for ships, airplanes, and missiles from World War II through the Cold War. Combining basic research and student training and supported by a network of corporate and military sponsors, Draper's laboratory was one of the proving grounds for post-World War II Big Science.

Draper received a B.A. in psychology from Stanford University in 1922. He then enrolled at MIT and earned a B.S. in electrochemical engineering in 1926. He remained at MIT to do graduate work in physics and soon demonstrated his precocity as both a researcher and entrepreneur. As a graduate student he became a national expert on aeronautical and meteorological research instruments. The Instruments Laboratory (I-Lab), which he founded in 1934, became a centre for both academic and commercial research, a combination that was not unusual at the time. It was through the I-Lab that Draper established a relationship with the Sperry Gyroscope Company (now part of Unisys Corporation). Though they would later become competitors, Sperry provided critical support for the fledgling laboratory and jobs for Draper's graduate students. Draper also operated a consulting business that further extended his academic and industrial connections. Appointed to the MIT faculty in 1935, he was promoted to professor after receiving his Doctor of Science degree in 1938.

With the start of World War II, Draper turned to developing antiaircraft weapons. The airplane had emerged as a critical weapon of modern warfare, and fighters proved too fast and agile for traditional fire-control systems. With support from Sperry and MIT, Draper and his students designed and built the Mark 14 gyroscopic lead-computing gunsight. Based on a radical new spring mechanism, the gunsight calculated an aircraft's future position, taking into account gravity, wind, and distance. Overcoming the problems posed by the production of the sight demanded that Sperry hire Draper's students to oversee the manufacturing process, while Draper trained naval officers in the newly renamed Confidential Instruments Development Laboratory on the use of the new sight. By war's end more than 85,000 Mark 14 sights had been built and installed on American and British warships, making it by far the most popular sight of its kind used by Allied navies during World War II.

After World War II Draper's interests expanded beyond the development of antiaircraft fire-control systems for capital ships and gunsights to the development of self-contained navigation systems for aircraft and missiles. During World War II radar and other radio- and microwave-based technologies had greatly increased the ability of aircraft to navigate to their targets under various weather conditions and with an unprecedented degree of accuracy. However, these systems were vulnerable to enemy jamming and provided foes with an electromagnetic phantom to track and attack. Other methods of aerial navigation, such as celestial navigation, produced no signals but depended upon the skillful use of instruments and the cooperation of the weather. As the Soviet Union became the main enemy of the United States in the postwar period, the development of a navigation system for aircraft and missiles that did not need external referents or trained humans became a national research priority. Working first with gyroscopes insulated in a climate-controlled viscous fluid and later with accelerometers, Draper developed entirely self-contained inertial guidance systems. These machines were so precise that they could compute a vehicle's exact position from its initial position and acceleration; needing no further inputs, they were invulnerable to enemy countermeasures. The first experimental systems for aircraft, Projects FEBE and SPIRE, were tested in 1949 and 1953. Production systems were installed in aircraft and submarines beginning in 1956 and in the Polaris missile in 1960. The "black boxes" of spinning gyroscopes and integrating circuits developed by Draper and his students were eventually deployed in the Air Force's Atlas, Titan, and Minuteman missiles and the Navy's Poseidon and Trident missiles, placing them at the core of the U.S. thermonuclear arsenal during the Cold War.

Inertial guidance provided a solution to critical technical problems in Cold War nuclear strategy. Equally important to its popularity and success was Draper's training of civilian and military engineers, who learned his methods, became disciples of self-contained navigation, made his systems work in the field, and awarded the I-Lab contracts. With the creation of the Weapons System Engineering Course in 1952, Draper institutionalized one mechanism for the development of a technological intelligentsia within the armed services and made the lab a centre for producing both guidance systems and the people to use them. Graduates of the program were among inertial guidance's most enthusiastic supporters and sources for Laboratory contracts, and they supervised the development of the nation's intercontinental and submarine-launched ballistic systems that used inertial systems. It was a Draper graduate, Robert Seamans, who gave the I-Lab the contract for the development of the Apollo program guidance system that successfully guided Neil Armstrong, Buzz Aldrin, and Michael Collins to the Moon and back.

Students, precision machinery, personal relationships, and federal patronage in civilian and military form made Draper a towering figure in 20th-century engineering and engineering education. Ironically, at the height of his success, in the late 1960s, both he and the I-Lab became the focus of inquiry into the effects of military patronage on MIT. After much protesting by antiwar activists and internal discussion among faculty and administrators, MIT decided in 1970 to divest itself of the laboratory. It was renamed the Charles Stark Draper Laboratory, Inc., and moved off campus in 1973. For a man who was first and foremost a teacher, it was the most undeserved of fates, especially at the institute whose modern form he had done so much to shape. Nonetheless, Draper's career reflected one of the fundamental changes in 20th-century academia: the transformation of academic research into big business supported by the armed services and major corporations. In partial recognition of the scope and significance of Draper's career, the National Academy of Engineering established the Charles Stark Draper Prize in 1988 to honour "innovative engineering achievement and its reduction to practice in ways that have contributed to human welfare and freedom."

WALT DISNEY

(b. December 5, 1901, Chicago, Ill., U.S.—d. December 15, 1966, Los Angeles, Calif.),

Walter Elias Disney, an American motion-picture and television producer and showman, became famous as a pioneer of animated cartoon films and as the creator of such cartoon characters as Mickey Mouse and Donald Duck. He also planned and built Disneyland, a huge amusement park that opened near Los Angeles in

1955, and before his death he had begun building a second such park, Walt Disney World, near Orlando, Florida. The Disney Company he founded has become one of the world's largest entertainment conglomerates.

EARLY LIFE

Walt Disney was the fourth son of Elias Disney, a peripatetic carpenter, farmer, and building contractor, and his wife, Flora Call, who had been a public school teacher. When Walt was little more than an infant, the family moved to a farm near Marceline, Missouri, a typical small Midwestern town, which is said to have furnished the inspiration and model for the Main Street, U.S.A., of Disneyland. There Walt began his schooling and first showed a taste and aptitude for drawing and painting with crayons and watercolours.

His restless father soon abandoned his efforts at farming and moved the family to Kansas City, Mo., where he bought a morning newspaper route and compelled his young sons to assist him in delivering papers. Walt later said that many of the habits and compulsions of his adult life stemmed from the disciplines and discomforts of helping his father with the paper route. In Kansas City the young Walt began to study cartooning with a correspondence school and later took classes at the Kansas City Art Institute and School of Design.

In 1917 the Disneys moved back to Chicago, and Walt entered McKinley High School, where he took photographs, made drawings for the school paper, and studied cartooning on the side, for he was hopeful of eventually achieving a job as a newspaper cartoonist. His progress was interrupted by World War I, in which he participated as an ambulance driver for the American Red Cross in France and Germany.

Returning to Kansas City in 1919, he found occasional employment as a draftsman and inker in commercial art studios, where he met Ub Iwerks, a young artist whose talents contributed greatly to Walt's early success.

FIRST ANIMATED CARTOONS

Dissatisfied with their progress, Disney and Iwerks started a small studio of their own in 1922 and acquired a second-hand movie camera with which they made one and two-minute animated advertising films for distribution to local movie theatres. They also did a series of animated cartoon sketches called *Laugh-O-grams* and the pilot film for a series of seven-minute fairy tales that combined both live action and animation, *Alice in Cartoonland*. A New York film distributor cheated the young producers, and Disney was forced to file for bankruptcy in 1923. He moved to California to pursue a career as a cinematographer, but the surprise success of the first *Alice* film compelled Disney and his brother Roy—a lifelong business partner—to reopen shop in Hollywood.

With Roy as business manager, Disney resumed the *Alice* series, persuading Iwerks to join him and assist with the drawing of the cartoons. They invented a character called Oswald the Lucky Rabbit, contracted for distribution of the films at $1,500 each, and propitiously launched their small enterprise. In 1927, just before the transition to sound in motion pictures, Disney and Iwerks experimented with a new character—a cheerful, energetic, and mischievous mouse called Mickey. They had planned two shorts, called *Plane Crazy* and *Gallopin' Gaucho*, that were to introduce Mickey Mouse when *The Jazz Singer*, a motion picture with the popular singer Al Jolson, brought the novelty of sound to the movies. Fully recognizing the possibilities for sound in animated-cartoon films, Disney quickly produced a third Mickey Mouse cartoon equipped with voices and music, entitled *Steamboat Willie*, and cast aside the other two soundless cartoon films. When it appeared in 1928, *Steamboat Willie* was a sensation.

The following year Disney started a new series called Silly Symphonies with a picture entitled *The Skeleton Dance*, in which a skeleton rises from the graveyard and does a grotesque, clattering dance set to music based on classical themes. Original and briskly syncopated, the film ensured popular acclaim for the series, but, with costs mounting because of the more complicated drawing and technical work, Disney's operation was continually in peril.

The growing popularity of Mickey Mouse and his girlfriend, Minnie, however, attested to the public's taste for the fantasy of little creatures with the speech, skills, and personality traits of human beings. (Disney himself provided the voice for Mickey until 1947.) This popularity led to the invention of other animal characters, such as Donald Duck and the dogs Pluto and Goofy. In 1933 Disney produced a short, *The Three Little Pigs*, which arrived in the midst of the Great Depression and took the country by storm. Its treatment of the fairy tale of the little pig who works hard and builds his house of brick against the huffing and puffing of a threatening wolf suited the need for fortitude in the face of economic disaster, and its song *Who's Afraid of the Big Bad Wolf?* was a happy taunting of adversity. It was in this period of economic hard times in the early 1930s that Disney fully endeared himself and his cartoons to audiences all over the world, and his operation began making money in spite of the Depression.

Disney had by that time gathered a staff of creative young people, who were headed by Iwerks. Colour was introduced in the Academy Award-winning Silly Symphonies film *Flowers and Trees* (1932), while other animal characters came and went in films such as *The Grasshopper and the Ants*

(1934) and *The Tortoise and the Hare* (1935). Roy franchised tie-in sales with the cartoons of Mickey Mouse and Donald Duck—watches, dolls, shirts, and tops—and reaped more wealth for the company.

FEATURE-LENGTH CARTOONS

Walt Disney was never one to rest or stand still. He had long thought of producing feature-length animated films in addition to the shorts. In 1934 he began work on a version of the classic fairy tale *Snow White and the Seven Dwarfs* (1937), a project that required great organization and coordination of studio talent and a task for which Disney possessed a unique capacity. While he actively engaged in all phases of creation in his films, he functioned chiefly as coordinator and final decision maker rather than as designer and artist. *Snow White* was widely acclaimed by critics and audiences alike as an amusing and sentimental romance. By animating substantially human figures in the characters of Snow White, the Prince, and the Wicked Queen and by forming caricatures of human figures in the seven dwarfs, Disney departed from the scope and techniques of the shorts and thus proved animation's effectiveness as a vehicle for feature-length stories.

While Disney continued to do short films presenting the anthropomorphic characters of his little animals, he was henceforth to develop a wide variety of full-length entertainment films, such as *Pinocchio* (1940), *Dumbo* (1941), and *Bambi* (1942). Disney also produced a totally unusual and exciting film—his multisegmented and stylized *Fantasia* (1940), in which cartoon figures and colour patterns were animated to the music of Igor Stravinsky, Paul Dukas, Pyotr Ilyich Tchaikovsky, and others. In 1940 Disney moved his company into a new studio in Burbank, Calif., abandoning the old plant it had occupied in the early days of growth.

MAJOR FILMS AND TELEVISION PRODUCTIONS

A strike by Disney animators in 1941 was a major setback for the company. Many top animators resigned, and it would be many years before the company produced animated features that lived up to the quality of its early 1940s classics. Disney's foray into films for the federal government during World War II helped the studio perfect methods of combining live-action and animation; the studio's commercial films using this hybrid technique include *The Reluctant Dragon* (1941), *Saludos Amigos* (1942), *The Three Caballeros* (1945), *Make Mine Music* (1946), and *Song of the South* (1946).

The Disney studio by that time was established as a big-business enterprise and began to produce a variety of entertainment films. One popular series, called *True-Life Adventures*, featured nature-based motion pictures such as *Seal Island* (1948), *Beaver Valley* (1950), and *The Living Desert* (1953). The Disney studio also began making full-length animation romances, such as *Cinderella* (1950), *Alice in Wonderland* (1951), and *Peter Pan* (1953), and produced low-budget, live-action films, including *The Absent-Minded Professor* (1961).

The Disney studio was among the first to foresee the potential of television as a popular-entertainment medium and to produce films directly for it. The *Zorro* and *Davy Crockett* series were very popular with children, and *Walt Disney's Wonderful World of Color* became a Sunday-night fixture. But the climax of Disney's career as a theatrical film producer came with his release in 1964 of the motion picture *Mary Poppins*, which won worldwide popularity.

DISNEYLAND

In the early 1950s Disney had initiated plans for a huge amusement park to be built near Los Angeles. When Disneyland opened in 1955, much of Disney's disposition toward nostalgic sentiment and fantasy was evident in its design and construction. It soon became a mecca for tourists from around the world. A second Disney park, Walt Disney World, near Orlando, Fla., which was under construction at the time of his death, opened in 1971.

ASSESSMENT

Disney's imagination and energy, his whimsical humour, and his gift for being attuned to the vagaries of popular taste inspired him to develop well-loved amusements for "children of all ages" throughout the world. Although some criticized his frequently saccharine subject matter and accused him of creating a virtual stylistic monopoly in American animation that discouraged experimentation, there is no denying his pathbreaking accomplishments. His achievement as a creator of entertainment for an almost unlimited public and as a highly ingenious merchandiser of his wares can rightly be compared to the most successful industrialists in history.

WILLIAM P. LEAR

(b. June 26, 1902, Hannibal, Mo., U.S. — d. May 14, 1978, Reno, Nev.)

William Powell Lear was a self-taught American electrical engineer and industrialist whose Lear Jet Corporation was the first mass-manufacturer of business jet aircraft in the world. Lear also developed the automobile radio, the eight-track stereo tape player for automobiles, and the miniature automatic pilot for aircraft.

The child of immigrant parents and a broken home, Lear said that at the age of 12 he had worked out a blue-print of his life, based upon profiting by inventing what people wanted. He held some 150 patents at his death.

After completing eighth grade, Lear quit school to become a mechanic and at the age of 16 joined the navy, lying about his age. During World War I, Lear studied radio and after his discharge designed the first practicable auto radio. Failing to secure the financial backing to pro-duce the radio himself, Lear sold the radio to the Motorola Company in 1924.

In 1934 he designed a universal radio amplifier (i.e., one that would work with any radio.) The Radio Corporation of America purchased the plans, giving Lear the capital he needed to expand his operations. He founded the Lear Avia Corporation in 1934 to make radio and navigational devices for aircraft. In 1939 he founded Lear, Inc. By 1939 more than half the private airplanes in the United States were using Lear radio and navigational equipment. In World War II, the company manufactured cowl-flap motors and other precision devices for Allied aircraft. After World War II, Lear, Inc., introduced a new, miniaturized autopilot that could be used on small fighter aircraft.

Between 1950 and 1962 the sales of Lear, Inc., rose to $90,000,000. New plants were added in the Midwest and on both coasts, and the company embarked on the manufacture of stereophonic sound systems and miniature communications satellites. Lear himself wanted to expand into low-priced, small jet aircraft for businessmen. When his board of directors would not approve the expenditure, Lear sold his share of the company and formed Lear Jet,

Inc., Wichita, Kan., which produced its first compact jet in 1963. The new company's jets became among the world's most popular private jet aircraft. Lear sold his interest in the corporation in 1967 and formed Lear Motors Corporation (1967–69) to produce a steam car.

FELIX WANKEL

(b. Aug. 13, 1902, Lahr, Ger.—d. Oct. 9, 1988, Lindau, W.Ger.)

German engineer Felix Wankel was the inventor of the Wankel rotary engine. The Wankel engine is radically different in structure from conventional reciprocating piston engines. Instead of pistons that move up and down in cylinders, the Wankel engine has a triangular orbiting rotor that turns in a closed chamber. Each quarter turn of the rotor completes an expansion or a compression of the gases inside the chamber, permitting the four functions characteristic of all internal-combustion engines—intake, compression, expansion, and exhaust—to be accomplished during one turn of the rotor. The only moving parts are the rotor and the output shaft. In theory, the advantages of this design include light weight, few moving parts, compactness, low initial cost, fewer repairs, and relatively smooth performance.

Wankel never earned an engineering degree and in fact never acquired a driver's license. The son of a forestry official in the Black Forest region of southern Germany, he grew up in straitened circumstances after his father was killed in World War I. As a young man, convinced that he could design a practical rotary engine (the concept was well known but usually dismissed as unworkable), he set up a small engineering business in Heidelberg while financing himself with other jobs such as bookselling. He was briefly a member of the Nazi Party before it rose to power. During the Nazi and World War II period he settled in Lindau, on

Lake Constance near the border with Switzerland, where he worked on designs for seals, unconventional rotary valves, and rotary engines for automobile and airplane engines. At various times he worked for the Daimler-Benz and BMW automobile companies as well as the German air force. At the end of the war his workshop was dismantled by the Allied authorities, and in 1951 he began working in Lindau with the research department of an engine manufacturer, NSU Motorenwerk AG. He completed his first design of a rotary engine for NSU in 1954, and prototype units were tested in 1957 and 1958. In 1961 Mazda, a Japanese automobile company, contracted with NSU to produce and develop the Wankel engine in Japan. Rotary-engined Mazda cars were introduced to the Japanese market in the 1960s and to the American market in 1971. Wankel established a series of his own research establishments at Lindau, where he continued to work under contract for various companies on the fundamental problems and future applications of the rotary engine. He received a number of honours from engineering societies in Germany and abroad, and in 1969 he was awarded an honorary doctorate from the Technical University of Munich. Committed all his life to antivivisectionism, Wankel in 1972 founded the annual or semiannual Felix Wankel Animal Welfare Research Award for papers and projects related to animal welfare and the cessation of experimentation on live animals.

JOHN VON NEUMANN

(b. Dec. 28, 1903, Budapest, Hung.—d. Feb. 8, 1957, Washington, D.C., U.S.)

John von Neumann (originally named János Neumann) was a Hungarian-born American mathematician. As an adult, he appended *von* to his surname; the hereditary title had been granted his father in 1913. Von Neumann grew from child prodigy to one of the world's foremost mathematicians by his mid-20s. Important work in set theory inaugurated a career that touched nearly every major branch of mathematics. Von Neumann's gift for applied mathematics took his work in directions that influenced quantum theory, automata theory, economics, and defense planning. Von Neumann pioneered game theory and, along with Alan Turing and Claude Shannon, was one of the conceptual inventors of the stored-program digital computer.

EARLY LIFE AND MATHEMATICAL CAREER

Von Neumann grew up in an affluent, highly assimilated Jewish family. His father, Miksa Neumann (Max Neumann), was a banker, and his mother, born Margit Kann (Margaret Kann), came from a family that had prospered selling farm equipment. He earned a degree in chemical engineering (1925) from the Swiss Federal Institute in Zürich and a doctorate in mathematics (1926) from the University of Budapest.

From 1926 to 1927 von Neumann did postdoctoral work under David Hilbert at the University of Göttingen. He then took positions as a Privatdozent ("private lecturer") at the Universities of Berlin (1927–29) and Hamburg (1929–30). The work with Hilbert culminated in von Neumann's book *The Mathematical Foundations of Quantum Mechanics* (1932), in which quantum states are treated as vectors in a Hilbert space. This mathematical synthesis reconciled the seemingly contradictory quantum mechanical formulations of Erwin Schrödinger and Werner Heisenberg. Von Neumann also claimed to prove that deterministic "hidden variables" cannot underlie quantum phenomena. This influential result pleased Niels Bohr and Heisenberg and played a strong role in convincing physicists to accept the indeterminacy of quantum theory. In contrast, the result dismayed Albert Einstein, who refused to abandon his belief in determinism.

In 1928 von Neumann published "Theory of Parlor Games," a key paper in the field of game theory. The nominal inspiration was the game of poker. Game theory focuses on the element of bluffing, a feature distinct from the pure logic of chess or the probability theory of roulette. Though von Neumann knew of the earlier work of the French mathematician Émile Borel, he gave the subject mathematical substance by proving the mini-max theorem. This asserts that for every finite, two-person zero-sum game, there is a rational outcome in the sense that two perfectly logical adversaries can arrive at a mutual choice of game strategies, confident that they could not expect to do better by choosing another strategy. In games like poker, the optimal strategy incorporates a chance element. Poker players must bluff occasionally—and unpredictably—in order to avoid exploitation by a savvier player.

In 1929 von Neumann was asked to lecture on quantum theory at Princeton University. This led to an appointment as visiting professor (1930–33). He was remembered as a mediocre teacher, prone to write quickly and erase the blackboard before students could copy what he had written. In 1933 von Neumann became one of the first professors at the Institute for Advanced Study (IAS), Princeton, N.J. The same year, Adolf Hitler came to power in Germany, and von Neumann relinquished his German academic posts. In a much-quoted comment on the Nazi regime, von Neumann wrote, "If these boys continue for only two more years . . . they will ruin German science for a generation—at least."

Though no longer a teacher, von Neumann became a Princeton legend. It was said that he played practical jokes on Einstein, could recite verbatim books that he had read years earlier, and could edit assembly-language computer code in his head. Von Neumann's natural diplomacy helped him move easily among Princeton's intelligentsia, where he often adopted a tactful modesty. He once said he felt he had not lived up to all that had been expected of him. Never much like the stereotypical mathematician, he was known as a wit, bon vivant, and aggressive driver—his frequent auto accidents led to one Princeton intersection being dubbed "von Neumann corner."

WORLD WAR II AND AFTER

In late 1943 von Neumann began work on the Manhattan Project at the invitation of J. Robert Oppenheimer. Von Neumann was an expert in the nonlinear physics of hydrodynamics and shock waves, an expertise that he had already applied to chemical explosives in the British war effort. At Los Alamos, N.M., von Neumann worked on Seth Neddermeyer's implosion design for an atomic bomb. This called for a hollow sphere containing fissionable plutonium to be symmetrically imploded in order to drive the plutonium into a critical mass at the centre. The implosion had to be so symmetrical that it was compared to crushing a beer can without splattering any beer. Adapting an idea proposed by James Tuck, von Neumann calculated that a "lens" of faster- and slower-burning chemical explosives could achieve the needed degree of symmetry. The Fat Man atomic bomb, dropped on the Japanese port of Nagasaki, used this design. Von Neumann participated in the selection of a Japanese target, arguing against bombing the Imperial Palace, Tokyo.

Overlapping with this work was von Neumann's magnum opus of applied math, *Theory of Games and Economic Behavior* (1944), cowritten with Princeton economist Oskar Morgenstern. Game theory had been orphaned since the 1928 publication of "Theory of Parlor Games," with neither von Neumann nor anyone else significantly developing it. The collaboration with Morgernstern burgeoned to 641 pages, the authors arguing for game theory as the "Newtonian science" underlying economic decisions. The book created a vogue for game theory among economists that has partly subsided. The theory has also had broad influence in fields ranging from evolutionary biology to defense planning.

In the postwar years, von Neumann spent increasing time as a consultant to government and industry. Starting in 1944, he contributed important ideas to the U.S. Army's hard-wired ENIAC computer, designed by J. Presper Eckert, Jr., and John W. Mauchly. Most important, von Neumann modified the ENIAC to run as a stored-program machine. He then lobbied to build an improved computer at the Institute for Advanced Study. The IAS machine, which began operating in 1951, used binary arithmetic—the ENIAC had used decimal numbers—and shared the same memory for code and data, a design that greatly facilitated the "conditional loops" at the heart of all subsequent coding. Von Neumann's publications on computer design (1945–51) created friction with Eckert and Mauchly, who sought to patent their contributions, and led to the independent construction of similar machines around the world. This established the merit of a single-processor, stored-program computer—the widespread architecture now known as a von Neumann machine.

Another important consultancy was at the RAND Corporation, a think tank charged with planning nuclear strategy for the U.S. Air Force. Von Neumann insisted on the value of game-theoretic thinking in defense policy. He supported development of the hydrogen bomb and was reported to have advocated a preventive nuclear strike to destroy the Soviet Union's nascent nuclear capability circa 1950. Despite his hawkish stance, von Neumann defended Oppenheimer against attacks on his patriotism and warned Edward Teller that his Livermore Laboratory (now the Lawrence Livermore National Laboratory) cofounders were "too reactionary." From 1954 until 1956, von Neumann served as a member of the Atomic Energy Commission and was an architect of the policy of nuclear deterrence developed by President Dwight D. Eisenhower's administration.

In his last years, von Neumann puzzled over the question of whether a machine could reproduce itself. Using an abstract model (a cellular automata), von Neumann outlined how a machine could reproduce itself from simple components. Key to this demonstration is that the machine reads its own "genetic" code, interpreting it first as instructions for constructing the machine exclusive of the code and second as data. In the second phase, the machine copies its code in order to create a completely "fertile" new machine. Conceptually, this work anticipated later discoveries in genetics.

Von Neumann was diagnosed with bone cancer in 1955. He continued to work even as his health deteriorated rapidly. In 1956 he received the Enrico Fermi Award. A lifelong agnostic, shortly before his death he converted to Roman Catholicism. With his pivotal work on quantum theory, the atomic bomb, and the computer, von Neumann likely exerted a greater influence on the modern world than any other mathematician of the 20th century.

CHESTER F. CARLSON

(b. Feb. 8, 1906, Seattle, Wash., U.S.—d. Sept. 19, 1968, New York, N.Y.)

American physicist Chester F. Carlson was the inventor of xerography (from the Greek words meaning "dry writing"), an electrostatic photocopying process that found applications ranging from office copying to reproducing out-of-print books.

By the age of 14 Carlson was supporting his invalid parents, yet he managed to earn a college degree from the California Institute of Technology, Pasadena, in 1930. After a short time spent with the Bell Telephone Company, he obtained a position with the patent department of P.R. Mallory Company, a New York electronics firm.

Plagued by the difficulty of getting copies of patent drawings and specifications, Carlson began in 1934 to look for a quick, convenient way to copy line drawings and text. Since numerous large corporations were already working on photographic or chemical copying processes, he turned to electrostatics for a solution to the problem. The basis of the process is photoconductivity, an increase in the ability of certain substances to allow an electric current to flow through them when struck by light. The chemical element selenium, for example, is a poor electrical conductor, but when light is absorbed by some of its electrons and a voltage is applied, these electrons are able to pass more freely from one atom to another. When the light is removed, their mobility falls. Xerography typically uses an aluminum drum coated with a layer of selenium. Light passed through the document to be copied, or reflected from its surface, reaches the selenium surface, onto which negatively charged particles of ink (i.e., the toner) are sprayed, forming an image of the document on the drum. A sheet of copy paper is passed close to the drum, and a positive electric charge under the sheet attracts the negatively charged ink particles, resulting in the transfer of the image to the copy paper. Heat is then momentarily applied to fuse the ink particles to the paper.

In 1938 Carlson and a research associate succeeded in making the first xerographic copy. Carlson obtained the first of many patents for the xerographic process in 1940 and for the next four years tried unsuccessfully to interest someone in developing and marketing his invention. More than 20 companies turned him down. Finally, in 1944, he persuaded Battelle Memorial Institute, Columbus, Ohio, a nonprofit industrial research organization, to undertake developmental work. In 1947 a small firm in Rochester, N.Y., the Haloid Company (later the Xerox Corporation), obtained the commercial rights to xerography, and 11 years later Xerox introduced its first office copier. Carlson's royalty rights and stock in Xerox Corporation made him a multimillionaire.

GRACE MURRAY HOPPER

(b. Dec. 9, 1906, New York, N.Y., U.S. — d. Jan. 1, 1992, Arlington, Va.)

Grace Murray Hopper (née Grace Brewster Murray) an American mathematician and rear admiral in the U.S. Navy, was a pioneer in developing computer technology, helping to devise UNIVAC I, the first commercial electronic computer, and naval applications for COBOL (*c*ommon-*b*usiness-*o*riented *l*anguage).

After graduating from Vassar College (B.A., 1928), Hooper attended Yale University (M.A., 1930; Ph.D., 1934). She taught mathematics at Vassar College, Poughkeepsie, N.Y., from 1931 to 1943 before joining the U.S. Naval Reserve. She became a lieutenant and was assigned to the Bureau of Ordnance's Computation Project at Harvard University (1944), where she worked on Mark I, the first

Grace Hopper, a pioneer in the field of computer programming, shown here at work on a UNIVAC mainframe. Smithsonian Institution No. 83-14874

large-scale automatic calculator and a precursor of electronic computers. She remained at Harvard as a civilian research fellow while maintaining her naval career as a reservist. After a moth infiltrated the circuits of Mark I, she coined the term *bug* to refer to unexplained computer failures.

In 1949 Hopper joined the Eckert-Mauchly Computer Corp., where she designed an improved compiler, which translated a programmer's instructions into computer codes. She remained with the firm when it was taken over by Remington Rand (1951) and by Sperry Rand Corp. (1955). In 1957 her division developed Flow-Matic, the first English-language data-processing compiler. She retired from the navy with the rank of commander in 1966, but she was recalled to active duty the following year to help standardize the navy's computer languages. At the age of 79, she was the oldest officer on active U.S. naval duty when she retired again in 1986. She was elected a fellow of the Institute of Electrical and Electronic Engineers (1962), was named the first computer science Man of the Year by the Data Processing Management Association (1969), and was awarded the National Medal of Technology (1991).

FRANK WHITTLE

(b. June 1, 1907, Coventry, Warwickshire, Eng. — d. August 8, 1996, Columbia, Md., U.S.)

Frank Whittle was an English aviation engineer and pilot who invented the jet engine.

The son of a mechanic, Whittle entered the Royal Air Force (RAF) as a boy apprentice and soon qualified as a pilot at the RAF College in Cranwell. He was posted to a fighter squadron in 1928 and served as a test pilot in 1931–32. He then pursued further studies at the RAF engineering school and at the University of Cambridge (1934–37). Early in his career Whittle recognized the potential demand for an aircraft that would be able to fly at great speed and height, and he first put forth his vision of jet propulsion in 1928, in his senior thesis at the RAF College. The young officer's ideas were ridiculed by the Air Ministry as impractical, however, and attracted support from neither the government nor private industry.

Whittle obtained his first patent for a turbo-jet engine in 1930, and in 1936 he joined with associates to found a company called Power Jets, Ltd. He tested his first jet engine on the ground in 1937. This event is customarily regarded as the invention of the jet engine, but the first operational jet engine was designed in Germany by Hans Pabst von Ohain and powered the first jet-aircraft flight on Aug. 27, 1939. The outbreak of World War II finally spurred the British government into supporting Whittle's development work. A jet engine of his invention was fitted to a specially built Gloster E.28/39 airframe, and the plane's maiden flight took place on May 15, 1941. The British government took over Power Jets, Ltd., in 1944, by which time Britain's Gloster Meteor jet aircraft were in service with the RAF, intercepting German V-1 rockets.

Whittle retired from the RAF in 1948 with the rank of air commodore, and that same year he was knighted. The British government eventually atoned for their earlier neglect by granting him a tax-free gift of £100,000. He was awarded the Order of Merit in 1986. In 1977 he became a research professor at the U.S. Naval Academy in Annapolis, Md. His book *Jet: The Story of a Pioneer* was published in 1953.

JOHN MAUCHLY AND J. PRESPER ECKERT

respectively, (b. Aug. 30, 1907, Cincinnati, Ohio, U.S.—d. Jan. 8, 1980, Ambler, Pa.); (b. April 9, 1919, Philadelphia, Pa., U.S.—d. June 3, 1995, Bryn Mawr, Pa.)

During World War II, U.S. government funding went to a project led by John Mauchly, J. Presper Eckert, and their colleagues at the Moore School of Electrical Engineering at the University of Pennsylvania. Their objective was an all-electronic computer, and work began in early 1943 on the Electronic Numerical Integrator and Computer (ENIAC). The next year, mathematician John von Neumann—already on full-time leave from the Institute for Advanced Studies in Princeton, N.J., for various government research projects (including the Manhattan Project)—began frequent consultations with the group.

Completed by February 1946, ENIAC was something less than the dream of a universal computer. Designed for the specific purpose of computing values for artillery range tables, it lacked some features that would have made it a more generally useful machine. For instance, it used plug-boards for communicating instructions to the machine. This had the advantage that, once the instructions were thus "programmed," the machine ran at electronic speed. The disadvantage was that it took days to rewire the machine for each new problem. This was such a liability that only with some generosity could ENIAC be called programmable. Nevertheless, it was the most powerful calculating device built to date and the first programmable general-purpose electronic digital computer.

ENIAC was also enormous. It occupied the 50-by-30-foot (15-by-9-metre) basement of the Moore School, where its 40 panels were arranged, U-shaped, along three walls. Each of the units was about 2 feet wide by 2 feet deep by 8 feet high (0.6 metre by 0.6 metre by 2.4 metres). With approximately 18,000 vacuum tubes, 70,000 resistors, 10,000 capacitors, 6,000 switches, and 1,500 relays, it was easily the most complex electronic system ever built. A portion of the machine is on exhibit at the Smithsonian Institution in Washington, D.C.

JOHN MAUCHLY

After completing his education, John William Mauchly entered the teaching profession, eventually becoming an associate professor of electrical engineering at the University of Pennsylvania, Philadelphia. During World War II Mauchly and Eckert, a graduate engineer, were asked to devise ways to accelerate the recomputation of artillery firing tables for the U.S. Army. They accordingly proposed the construction of a general-purpose digital computer that would handle data in coded form; by 1946 they completed ENIAC, a huge machine containing more than 18,000 vacuum tubes. ENIAC was first used by the U.S. Army at its Aberdeen Proving Ground in Maryland in 1947 for ballistics tests.

The following year Mauchly and Eckert formed a computer-manufacturing firm, and in 1949 they announced the Binary Automatic Computer (BINAC), which used magnetic tape instead of punched cards. In 1950 the Eckert–Mauchly Computer Corporation was acquired by Remington Rand, Inc. (later Sperry Rand Corporation), Mauchly becoming director of special projects. The third computer after BINAC was the Universal Automatic Computer (UNIVAC I), specially designed to handle business data. Mauchly continued his work in the computer field, winning many honours. He served as president (1959–65) and chairman of the board (1965–69) of Mauchly Associates, Inc., and as president of Dynatrend, Inc. (1968–80) and of Marketrend, Inc. (1970–80).

J. PRESPER ECKERT

John Presper Eckert, Jr., was educated at the Moore School of Electrical Engineering at the University of Pennsylvania,

Philadelphia (B.S., 1941; M.S., 1943), where he and his professor, Mauchly, made several valuable improvements in computing equipment. In 1946 the pair fulfilled a government contract to build a digital computer, which they called ENIAC. In primitive form, ENIAC contained virtually all the circuitry used in present-day high-speed digital computers. It was used by the U.S. Army for military calculations.

In 1948 Eckert and Mauchly established a computer-manufacturing firm; a year later, they introduced BINAC, which stored information on magnetic tape rather than on punched cards. Designed to handle business data, UNIVAC I, Eckert and Mauchly's third model, found many uses in commerce and may be said to have started the computer boom. Between 1948 and 1966 Eckert received 85 patents, mostly for electronic inventions.

Eckert remained in executive positions at his company when it was acquired by Remington Rand, Inc., in 1950 and when that firm was, in 1955, merged into the Sperry Rand Corp. (later Unisys Corp.). Eckert was elected to the National Academy of Engineering in 1967 and was awarded the National Medal of Science in 1969.

EDWARD TELLER

(b. Jan. 15, 1908, Budapest, Hung., Austria-Hung.—d. Sept. 9, 2003, Stanford, Calif., U.S.)

Edward Teller was a Hungarian-born American nuclear physicist who participated in the production of the first atomic bomb (1945) and who led the development of the world's first thermonuclear weapon, the hydrogen bomb.

Teller, born Ede Teller, was from a family of prosperous Hungarian Jews. After attending schools in Budapest, he earned a degree in chemical engineering at the Institute of

Technology in Karlsruhe, Ger. He then went to Munich and Leipzig to earn a Ph.D. in physical chemistry (1930). His doctoral thesis, on the hydrogen molecular ion, helped lay the foundation for a theory of molecular orbitals that remains widely accepted today. While a student in Munich, Teller fell under a moving streetcar and lost his right foot, which was replaced with an artificial one.

During the years of the Weimar Republic, Teller was absorbed with atomic physics, first studying under Niels Bohr in Copenhagen and then teaching at the University of Göttingen (1931–33). In 1935 Teller and his bride, Augusta Harkanyi, went to the United States, where he taught at George Washington University in Washington, D.C. Together with his colleague George Gamow, he established new rules for classifying the ways subatomic particles can escape the nucleus during radioactive decay. Following Bohr's stunning report on the fission of the uranium atom in 1939 and inspired by the words of Pres. Franklin D. Roosevelt, who had called for scientists to act to defend the United States against Nazism, Teller resolved to devote his energies to developing nuclear weapons.

By 1941 Teller had taken out U.S. citizenship and joined Enrico Fermi's team at the University of Chicago in the epochal experiment to produce the first self-sustaining nuclear chain reaction. Teller then accepted an invitation from the University of California at Berkeley to work on theoretical studies on the atomic bomb with J. Robert Oppenheimer; and when Oppenheimer set up the secret Los Alamos Scientific Laboratory in New Mexico in 1943, Teller was among the first men recruited. Although the Los Alamos assignment was to build a fission bomb, Teller digressed more and more from the main line of research to continue his own inquiries into a potentially much more powerful thermonuclear hydrogen fusion bomb. At war's end he wanted the U.S. government's nuclear weapons development priorities shifted to the hydrogen bomb. Hiroshima, however, had had a profound effect on Oppenheimer and other Manhattan Project scientists, and few had the desire to continue in nuclear weapons research.

Teller accepted a position with the Institute for Nuclear Studies at the University of Chicago in 1946 but returned to Los Alamos as a consultant for extended periods. The Soviet Union's explosion of an atomic bomb in 1949 made him more determined that the United States have a hydrogen bomb, but the Atomic Energy Commission's general advisory committee, which was headed by Oppenheimer, voted against a crash program to develop one. The debate was settled by the confession of the British atomic scientist Klaus Fuchs that he had been spying for the Soviet Union since 1942. Fuchs had known of the American interest in a hydrogen bomb and had passed along early American data on it to the Soviets. In response, President Harry Truman ordered the go-ahead on the weapon, and Teller laboured on at Los Alamos to make it a reality.

Teller and his colleagues at Los Alamos made little actual progress in designing a workable thermonuclear device until early in 1951, when the physicist Stanislaw Marcin Ulam proposed to use the mechanical shock of an atomic bomb to compress a second fissile core and make it explode; the resulting high density would make the burning of the second core's thermonuclear fuel much more efficient. Teller in response suggested that radiation, rather than mechanical shock, from the atomic bomb's explosion be used to compress and ignite the thermonuclear second core. Together these new ideas provided a firm basis for a fusion weapon, and a device using the

Teller-Ulam configuration, as it is now known, was successfully tested at Enewetak atoll in the Pacific on Nov. 1, 1952; it yielded an explosion equivalent to 10 million tons (10 megatons) of TNT.

Teller was subsequently credited with developing the world's first thermonuclear weapon, and he became known in the United States as "the father of the H-bomb." Ulam's key role in conceiving the bomb design did not emerge from classified government documents and other sources until nearly three decades after the event. Still, Teller's stubborn pursuit of the weapon in the face of skepticism, and even hostility, from many of his peers played a major role in the bomb's development.

At the U.S. government hearings held in 1954 to determine whether Oppenheimer was a security risk, Teller's testimony was decidedly unsympathetic to his former chief. "I would feel personally more secure," he told the inquiry board, "if public matters would rest in other hands." After the hearings' end, Oppenheimer's security clearance was revoked, and his career as a science administrator was at an end. Although Teller's testimony was by no means the decisive factor in this outcome, many prominent American nuclear physicists never forgave him for what they viewed as his betrayal of Oppenheimer.

Teller was instrumental in the creation of the United States' second nuclear weapons laboratory, the Lawrence Livermore Laboratory, in Livermore, Calif., in 1952. For almost the next four decades it was the United States' chief factory for making thermonuclear weapons. Teller was associate director of Livermore from 1954 to 1958 and from 1960 to 1975, and he was its director in 1958–60. Concurrently he was professor of physics at the University of California at Berkeley from 1953 to 1960 and was professor-at-large there until 1970.

A staunch anticommunist, Teller devoted much time in the 1960s to his crusade to keep the United States ahead of the Soviet Union in nuclear arms. He opposed the 1963 Nuclear Test Ban Treaty, which banned nuclear weapons testing in the atmosphere, and he was a champion of Project Plowshare, an unsuccessful federal government program to find peaceful uses for atomic explosives. In the 1970s Teller remained a prominent government adviser on nuclear weapons policy, and in 1982–83 he was a major influence in President Ronald Reagan's proposal of the Strategic Defense Initiative, an attempt to create a defense system against nuclear attacks by the Soviet Union. In 2003 Teller was awarded the Presidential Medal of Freedom.

MICHAEL DEBAKEY

(b. Sept. 7, 1908, Lake Charles, La., U.S.—d. July 11, 2008, Houston, Texas)

Michael Ellis DeBakey was an American cardiovascular surgeon, educator, international medical statesman, and pioneer in surgical procedures for treatment of defects and diseases of the cardiovascular system.

In 1932 DeBakey devised the "roller pump," an essential component of the heart-lung machine that permitted open-heart surgery. He also developed an efficient method of correcting aortic aneurysms by grafting frozen blood vessels to replace diseased vessels. By 1953 DeBakey had developed a technique of using plastic tubing (Dacron) instead of arterial homographs to replace diseased vessels. In 1953 he performed the first successful carotid endarterectomy for stroke, in 1964 the first successful coronary artery bypass, and in 1966 the first successful implantation of a ventricular assist device.

DeBakey received his B.S. (1930), M.D. (1932), and M.S. (1935) degrees from Tulane University School of Medicine in New Orleans. After volunteering for military service during World War II, his work with the U.S. Surgeon General's office led to the development of mobile army surgical hospitals (MASH units) and the Department of Veterans Affairs (VA) hospital research system. In 1948 he became professor of surgery and chairman of the department of surgery at Baylor College of Medicine in Houston, where he later served as president (1969–79) and then as chancellor (1979–96).

DeBakey received numerous national and international awards, including the American Medical Association Distinguished Service Award (1959), the Albert Lasker Award for Clinical Research (1963; corecipient), the Eleanor Roosevelt Humanities Award (1969), the Presidential Medal of Freedom with Distinction (1969), the U.S.S.R. Academy of Sciences 50th Anniversary Jubilee Medal (1973), and the Presidential National Medal of Science (1987). He received more than 50 honorary degrees from universities throughout the world. In 1992 he was introduced into the Academy of Athens, a society of scholars generally restricted to Greeks who have made significant contributions to the arts, sciences, or literature. He edited the *Yearbook of Surgery* (1958–70), was the founding editor of the *Journal of Vascular Surgery*, and served on many medical editorial boards. Among his more than 1,600 professional and lay publications is the *The New Living Heart* (1997). DeBakey later received the Denton A. Cooley Cardiovascular Surgical Society's lifetime achievement award (2007) and was bestowed with the highest and most distinguished civilian award given by the U.S. Congress, the Congressional Gold Medal of Honor (2008).

WILLARD LIBBY

(b. Dec. 17, 1908, Grand Valley, Colo., U.S.—d. Sept. 8, 1980, Los Angeles, Calif.)

Willard Frank Libby was an American chemist whose technique of carbon-14 (or radiocarbon) dating provided an extremely valuable tool for archaeologists, anthropologists, and earth scientists. For this development he was honoured with the Nobel Prize for Chemistry in 1960.

Libby, the son of farmer Ora Edward Libby and his wife, Eva May (née Rivers), attended the University of California at Berkeley, where he received a bachelor's degree (1931) and a doctorate (1933). After graduation, he joined the faculty at Berkeley, where he rose through the ranks from instructor (1933) to assistant professor (1938) to associate professor (1945). In 1940 he married Leonor Hickey, by whom he had twin daughters. In 1966 he was divorced and married Leona Woods Marshall, a staff member at the RAND Corporation of Santa Monica, Calif.

In 1941 Libby received a Guggenheim fellowship to work at Princeton University in New Jersey, but his work was interrupted by the entry of the United States into World War II. He was sent on leave to the Columbia War Research Division of Columbia University in New York City, where he worked with Nobel chemistry laureate Harold C. Urey until 1945. Libby became professor of chemistry at the Institute for Nuclear Studies (now the Enrico Fermi Institute for Nuclear Studies) and the department of chemistry at the University of Chicago (1945–59). He was appointed by Pres. Dwight D. Eisenhower to the U.S. Atomic Energy Commission (1955–59). From 1959 Libby was a professor of chemistry at the University of California, Los Angeles, and director of its Institute of Geophysics and Planetary Physics (from 1962) until his death. He was the recipient of numerous honours, awards, and honourary degrees.

During the late 1950s, Libby and physicist Edward Teller, both committed to the Cold War and both prominent advocates of nuclear weapons testing, opposed Nobel chemistry and peace laureate Linus Pauling's petition for a ban on nuclear weapons. To prove the survivability of nuclear war, Libby built a fallout shelter at his house, an event that was widely publicized. The shelter and house burned down several weeks later, however, which caused physicist and nuclear testing critic Leo Szilard to joke, "This proves not only that there is a God but that he has a sense of humor."

While associated with the Manhattan Project (1941–45), Libby helped develop a method for separating uranium isotopes by gaseous diffusion, an essential step in the creation of the atomic bomb. In 1946 he showed that cosmic rays in the upper atmosphere produce traces of tritium, the heaviest isotope of hydrogen, which can be used as a tracer for atmospheric water. By measuring tritium concentrations, he developed a method for dating well water and wine, as well as for measuring circulation patterns of water and the mixing of ocean waters.

Because it had been known since 1939 that cosmic rays create showers of neutrons on striking atoms in the atmosphere, and because the atmosphere contains about 78 percent nitrogen, which absorbs neutrons to decay into the radioactive isotope carbon-14, Libby concluded that traces of carbon-14 should always exist in atmospheric carbon dioxide. Also, because carbon dioxide is continuously absorbed by plants and becomes part of their tissues, plants should contain traces of carbon-14. Since animals consume plants, animals should likewise contain traces of carbon-14. After a plant or other organism dies, no additional carbon-14 should be incorporated into its tissues, while that which is already present should decay at a constant rate. The half-life of carbon-14 was determined by its codiscoverer, chemist Martin D. Kamen, to be 5,730 years, which, compared with the age of the Earth, is a short time but one long enough for the production and decay of carbon-14 to reach equilibrium. In his Nobel presentation speech, Swedish chemist Arne Westgren summarized Libby's method: "Because the activity of the carbon atoms decreases at a known rate, it should be possible, by measuring the remaining activity, to determine the time elapsed since death, if this occurred during the period between approximately 500 and 30,000 years ago."

Libby verified the accuracy of his method by applying it to samples of fir and redwood trees whose ages had already been found by counting their annual rings and to artifacts, such as wood from the funerary boat of Pharaoh Sesostris III, whose ages were already known. By measuring the radioactivity of plant and animal material obtained globally from the North Pole to the South Pole, he showed that the carbon-14 produced by cosmic-ray bombardment varied little with latitude. On March 4, 1947, Libby and his students obtained the first age determination using the carbon-14 dating technique. He also dated linen wrappings from the Dead Sea Scrolls, bread from Pompeii buried in the eruption of Vesuvius (79 CE), charcoal from a Stonehenge campsite, and corncobs from a New Mexico cave, and he showed that the last North American ice age ended about 10,000 years ago, not 25,000 years ago as previously believed by geologists. The most publicized and controversial case of radiocarbon dating is probably that of the Shroud of Turin, which believers claim once covered the body of Jesus Christ but which Libby's method applied by others shows to be from a period between 1260 and 1390. In nominating Libby for the Nobel Prize, one scientist stated, "Seldom has a single discovery in chemistry had such an impact on the thinking in so many fields of human endeavour. Seldom has a single discovery generated such wide public interest."

EDWIN HERBERT LAND

(b. May 7, 1909, Bridgeport, Conn., U.S.—d. March 1, 1991, Cambridge, Mass.)

Edwin Herbert Land was an American inventor and phys-icist whose one-step process for developing and printing photographs culminated in a revolution in photography unparalleled since the advent of roll film.

While a student at Harvard University, Land became interested in polarized light, i.e., light in which all rays are aligned in the same plane. He took a leave of absence, and, after intensive study and experimentation, succeeded (1932) in aligning submicroscopic crystals of iodoquinine sulfate and embedding them in a sheet of plastic. The resulting polarizer, for which he envisioned numerous uses and which he dubbed Polaroid J sheet, was a tremendous advance. It allowed the use of almost any size of polarizer and significantly reduced the cost.

With George Wheelwright III, a Harvard physics instructor, Land founded the Land-Wheelwright Laboratories, Boston, in 1932. He developed and, in 1936, began to use numerous types of Polaroid material in sunglasses and other optical devices. Polaroid was later used in camera filters and other optical equipment.

Land founded the Polaroid Corporation, Cambridge, Mass., in 1937. Four years later he developed a widely used, three-dimensional motion-picture process based on polarized light. During World War II he applied the polarizing principle to various types of military equipment.

Land began work on an instantaneous developing film after the war. In 1947 he demonstrated a camera (known as the Polaroid Land Camera) that produced a finished print in 60 seconds. The Land photographic process soon found numerous commercial, military, and scientific applications. Many innovations were made in the following years, including the development of a colour process. Land's Polaroid Land cameras, which were able to produce developed photographs within one minute after the exposure, became some of the most popular cameras in the world.

Land's interest in light and colour resulted in a new theory of colour perception. In a series of experiments he revealed certain conflicts in the classical theory of colour perception. He found that the colour perceived is not dependent on the relative amounts of blue, green, and red light entering the eye; he proposed that at least three independent image-forming mechanisms, which he called retinexes, are sensitive to different colours and work in conjunction to indicate the colour seen.

Land received more than 500 patents for his innovations in light and plastics. In 1980 he retired as chief executive officer of Polaroid but remained active in the field of light and colour research by working with the Rowland Institute of Science, a nonprofit centre supported by the Rowland Foundation, Inc., a corporation that Land founded in 1960. Under Land's direction, Rowland researchers discovered that perception of light and colour is regulated essentially by the brain, rather than through a spectrum system in the retina of the eye, as was previously believed.

VIRGINIA APGAR

(b. June 7, 1909, Westfield, N.J., U.S.—d. Aug. 7, 1974, New York, N.Y.)

Virginia Apgar, an American physician, anesthesiologist, and medical researcher, developed the Apgar Score System, a method of evaluating an infant shortly after birth to assess its well-being and to determine if any immediate medical intervention is required.

Apgar graduated from Mount Holyoke College in 1929 and from the Columbia University College of Physicians and Surgeons in 1933. After an internship at Presbyterian Hospital, New York City, she held residencies in the relatively new specialty of anesthesiology at the University of Wisconsin and then at Bellevue Hospital, New York City, in 1935–37. In 1937 she became the first female board-certified anesthesiologist. The first professor of anesthesiology at the College of Physicians and Surgeons (1949–59), she was also the first female physician to attain the rank of full professor there. Additionally, from 1938 she was director of the department of anesthesiology at Columbia-Presbyterian Medical Center.

An interest in obstetric procedure, and particularly in the treatment of the newborn, led her to develop a simple system for quickly evaluating the condition and viability of newly delivered infants. As finally presented in 1952, the Apgar Score System relies on five simple observations to be made by delivery room personnel (nurses or interns) of the infant within one minute of birth and—depending on the results of the first observation—periodically thereafter. The Apgar Score System soon came into general use throughout the United States and was adopted by several other countries.

In 1959 Apgar left Columbia and took a degree in public health from Johns Hopkins University. She headed the division of congenital malformations at the National Foundation-March of Dimes from 1959–67. She was promoted to director of basic research at the National Foundation (1967–72), and she later became senior vice president for medical affairs (1973–74). She cowrote the book *Is My Baby All Right?* (1972) with Joan Beck.

LEO FENDER

(b. Aug. 10, 1909, Anaheim, Calif., U.S. — d. March 21, 1991, Fullerton, Calif.)

Clarence Leo Fender was an American inventor and manufacturer of electronic musical instruments.

Together with George Fullerton, Fender developed the first mass-produced solid-body electric guitar, in 1948. Called the Fender Broadcaster (renamed the Telecaster in 1950), it was produced under the auspices of the Fender Electric Instruments Company, which Fender had formed in 1946. In 1951 the Fender Precision Bass, the world's first electric bass guitar, was unveiled, and in 1954 the Fender Stratocaster was put on the market. More stylish and technically improved than the Telecaster, the Stratocaster was the first guitar to feature three electric pickups (instead of two) and the tremolo arm used for vibrato effects. Its clean, sharp sound earned it a loyal following among guitarists, rivaled only by that of Gibson's eponymous Les Paul, and it became the signature instrument of Jeff Beck, Eric Clapton, Jimi Hendrix, and others.

Fender, who never learned to play the instrument he revolutionized, sold his manufacturing and distribution companies to CBS Corporation in 1965, a concession to his failing health. When his physical condition improved a few years later, he returned to the company as a design consultant and continued to indulge his inventive and entrepreneurial inclinations well into the 1980s.

WILLIAM SHOCKLEY, JOHN BARDEEN, AND WALTER BRATTAIN

respectively, (b. Feb. 13, 1910, London, Eng.—d. Aug. 12, 1989, Palo Alto, Calif., U.S.); (b. May 23, 1908, Madison, Wis., U.S.—d. Jan. 30, 1991, Boston, Mass.); (b. Feb. 10, 1902, Amoy, China—d. Oct. 13, 1987, Seattle, Wash., U.S.)

Electron tubes are bulky and fragile, and they consume large amounts of power to heat their cathode filaments and generate streams of electrons; also, they often burn out after several thousand hours of operation. Electromechanical switches, or relays, are slow and can become stuck in the on or off position. For applications requiring thousands of tubes or switches, such as the nationwide telephone systems developing around the world in the 1940s and the first electronic digital computers, this meant constant vigilance was needed to minimize the inevitable breakdowns.

An alternative was found in semiconductors, materials such as silicon or germanium whose electrical conductivity lies midway between that of insulators such as glass and conductors such as aluminum. The conductive properties of semiconductors can be controlled by "doping" them with select impurities, and a few visionaries had seen the potential of such devices for telecommunications and computers. Executives at Bell Telephone Laboratories, for instance, recognized that semiconductors might lead to solid-state alternatives to the electron-tube amplifiers and electromechanical switches employed throughout the nationwide Bell telephone system. With the close of World War II, Bell Labs created a new solid-state research group headed by solid-state physicist William B. Shockley.

Shockley suggested that silicon and germanium semi-conductors could be used to make a field-effect amplifier. He reasoned that an electric field from a third electrode could increase the conductivity of a sliver of semiconductor material just beneath it and thereby allow usable current to flow through the sliver. But attempts to fabricate such a device by Walter H. Brattain, an experimental physicist already working at Bell Labs, and others in Shockley's group failed. The following March, John Bardeen, a theo-retical physicist whom Shockley had hired for his group, offered a possible explanation. Perhaps electrons drawn to the semiconductor surface by the electric field were blocking the penetration of this field into the bulk material, thereby preventing it from influencing the conductivity.

Working closely together, Bardeen and Brattain invented the first successful semiconductor amplifier, called the point-contact transistor, on Dec. 16, 1947. Their weird-looking device had not one but two closely spaced metal wires jabbing into the surface of a semiconductor—in this case, germanium. The input signal on one of these wires (the emitter) boosted the conductivity of the germanium beneath both of them, thus modulating the output signal on the other wire (the collector). Observers present at a demonstration of this device the following week could hear amplified voices in the earphones that it powered. Shockley, not to be outdone by members of his own group, conceived yet another way to fabricate a semiconductor amplifier the very next month, on Jan. 23, 1948. His junc-tion transistor was basically a three-layer sandwich of germanium or silicon in which the adjacent layers would be doped with different impurities to induce distinct electrical characteristics.

The name *transistor*, a combination of *transfer* and *resistor*, was coined for these devices in May 1948 by Bell Labs electrical engineer John Robinson Pierce, who was also a

WILLIAM SHOCKLEY, JOHN BARDEEN, AND WALTER BRATTAIN

science-fiction author in his spare time. A month later Bell Labs announced the revolutionary invention in a press conference held at its New York City headquarters, heralding Bardeen, Brattain, and Shockley as the three coinventors of the transistor. The three were awarded the 1956 Nobel Prize for Physics for their invention, which ushered in the age of microminiature electronics.

WILLIAM SHOCKLEY

William Bradford Shockley studied physics at the California Institute of Technology (B.S., 1932) and at Harvard University (Ph.D., 1936). He joined the technical staff of Bell Labs in 1936 and there began experiments with semiconductors that ultimately led to the invention and development of the transistor. During World War II, he served as director of research for the Antisubmarine Warfare Operations Research Group of the U.S. Navy.

After the war, Shockley returned to Bell Labs as director of its research program on solid-state physics. Working with Bardeen and Brattain, he resumed his attempts to use semiconductors as amplifiers and controllers of electronic signals. The three men invented the point-contact transistor in 1947 and a more effective device, the junction transistor, in 1948. Shockley was deputy director of the Weapons Systems Evaluation Group of the Department of Defense in 1954–55. He joined Beckman Instruments, Inc., to establish the Shockley Semiconductor Laboratory in 1955. In 1958 he became lecturer at Stanford University, California, and in 1963 he became the first Poniatoff professor of engineering science there (emeritus, 1974). He wrote *Electrons and Holes in Semiconductors* (1950).

During the late 1960s Shockley became a figure of some controversy because of his widely debated views on the intellectual differences between races. He held that standardized intelligence tests reflect a genetic factor in intellectual capacity and that tests for IQ (intelligence quotient) reveal that blacks are inferior to whites. He further concluded that the higher rate of reproduction among blacks had a retrogressive effect on evolution.

JOHN BARDEEN

Two-time Nobelist John Bardeen earned bachelor's and master's degrees in electrical engineering from the University of Wisconsin, Madison and obtained his doctorate in 1936 in mathematical physics from Princeton University. A staff member of the University of Minnesota, Minn., from 1938 to 1941, he served as principal physicist at the U.S. Naval Ordnance Laboratory in Washington, D.C., during World War II.

After the war Bardeen joined (1945) Bell Labs in Murray Hill, N.J., where he, Brattain, and Shockley conducted research on the electron-conducting properties of semiconductors. On Dec. 23, 1947, they unveiled the transistor, which ushered in the electronic revolution. The transistor replaced the larger and bulkier vacuum tube and provided the technology for miniaturizing the electronic switches and other components needed in the construction of computers. Bardeen's role in the invention of the transistor brought him his first Nobel Prize for Physics in 1956.

In the early 1950s Bardeen resumed research he had begun in the 1930s on superconductivity, and his investigations provided a theoretical explanation of the disappearance of electrical resistance in materials at temperatures close to absolute zero. The BCS theory of superconductivity (from the initials of Bardeen, Leon N. Cooper, and John R. Schrieffer) was first advanced in 1957 and became the basis for all later theoretical work in superconductivity. In 1972, with Cooper and Schrieffer,

Bardeen was awarded his second Nobel Prize for Physics, for development of the theory of superconductivity. Bardeen was also the author of a theory explaining certain properties of semiconductors. He served as a professor of electrical engineering and physics at the University of Illinois, Urbana-Champaign, from 1951 to 1975.

WALTER BRATTAIN

Walter Houser Brattain earned a Ph.D. from the University of Minnesota, and in 1929 he became a research physicist for Bell Labs. His chief field of research involved the surface properties of solids, particularly the atomic structure of a material at the surface, which usually differs from its atomic structure in the interior. He, Shockley, and Bardeen invented the transistor in 1947. After leaving Bell Labs in 1967, Brattain served as adjunct professor at Whitman College, Walla Walla, Wash. (1967–72), then was designated overseer emeritus. He was granted a number of patents and wrote many articles on solid-state physics.

WERNHER VON BRAUN

(b. March 23, 1912, Wirsitz, Ger. — d. June 16, 1977, Alexandria, Va., U.S.)

W ernher von Braun was a German engineer who played a prominent role in all aspects of rocketry and space exploration, first in Germany and, after World War II, in the United States.

EARLY LIFE

Braun was born into a prosperous aristocratic family. His mother encouraged young Wernher's curiosity by giving him a telescope upon his confirmation in the Lutheran church. Braun's early interest in astronomy and the realm of space never left him thereafter. In 1920 his family moved to the seat of government in Berlin. He did not do well in school, particularly in physics and mathematics. A turning point in his life occurred in 1925 when he acquired a copy of *Die Rakete zu den Planetenräumen* ("The Rocket into Interplanetary Space") by a rocket pioneer, Hermann Oberth. Frustrated by his inability to understand the mathematics, he applied himself at school until he led his class.

In the spring of 1930, while enrolled in the Berlin Institute of Technology, Braun joined the German Society for Space Travel. In his spare time he assisted Oberth in liquid-fueled rocket motor tests. In 1932 he was graduated from the Technical Institute with a B.S. degree in mechanical engineering and entered Berlin University.

By the fall of 1932 the rocket society was experiencing grave financial difficulties. At that time Capt. Walter R. Dornberger (later major general) was in charge of solid-fuel rocket research and development in the Ordnance Department of Germany's 100,000-man armed forces, the Reichswehr. He recognized the military potential of liquid-fueled rockets and the ability of Braun. Dornberger arranged a research grant

Test launch of a V-2 rocket. Camera Press

from the Ordnance Department for Braun, who then did research at a small development station that was set up adjacent to Dornberger's existing solid-fuel rocket test facility at the Kummersdorf Army Proving Grounds near Berlin. Two years later Braun received a Ph.D. in physics from the University of Berlin. His thesis, which, for reasons of military security, bore the nondescript title "About Combustion Tests," contained the theoretical investigation and developmental experiments on 300- and 660-pound-thrust rocket engines.

By December 1934 Braun's group, which then included one additional engineer and three mechanics, had successfully launched two rockets that rose vertically to more than 1.5 miles (2.4 km). But by this time there was no longer a German rocket society; rocket tests had been forbidden by decree, and the only way open to such research was through the military forces.

Since the test grounds near Berlin had become too small, a large military development facility was erected at the village of Peenemünde in northeastern Germany on the Baltic Sea, with Dornberger as the military commander and Braun as the technical director. Liquid-fueled rocket aircraft and jet-assisted takeoffs were successfully demonstrated, and the long-range ballistic missile A-4 and the supersonic anti-aircraft missile Wasserfall were developed. The A-4 was designated by the Propaganda Ministry as V-2, meaning Vengeance Weapon 2. By 1944 the level of technology of the rockets and missiles being tested at Peenemünde was many years ahead of that available in any other country.

WORK IN THE UNITED STATES

Braun always recognized the value of the work of U.S. rocket pioneer Robert H. Goddard. "Until 1936," said

Braun, "Goddard was ahead of us all." At the end of World War II, Braun, his younger brother Magnus, Dornberger, and the entire German rocket development team surrendered to U.S. troops. Within a few months Braun and about 100 members of his group were at the U.S. Army Ordnance Corps test site at White Sands, N.M., where they tested, assembled, and supervised the launching of captured V-2s for high-altitude research purposes. Developmental studies were made of advanced ramjet and rocket missiles. At the end of the war the United States had entered the field of guided missiles with practically no previous experience. The technical competence of Braun's group was outstanding. "After all," he said, "if we are good, it's because we've had 15 more years of experience in making mistakes and learning from them!"

Moving to Huntsville, Ala., in 1952, Braun became technical director (later chief) of the U.S. Army ballistic-weapon program. Under his leadership, the Redstone, Jupiter-C, Juno, and Pershing missiles were developed. In 1955 he became a U.S. citizen and, characteristically, accepted citizenship wholeheartedly. During the 1950s Braun became a national and international focal point for the promotion of space flight. He was the author or coauthor of popular articles and books and made addresses on the subject.

In 1954 a secret army–navy project to launch an Earth satellite, Project Orbiter, was thwarted. The situation was changed by the launching of Sputnik 1 by the Soviet Union on Oct. 4, 1957, followed by Sputnik 2 on November 3. Given leave to proceed on November 8, Braun and his army group launched the first U.S. satellite, Explorer 1, on Jan. 31, 1958.

After the National Aeronautics and Space Administration (NASA) was formed to carry out the U.S. space program, Braun and his organization were transferred from the army to that agency. As director of the NASA George C. Marshall Space Flight Center in Huntsville, Braun led the development of the large space launch vehicles, Saturn I, IB, and V. The engineering success of each of the Saturn class of space boosters, which contained millions of individual parts, remains unparalleled in rocket history. Each was launched successfully and on time and met safe performance requirements.

In March 1970 Braun was transferred to NASA head-quarters in Washington as deputy associate administrator for planning. He resigned from the agency in 1972 to become vice president at Fairchild Industries, Inc., an aerospace company. In 1975 he founded the National Space Institute, a private organization whose objective was to gain public support and understanding of space activities.

In attempting to justify his involvement in the development of the German V-2 rocket, Braun stated that patriotic motives outweighed whatever qualms he had about the moral implications of his nation's policies under Hitler. He also emphasized the innate impartiality of scientific research, which in itself has no moral dimensions until its products are put to use by the larger society. During his later career Braun received numerous high awards from U.S. government agencies and from professional societies in the United States and other countries.

CHARLES TOWNES

(b. July 28, 1915, Greenville, S.C., U.S.)

American physicist Charles Hard Townes was a joint winner with the Soviet physicists Aleksandr M. Prokhorov and Nikolay G. Basov of the Nobel Prize for Physics in 1964 for his role in the invention of the maser and the laser.

Townes studied at Furman University (B.A., B.S., 1935), Duke University (M.A., 1937), and the California Institute of Technology (Ph.D., 1939). In 1939 he joined the technical staff of Bell Telephone Laboratories, Inc., where he worked until 1948, when he joined the faculty of Columbia University. Three years later he conceived the idea of using ammonia molecules to amplify microwave radiation. In December 1953 Townes and two students demonstrated a working device that focused "excited" molecules in a resonant microwave cavity, where they emitted a pure microwave frequency. Townes named the device a maser, an acronym for "microwave amplification by stimulated emission of radiation." (At this time Prokhorov and Basov of the P.N. Lebedev Physical Institute in Moscow independently described the theory of maser operation.)

An intense burst of maser research followed in the mid-1950s, but masers found only a limited range of applications as low-noise microwave amplifiers and atomic clocks. In 1957 Townes proposed to his brother-in-law and former postdoctoral student at Columbia University, Arthur L. Schawlow (then at Bell Labs), that they try to extend maser action to the much shorter wavelengths of infrared or visible light. Townes also had discussions with a graduate student at Columbia University, Gordon Gould, who quickly developed his own laser ideas. Townes and Schawlow published their ideas for an "optical maser" in a seminal paper in the Dec. 15, 1958, issue of *Physical Review*. Meanwhile, Gould coined the word *laser* and wrote a patent application. Whether Townes or Gould should be credited as the "inventor" of the laser thus became a matter of intense debate and led to years of litigation. Eventually, Gould received a series of four patents starting in 1977 that earned him millions of dollars in royalties.

From 1959 to 1961 Townes served as vice president and director of research of the Institute for Defense Analyses, Washington, D.C. He then was appointed provost and professor of physics at Massachusetts Institute of Technology, Cambridge. In 1967 he became a professor at the University of California, Berkeley, where he initiated a program of radio and infrared astronomy leading to the discovery of complex molecules (ammonia and water) in the interstellar medium. He became professor emeritus in 1986.

GERTRUDE B. ELION

(b. Jan. 23, 1918, New York, N.Y., U.S.—d. Feb. 21, 1999, Chapel Hill, N.C.)

Gertrude Belle Elion was an American pharmacologist who, along with George H. Hitchings and Sir James W. Black, received the Nobel Prize for Physiology or Medicine in 1988 for their development of drugs used to treat several major diseases.

Elion was the daughter of immigrants. She graduated from Hunter College in New York City with a degree in biochemistry in 1937. Unable to obtain a graduate research position because she was a woman, she found work as a lab assistant at the New York Hospital School of Nursing (1937), an assistant organic chemist at the Denver Chemical Manufacturing Company (1938–39), a chemistry and physics teacher in New York City high schools (1940–42), and a research chemist at Johnson & Johnson (1943–44). During this time she also took classes at New York University (M.S., 1941). Unable to devote herself to full-time studies, Elion never received a Ph.D.

In 1944 Elion joined the Burroughs Wellcome Laboratories (later part of Glaxo Wellcome; today known as GlaxoSmithKline). There she was first the assistant and then the colleague of Hitchings, with whom she worked for the next four decades. Elion and Hitchings developed an array of new drugs that were effective against leukemia, autoimmune disorders, urinary-tract infections, gout, malaria, and viral herpes. Their success was due primarily to their innovative research methods, which marked a radical departure from the trial-and-error approach taken by previous pharmacologists. Elion and Hitchings pointedly examined the difference between the biochemistry of normal human cells and those of cancer cells, bacteria, viruses, and other pathogens (disease-causing agents). They then used this information to formulate drugs that could kill or inhibit the reproduction of a particular pathogen, leaving the human host's normal cells undamaged. The two researchers' new emphasis on understanding basic biochemical and physiological processes enabled them to eliminate much guesswork and wasted effort typical previously in developing new therapeutic drugs.

Though Elion officially retired in 1983, she helped oversee the development of azidothymidine (AZT), the first drug used in the treatment of AIDS. In 1991 she was awarded a National Medal of Science and was inducted into the National Women's Hall of Fame.

FREDERICK SANGER

(b. Aug. 13, 1918, Rendcombe, Gloucestershire, Eng.)

English biochemist Frederick Sanger was twice the recipient of the Nobel Prize for Chemistry. He was awarded the prize in 1958 for his determination of the structure of the insulin molecule. He shared the prize (with Paul Berg and Walter Gilbert) in 1980 for his determination of base sequences in nucleic acids.

Sanger was only the fourth two-time recipient of the Nobel Prize.

EDUCATION

Sanger was the middle child of Frederick Sanger, a medical practitioner, and Cicely Crewsdon Sanger, the daughter of a wealthy cotton manufacturer. The family expected him to follow in his father's footsteps and become a medical doctor. After much thought, he decided to become a scientist. In 1936 Sanger entered St. John's College, Cambridge. He initially concentrated on chemistry and physics, but he was later attracted to the new field of bio-

chemistry. He received a bachelor's degree in 1939 and stayed at Cambridge an additional year to take an advanced course in biochemistry. He and Joan Howe married in 1940 and subsequently had three children.

Because of his Quaker upbringing, Sanger was a conscientious objector and was assigned as an orderly to a hospital near Bristol when World War II began. He soon decided to visit Cambridge to see if he could enter the doctoral program in biochemistry. Several researchers there

The noted biochemist Frederick Sanger, seen here, was only the fourth person to ever win the Nobel Prize twice. Getty/Keystone were interested in having a student, especially one who did not need money. He studied lysine metabolism with biochemist Albert Neuberger. They also had a project in support of the war effort, analyzing nitrogen from potatoes. Sanger received a doctorate in 1943.

INSULIN RESEARCH

Biochemist Albert C. Chibnall and his protein research group moved from Imperial College in London to the safer wartime environment of the biochemistry department at Cambridge. Two schools of thought existed among protein researchers at the time. One group thought proteins were complex mixtures that would not readily lend themselves to chemical analysis. Chibnall was in the other group, which considered a given protein to be a distinct chemical compound.

Chibnall was studying insulin when Sanger joined the group. At Chibnall's suggestion, Sanger set out to identify and quantify the free-amino groups of insulin. Sanger developed a method using dinitrofluorobenzene to produce yellow-coloured derivatives of amino groups. Information about a new separation technique, partition chromatography, had recently been published. In a pattern that typified Sanger's career, he immediately recognized the utility of the new technique in separating the hydrolysis products of the treated protein. He identified two terminal amino groups for insulin, phenylalanine and glycine, suggesting that insulin is composed of two types of chains. Working with his first graduate student, Rodney Porter, Sanger used the method to study the amino terminal groups of several other proteins. (Porter later shared the 1972 Nobel Prize for Physiology or Medicine for his work in determining the chemical structure of antibodies.)

On the assumption that insulin chains are held together by disulphide linkages, Sanger oxidized the chains and separated two fractions. One fraction had phenylalanine at its amino terminus; the other had glycine. Whereas complete acid hydrolysis degraded insulin to its constituent amino acids, partial acid hydrolysis generated insulin peptides composed of several amino acids. Using another recently introduced technique, paper chromatography, Sanger was able to sequence the amino-terminal peptides of each chain, demonstrating for the first time that a protein has a specific sequence at a specific site. A combination of partial acid hydrolysis and enzymatic hydrolysis allowed Sanger and the Austrian biochemist Hans Tuppy to determine the complete sequence of amino acids in the phenylalanine chain of insulin. Similarly, Sanger and the Australian biochemist E.O.P. Thompson determined the sequence of the glycine chain.

Two problems remained: the distribution of the amide groups and the location of the disulphide linkages. With the completion of those two puzzles in 1954, Sanger had deduced the structure of insulin. For being the first person to sequence a protein, Sanger was awarded the 1958 Nobel Prize for Chemistry.

Sanger and his coworkers continued their studies of insulin, sequencing insulin from several other species and comparing the results. Utilizing newly introduced radiolabeling techniques, Sanger mapped the amino acid sequences of the active centres from several enzymes. One of these studies was conducted with another graduate student, Argentine-born immunologist César Milstein. (Milstein later shared the 1984 Nobel Prize for Physiology or Medicine for discovering the principle for the production of monoclonal antibodies.)

RNA Research

In 1962 the Medical Research Council opened its new laboratory of molecular biology in Cambridge. The Austrian-born British biochemist Max Perutz, British biochemist John Kendrew, and British biophysicist Francis Crick moved to the new laboratory. Sanger joined them as head of the protein division. It was a banner year for the group, as Perutz and Kendrew shared the 1962 Nobel Prize for Chemistry and Crick shared the 1962 Nobel Prize for Physiology or Medicine with the American geneticist James D. Watson and the New Zealand-born British biophysicist Maurice Wilkins for the discovery of DNA (deoxyribonucleic acid).

Sanger's interaction with nucleic acid groups at the new laboratory led to his pursuing studies on ribonucleic acid (RNA). RNA molecules are much larger than proteins, so obtaining molecules small enough for technique development was difficult. The American biochemist Robert W. Holley and his coworkers were the first to sequence RNA when they sequenced alanine-transfer RNA. They used partial hydrolysis methods somewhat like those Sanger had used for insulin. Unlike other RNA types, transfer RNAs have many unusual nucleotides. This partial hydrolysis method would not work well with other RNA molecules, which contain only four types of nucleotides, so a new strategy was needed.

The goal of Sanger's lab was to sequence a messenger RNA and determine the genetic code, thereby solving the puzzle of how groups of nucleotides code for amino acids. Working with British biochemists George G. Brownlee and Bart G. Barrell, Sanger developed a two-dimensional electrophoresis method for sequencing RNA. By the time the sequence methods were worked out, the code had been broken by other researchers, mainly the American biochemist Marshall Nirenberg and the Indian-born American biochemist Har Gobind Khorana, using in vitro protein synthesis techniques. The RNA sequence work of Sanger's group did confirm the genetic code.

DNA RESEARCH

By the early 1970s, Sanger was interested in deoxyribonucleic acid (DNA). DNA sequence studies had not developed because of the immense size of DNA molecules and the lack of suitable enzymes to cleave DNA into smaller pieces. Building on the enzyme copying approach used by the Swiss chemist Charles Weissmann in his studies on bacteriophage RNA, Sanger began using the enzyme DNA polymerase to make new strands of DNA from single-strand templates, introducing radioactive nucleotides into the new DNA. DNA polymerase requires a primer that can bind to a known region of the template strand. Early success was limited by the lack of suitable primers. Sanger and British colleague Alan R. Coulson developed the "plus and minus" method for rapid DNA sequencing. It represented a radical departure from earlier methods in that it did not utilize partial hydrolysis. Instead, it generated a series of DNA molecules of varying lengths that could be separated by using polyacrylamide gel electrophoresis. For both plus and minus systems, DNA was synthesized from templates to generate random sets of DNA molecules from very short to very long. When both plus and minus sets were separated on the same gel, the sequence could be read from either system, one confirming the other. In 1977 Sanger's group used this system to deduce most of the DNA sequence of bacteriophage ΦX174, the first complete genome to be sequenced.

A few problems remained with the plus and minus system. Sanger, Coulson, and British colleague Steve Nicklen developed a similar procedure using dideoxynucleotide chain-terminating inhibitors. DNA was synthesized until an inhibitor molecule was incorporated into the growing DNA chain. Using four reactions, each with a different inhibitor, sets of DNA fragments were generated ending in every nucleotide. For example, in the A reaction, a series of DNA fragments ending in A (adenine) was generated. In the C reaction, a series of DNA fragments ending in C (cytosine) was generated, and so on for G (guanine) and T (thymine). When the four reactions were separated side by side on a gel and an autoradiograph developed, the sequence was read from the film. Sanger and his coworkers used the dideoxy method to sequence human mitochondrial DNA, the first human gene to be sequenced. For his contributions to DNA sequencing methods, Sanger shared the 1980 Nobel Prize for Chemistry. He retired in 1983.

ADDITIONAL HONOURS

Sanger's additional honours included election as a fellow of the Royal Society (1954), being named a Commander of the Order of the British Empire (1963), the Royal Society's Royal Medal (1969), the Royal Society's Copley Medal (1977), election to the Order of the Companions of Honour (1981), and the Order of Merit (1986). In 1992 the Wellcome Trust and the British Medical Research Council established a genome research centre, honoring Sanger by naming it the Wellcome Trust Sanger Institute.

TOM KILBURN

(b. Aug. 11, 1921, Dewsbury, Yorkshire, Eng.—d. Jan. 17, 2001, Manchester)

Tom Kilburn was an English engineer and coinventor of the first working computer memory. He also designed and built the first stored-program computer and led a team that produced a succession of pioneering computers over the next 25 years.

In 1942 Kilburn graduated from the University of Cambridge with a degree in mathematics. He immediately converted, however, to electronics research when he was recruited to join Frederic Williams's wartime radar group at the Telecommunications Research Establishment (TRE). In December 1946 Williams left TRE to become a professor at the University of Manchester, and Kilburn accompanied him in order to help develop an electronic storage system for electronic computers. They devised a storage device—later known as the Williams tube—based on cathode-ray tubes. A working model was completed late in 1947, and by June 1948 they had incorporated it in a small electronic computer that they built to prove the device's effectiveness. The computer was called the Small Scale Experimental Machine (SSEM) or just "Baby." It was the world's first working stored-program computer, and the Williams tube became one of the two standard methods of storage used by computers worldwide until the advent of magnetic-core storage in the mid-1950s. By April 1949 the SSEM had developed into a full-sized machine, and by October 1949 secondary storage had been added (using a magnetic drum). This machine, the Manchester Mark I, was the prototype for the Ferranti Mark I, manufactured by Ferranti, Ltd.

From 1951 Kilburn formally led the computer group within Williams's electrical engineering department. In 1953 the group completed an experimental computer using transistors instead of vacuum tubes. In 1954 the group completed MEG, which provided floating-point arithmetic (calculations using exponential notation—e.g., 3.27×10^{17}) and was manufactured by Ferranti as the Mercury beginning in 1957.

In 1956 Kilburn started his most ambitious project, MUSE, renamed Atlas when Ferranti joined the project in 1959. In parallel with two similar projects in the United States (LARC and Stretch) but largely independent of them, Atlas made the massive jump from running one program at a time to multiprogramming. With multiprogramming a computer can "interleave" several programs, allocating various computer resources (memory, storage, input, and output) to each program through an operating system. Atlas was also the first computer to employ a technique, now known as virtual memory or virtual storage, of using some slower external memory (such as magnetic drums) as though it were an extension of the computer's faster internal memory. Operational by 1962, Atlas was probably the most sophisticated computer of its time.

In 1964 Kilburn created the first department of computer science in the United Kingdom. In 1966 he started his last computer project, MU5. Operational by 1972, MU5 pioneered an architecture geared to the requirements of high-level languages (languages with more humanlike syntax).

Kilburn was made a professor in 1960 and was elected a fellow of the Royal Society in 1965. He retired in 1981.

STEPHANIE KWOLEK

(b. July 23, 1923, New Kensington, Pa., U.S.)

American chemist Stephanie Louise Kwolek was a pioneer in polymer research whose work yielded Kevlar, an ultrastrong and ultrathick material best known for its use in bulletproof vests.

Kwolek's father, a foundry worker, died when she was 10 years old, and her mother raised her and a brother alone. In 1946 she received a Bachelor of Science degree in chemistry from the Carnegie Institute of Technology (now

Carnegie Mellon University), Pittsburgh, Penn. Intending eventually to go to medical school, she went to work as a laboratory chemist at the rayon department of the DuPont Company in Buffalo, New York. DuPont had introduced nylon just before World War II, and in the postwar years the company resumed its drive into the highly competitive market of synthetic fibres. Kwolek thus became engaged in basic research in a new and fast-growing field, and as a consequence she never left employment with DuPont. She moved with the company's Pioneering Research Laboratory to Wilmington, Del., in 1950 and retired with the rank of research associate in 1986. Having accumulated many patents and awards in her career, she continued in retirement to work as a consultant and public speaker.

Kwolek is best known for her work during the 1950s and '60s with aramids, or "aromatic polyamides," a type of polymer that can be made into strong, stiff, and flame-resistant fibres. Her laboratory work in aramids was conducted under the supervision of research fellow Paul W. Morgan, who calculated that the aramids would form stiff fibres owing to the presence of bulky benzene (or "aromatic") rings in their molecular chains but that they would have to be prepared from solution because they melt only at very high temperatures. Kwolek determined the solvents and polymerization conditions suitable for producing poly-m-phenylene isophthalamide, a compound that DuPont released in 1961 as a flame-resistant fibre with the trade name Nomex. She then extended her work into poly-p-benzamide and poly-p-phenylene terephthalamide, which she noted adopted highly regular rodlike molecular arrangements in solution. From these two "liquid crystal polymers" (the first ever prepared), fibres were spun that displayed unprecedented stiffness and tensile strength. Poly-p-phenylene terephthalamide was released commercially in 1971 with the trade name Kevlar, a fibre that finds use in high-strength tire cord, reinforced boat hulls and other structural parts, and lightweight bulletproof vests.

DOUGLAS ENGELBART

(b. Jan. 30, 1925, near Portland, Ore., U.S.)

Douglas Engelbart was an American inventor whose work beginning in the 1950s led to his patent for the computer mouse, the development of the basic graphical user interface, and groupware.

Engelbart grew up on a farm near Portland. Following two years of enlisted service as a radar technician for the U.S. Navy in World War II, he completed his bachelor's degree in electrical engineering at Oregon State University in 1948. He soon became dissatisfied with his electrical engineering job at the Ames Research Center, located in Moffett Field, Calif., and in December 1950 had the inspiration that would drive the rest of his professional life.

Engelbart's dream was to use computers to connect individuals in a network that would allow them to share and update information in "real time." He combined this idea of collaborative software, or groupware, with his experience interpreting radar displays and with ideas he gleaned from an *Atlantic Monthly* article by Vannevar Bush, "As We May Think," to envision networked computers employing a graphical user interface. After receiving a Ph.D. in electrical engineering from the University of California at Berkeley in 1955, he stayed on as an acting assistant professor for a year before accepting a position with the Stanford Research Institute (SRI) in Stanford, Calif.

In 1963 Engelbart was given funding by SRI to start his own research laboratory, the Augmentation Research Center, where he worked on inventing and perfecting various devices—such as the computer mouse, the multiple window display, and hypermedia (the linking of texts, images, video, and sound files within a single document)—for inputting, manipulating, and displaying data. Together with a colleague at SRI, William English, he eventually perfected a variety of input devices—including joysticks, light pens, and track balls—that are now common. Prior to Engelbart's inventions, laborious and error-prone keypunch cards or manually set electronic switches were necessary to control computers, and data had to be printed before it could be viewed. His work made it possible for ordinary people to use computers.

Early in 1967 Engelbart's laboratory became the second site on the Advanced Research Projects Agency Network (ARPANET), the primary precursor to the Internet. On Dec. 9, 1968, at a computer conference in San Francisco, Engelbart demonstrated a working real-time collaborative computer system known as NLS (oNLine System). Using NLS, he and English (back at Stanford) worked on a shared document in one window (using keyboard and mouse input devices) while at the same time conducting the world's first public computer video conference in another window. Engelbart continued his research, building increasingly sophisticated input and display devices and improving the graphical user interface, but because of budget cuts at SRI most of his research staff migrated to other institutions such as Xerox Corporation's Palo Alto Research Center in Palo Alto, California.

In 1977 SRI sold Engelbart's NLS groupware system to Tymshare, Inc., a telephone networking company that renamed it Augment and sought to make it into a commercially viable office automation system. As the last remaining member of his research laboratory, and with SRI showing no further interest in his work, Engelbart joined Tymshare. In 1984 Tymshare was acquired by the

McDonnell Douglas Corporation, where Engelbart worked on information systems. In 1989 he founded the Bootstrap Institute, a research and consulting firm. Over the following decade he finally began to receive recognition for his innovations, including the 1997 Turing Award, a major achievement in computer science.

ROBERT NOYCE

(b. Dec. 12, 1927, Burlington, Iowa, U.S.—d. June 3, 1990, Austin, Texas)

American engineer Robert Norton Noyce was coinventor of the integrated circuit, a system of interconnected transistors on a single silicon microchip.

EDUCATION

In 1939 the Noyce family moved to Grinnell, Iowa, where the father had accepted a position as a Congregational minister and where the son began to demonstrate the traits of an inventor and tinkerer. Noyce majored in physics at Grinnell College (B.A., 1949) and earned a doctorate in solid state physics from the Massachusetts Institute of Technology (MIT; Ph.D., 1953), for a dissertation related to the technology he found most fascinating, the transistor.

SHOCKLEY SEMICONDUCTOR LABORATORY

Developed at Bell Laboratories in 1947, the transistor had figured in Noyce's imagination since he saw an early one in a college physics class. In 1956, while working for Philco Corporation, Noyce met William Shockley, one of the transistor's Nobel Prize-winning inventors. Shockley was recruiting researchers for Shockley Semiconductor Laboratory, a company that he had started in Palo Alto,

Calif., to produce high-speed transistors. Noyce jumped at the opportunity, renting a house in Palo Alto even before his official job interview.

By early 1957, however, engineers at the new company had rebelled and attempted to force Shockley out of his management position, arguing that his poor management delayed production and adversely affected morale. Noyce and seven colleagues, among them Gordon Moore, resigned after failing to remove Shockley. With Noyce as their leader, the group—labeled the "traitorous eight" by Shockley— successfully negotiated with the Fairchild Camera and Instrument Company to form a new company, Fairchild Semiconductor Corporation, located in Santa Clara.

FAIRCHILD SEMICONDUCTOR CORPORATION AND THE INTEGRATED CIRCUIT

In 1958 Jean Hoerni, another Fairchild Semiconductor founder, engineered a process to place a layer of silicon oxide on top of transistors, sealing out dirt, dust, and other contaminants. For Noyce, Hoerni's process made a fundamental innovation possible. At that time, Fairchild produced transistors and other elements on large silicon wafers, cut the components out of the wafer, and later connected individual components with wires. However, as the number of connections increased, it became progressively more difficult to solder in ever smaller spaces. Noyce realized that cutting the wafer apart was unnecessary; instead, he could manufacture an entire circuit—complete with transistors, resistors, and other elements—on a single silicon wafer, the integrated circuit (IC). In this sense, Noyce and coinventor Jack Kilby, who was working at Texas Instruments, Inc., thought along similar lines. They both saw the importance of the wafer, and each of their companies received patents on various aspects of IC design and manufacture. But Noyce saw further. Noyce saw that the solution to the problem of connecting the components was to evaporate lines of conductive metal (the "wires") directly onto the silicon wafer's surface, a technique known as the planar process. Kilby and Noyce share credit for independently inventing the integrated circuit. However, after much litigation, Fairchild Semiconductor was granted the patent on the planar process, the basic technique used by subsequent manufacturers. The patent made both Noyce and Fairchild wealthy.

INTEL CORPORATION

In 1968 Noyce and Moore left Fairchild Semiconductor to start their own company. Soon they were joined by Andrew Grove, another Fairchild colleague, and formed Intel Corporation. In 1971 Intel introduced the first microprocessor, which combined on a single silicon chip the circuitry for both information storage and information processing. Intel quickly became the leading producer of microprocessor chips.

Noyce served as president of Intel until 1975 and then as chairman of the board of directors before stepping down in 1978 to become chairman of the Semiconductor Industry Association (SIA).

STATESMAN

The SIA was formed to address the growing economic concerns of the American semiconductor industry, especially with respect to foreign competition. Noyce played an important role in establishing Sematech, a joint industry-government consortium formed with sometimes conflicting goals—research to keep the American semiconductor industry at the forefront and efforts to maintain a domestic semiconductor manufacturing capacity. Noyce became Sematech, Inc.'s, first president in 1988.

Noyce held 16 patents and was awarded the National Medal of Science in 1979. A lifelong swimmer (and former Iowa state diving champion), Noyce died of a heart attack following a morning swim in 1990.

RON TOOMER

(b. May 31, 1930, Pasadena, Calif., U.S.)

Ronald Valentine Toomer is an American engineer and roller coaster designer who could be considered the sovereign of steel coasters. His work with Arrow Dynamics (founded as Arrow Development Company in 1946) brought to life such influential steel thrillers as the tubular track Runaway Mine Ride (1966), the inverted helix-shaped Corkscrew (1975), and the first suspended coasters of the 1980s.

A mechanical engineering graduate of the University of Nevada–Reno (1961, B.S.), Toomer was involved in the first U.S. satellite launches and served on the team that designed the heat shield for the Apollo spacecraft. During his stint in the space program, Toomer met a coworker who had previously been a welder for the Arrow Development Company. In 1965 Toomer joined the company and was hired to work on the design of the Runaway Mine Ride, the world's first all-steel coaster. Toomer's tool of choice (and necessity): the slide rule. "A big part of the attraction of roller coasters is that people know that unlike with hang-gliding or skydiving, the train is definitely going to come back," Toomer said.

In more than 30 years in the amusement industry, Toomer designed more than 80 steel coasters worldwide. In 1975 he built one of the first looping coasters of the modern era—the Corkscrew at Knott's Berry Farm (Buena

Park, Calif.), which was followed the next year by one at Cedar Point (Sandusky, Ohio). The Corkscrew brought 360-degree rolls to coaster design for the first time. Other achievements by Toomer included Cedar Point's beloved Magnum XL-200 (1989), an out-and-back coaster that was the first to top 200 feet (60 metres), and also the first suspended coasters, Big Bad Wolf (1984) at Busch Gardens, Williamsburg, Va., and Cedar Point's Iron Dragon (1987). All this time he gained fame for never riding his own creations, declaring, "I've had a bad motion sickness problem since I was a little kid. But I've ridden enough of them to know what happens and how it feels."

Toomer became president of Arrow Dynamics in 1986, at about the time that the company was developing the innovative Pipeline coaster, on which the cars execute a snap roll of 182 degrees around their longitudinal axis. Unfortunately, the highly complex project ran out of funds before it could be realized as anything more than a prototype. In the 1990s Toomer held posts as chairman of the board and as director. In 2000 he was inducted into the International Association of Amusement Parks and Attractions Hall of Fame.

HEINRICH ROHRER AND GERD BINNIG

respectively, (b. June 6, 1933, Buchs, Sankt Gallen canton, Switz.); (b. July 20, 1947, Frankfurt am Main, W.Ger.)

The scanning tunneling microscope (STM) appeared in 1981 when Swiss physicists Gerd Binnig and Heinrich Rohrer set out to build a tool for studying the local conductivity of surfaces. Its principle of operation is based on the quantum mechanical phenomenon known as tunneling, in which the wavelike properties of electrons permit them to "tunnel" beyond the surface of a solid into regions of space that are forbidden to them under the rules of classical physics. The probability of finding such tunneling electrons decreases exponentially as the distance from the surface increases. The STM makes use of this extreme sensitivity to distance. The sharp tip of a tungsten needle is positioned a few angstroms from the sample surface. A small voltage is applied between the probe tip and the surface, causing electrons to tunnel across the gap. As the probe is scanned over the surface, it registers variations in the tunneling current, and this information can be processed to provide a topographical image of the surface.

Binnig and Rohrer chose the surface of gold for their first image. When the image was displayed on the screen of a television monitor, they saw rows of precisely spaced atoms and observed broad terraces separated by steps one atom in height. Binnig and Rohrer had discovered in the STM a simple method for creating a direct image of the atomic structure of surfaces. Their discovery opened a new era for surface science, and their impressive achievement was recognized with the award of half the Nobel Prize for Physics in 1986. (Ernst Ruska, a German electrical engineer who invented the electron microscope, received the other half of the prize.)

HEINRICH ROHRER

Heinrich Rohrer was educated at the Swiss Federal Institute of Technology in Zürich and received his Ph.D. there in 1960. In 1963, after a period of postdoctoral work at Rutgers University in New Jersey, he joined the IBM Zürich Research Laboratory, where he remained until his retirement in 1997. Binnig also joined the laboratory, and it was there that the two men designed and built the first STM. This instrument is equipped with a tiny tungsten probe whose tip, only about one or two atoms wide, is brought to within five or ten atoms' distance of the surface of a conducting or semiconducting material. (An atom is equal to about one angstrom, or one ten-billionth of a metre.) When the electric potential of the tip is made to differ by a few volts from that of the surface, quantum mechanical effects cause a measurable electric current to cross the gap. The strength of this current is extremely sensitive to the distance between the probe and the surface, and as the probe's tip scans the surface, it can be kept a fixed distance away by raising and lowering it so as to hold the current constant. A record of the elevation of the probe is a topographical map of the surface under study, on which the contour intervals are so small that the individual atoms making up the surface are clearly recognizable.

GERD BINNIG

The German-born Gerd Binnig graduated from Johann Wolfgang Goethe University in Frankfurt in 1973 and received a doctorate from the University of Frankfurt in 1978. He then joined the IBM Zürich Research Laboratory, where he and Rohrer designed and built the first STM. In 1985–86 Binnig joined a physics research group at IBM's Almaden Research Center in San Jose, Calif., and in 1987–95 he directed an IBM research group at the University of Munich. He then returned to Zürich.

About the time Binnig shared the Nobel Prize with Rohrer for the invention of the STM, he developed the concept of atomic force microscopy. An atomic force microscope profiles a sample by dragging a stylus only a few atoms wide across the surface of the sample and measuring the force between the stylus and the surface. The resulting signal can be translated into a description of the surface topography. This surface-force scan can be converted into a three-dimensional surface image.

Binnig's involvement in the invention of the STM stimulated an interest in the creative process. In 1989 he published the book *Aus dem Nichts* ("Out of Nothing"), which posited that creativity grows from disorder. Binnig went on to articulate what he called "fractal Darwinism," a theory that new ideas or devices evolve through complex interactions on multiple scales, from the social group to the individual and from broad concepts to specific problems.

PAUL LAUTERBUR AND PETER MANSFIELD

respectively, (b. May 6, 1929, Sidney, Ohio, U.S.—d. March 27, 2007, Urbana, Ill.); (b. Oct. 9, 1933, London, Eng.)

The 2003 Nobel Prize for Physiology or Medicine was awarded to two pioneers of magnetic resonance imaging (MRI), a computerized scanning technology that produces images of internal body structures, especially those comprising soft tissues. The recipients were chemist Paul Lauterbur of the University of Illinois at Urbana-Champaign and physicist Sir Peter Mansfield of the University of Nottingham, Eng.

"A great advantage with MRI is that it is harmless according to all present knowledge," stated the Nobel Assembly at the Karolinska Institute in Stockholm, which awarded the prize. Unlike X-ray and computed tomography (CT) examinations, MRI avoided the use of potentially harmful ionizing radiation; rather, it produced its images with magnetic fields and radio waves. MRI scans spared patients not only many X-ray examinations but also surgical procedures and invasive tests formerly needed to diagnose diseases and follow up after treatments. More than 60 million MRI procedures were performed in 2002 alone, according to the Nobel Assembly.

PAUL LAUTERBUR

Paul Christian Lauterbur received a Ph.D. in chemistry from the University of Pittsburgh in 1962. He served as a professor at the University of New York at Stony Brook from 1969 to 1985, when he accepted the position of professor at the University of Illinois at Urbana-Champaign and director of its Biomedical Magnetic Resonance Laboratory.

Lauterbur began work in the early 1970s, when the technology underpinning MRI was a laboratory research tool. Called nuclear magnetic resonance (NMR) spectroscopy, it involves putting a sample to be analyzed in a strong magnetic field and then irradiating it with weak radio waves at the appropriate frequency. In the presence of the magnetic field, the nuclei of certain atoms—for example, ordinary hydrogen—absorb the radio energy; i.e., they show resonance at that particular frequency. Because the resonance frequency depends on the kind of nuclei and is influenced by the presence of nearby atoms, absorption measurements (absorption signal spectra) can provide information about the molecular structure of various solids and liquids. When the nuclei return to their previous energy levels, they emit energy, which carries additional information. NMR spectroscopy has remained a key tool in chemical analysis.

When studying molecules with NMR, chemists always had tried to maintain a steady magnetic field because variations made the absorption signals fuzzy. Lauterbur realized that if the magnetic field was deliberately made nonuniform, information contained in the signal distortions could be used to create two-dimensional images of a sample's internal structure. While at Stony Brook, he worked evenings developing his idea, using an NMR unit borrowed from campus chemists. His discovery laid the groundwork for the development of MRI as Mansfield transformed Lauterbur's work into a practical medical tool.

PETER MANSFIELD

Peter Mansfield received a Ph.D. in physics from the University of London in 1962. Following two years as a research associate in the United States, he joined the faculty of the University of Nottingham, where he became professor in 1979. Mansfield was knighted in 1993.

Mansfield's prize-winning work expanded upon Lauterbur's earlier discoveries regarding NMR. MRI imaging succeeds because the human body is about two-thirds water, whose molecules are made of hydrogen and oxygen atoms. There are differences in the amount of water present in different organs and tissues. In addition, the amount of water often changes when body structures become injured or diseased; those variations show up in MRI images. When the body is exposed to MRI's magnetic field and its pulses of radio waves, the nucleus of each hydrogen atom in water absorbs energy; it then emits the energy in the form of radio waves, or resonance signals, as it returns to its previous energy level. Electronic devices detect the myriad resonance signals from all the hydrogen nuclei in the tissue being examined, and computer processing builds cross-sectional images of internal body structures, based on differences in water content and movements of water molecules. Computer processing also can stack the cross sections in sequence to create three-dimensional, solid images. Because MRI does not have the harmful side effects of X-ray or computed tomography (CT) examinations and is noninvasive, the technology proved an invaluable tool in medicine.

Mansfield's research helped transform Lauterbur's discoveries into a practical technology in medicine by developing a way of using the nonuniformities, or gradients, introduced in the magnetic field to identify differences in the resonance signals more precisely. He also created new mathematical methods for quickly analyzing information in the signal and showed how to attain extremely rapid imaging.

ROBERT KAHN AND VINT CERF

respectively, (b. Dec. 23, 1938, Brooklyn, N.Y., U.S.); (b. June 23, 1943, New Haven, Conn., U.S.)

The Internet grew out of funding by the U.S. Advanced Research Projects Agency (ARPA), later renamed the Defense Advanced Research Projects Agency (DARPA), to develop a communication system among government and academic computer-research laboratories. First, DARPA established a program to investigate the interconnection of "heterogeneous networks." This program, called Internetting, was based on the newly introduced concept of open architecture networking, in which networks with defined standard interfaces would be interconnected by "gateways."

In order for the concept to work, a new protocol had to be designed and developed; indeed, a system architecture was also required. In 1974 computer scientist Vint Cerf, then at Stanford University in California, and electrical engineer Robert Kahn, then at DARPA, collaborated on a paper that first described such a protocol and system architecture—namely, the transmission control protocol (TCP), which enabled different types of machines on networks all over the world to route and assemble data packets. TCP, which originally included the Internet protocol (IP), a global addressing mechanism that allowed routers to get data packets to their ultimate destination, formed the TCP/IP standard, which was adopted by the U.S. Department of Defense in 1980. TCP/IP is now the standard Internet communications protocol that allows digital computers to communicate over long distances. In acknowledgement of their role as two of the principal architects of the Internet, Kahn and Cerf received the 2004 A.M. Turing Award from the Association for Computing Machinery.

ROBERT KAHN

After receiving an engineering degree from City College of New York in 1960, Robert Elliot Kahn received his M.A. (1962) and Ph.D. (1964) in electrical engineering from Princeton University. Immediately after completing his doctorate, Kahn worked for Bell Laboratories and subsequently served as an assistant professor of electrical engineering at the Massachusetts Institute of Technology (MIT) from 1964–66. However, it was his role as a senior scientist at Bolt Beranek & Newman (BB&N), an engineering consulting firm located in Cambridge, Mass., that brought Kahn into contact with the planning for a new kind of computer network, the Advanced Research Project Network (ARPANET).

ARPANET was named for its sponsor, the Defense Advanced Research Projects Agency, or DARPA. The network was based on a radically different architecture known as packet switching, in which messages were split into multiple "packets" that traveled independently over many different circuits to their common destination. But the ARPANET was more than a predecessor to the

Internet—it was the common technological context in which an entire generation of computer scientists came of age. While at BB&N, Kahn had two major accomplishments. First, he was part of a group that designed the network's Interface Message Processor, which would mediate between the network and each institution's host computer. Second, and perhaps more important, in 1972 Kahn helped organize the first International Conference on Computer Communication, which served as the ARPANET's public debut.

In 1972 Kahn left BB&N for DARPA's Information Processing Techniques Office (IPTO). Here he confronted a set of problems related to the deployment of packet switching technology in military radio and satellite communications. However, the real technical problem lay in connecting these disparate military networks— hence the name Internet for a network of networks. As program manager and later director of the IPTO, Kahn worked closely with Cerf and others on the development of the Internet's technical protocol, TCP/IP, which separated packet error checking (TCP) from issues related to domains and destinations (IP). The protocol is the basis for the Internet's open architecture, which permits any computer with the appropriate connection to enter the network. In addition to his work on the Internet, Kahn was the designer of the U.S. military's Strategic Computing Initiative during the administration of President Ronald Reagan. Kahn also coined the phrase "national information infrastructure" during this period.

Upon leaving IPTO in 1985, Kahn served as president of the Corporation for the National Research Initiatives, a not-for-profit group located in Reston, Va., and dedicated to the development of network technologies for the public. In 2001 he was among four individuals honoured by the National Academy of Engineering with the

Charles Stark Draper Prize for his role in developing the Internet.

VINT CERF

In 1965 Vinton Gray Cerf received his bachelor's degree in mathematics from Stanford University, Calif., U.S. He then worked for IBM as a systems engineer before attending the University of California at Los Angeles (UCLA), where he earned a master's degree in computer science in 1970. He returned to Stanford and completed his doctorate in computer science in 1972.

While at UCLA, Cerf wrote the communication protocol for the ARPANET, the first computer network based on packet switching, a heretofore untested technology. (In contrast to ordinary telephone communications, in which a specific circuit must be dedicated to the transmission, packet switching splits a message into "packets" that travel independently over many different circuits.) UCLA was among the four original ARPANET nodes. While working on the protocol, Cerf met Kahn, an electrical engineer who was then a senior scientist at Bolt Beranek & Newman. Cerf's professional relationship with Kahn was among the most important of his career.

In 1972 Kahn moved to DARPA as a program manager in the IPTO, where he began to envision a network of packet-switching networks—essentially, what would become the Internet. In 1973 Kahn approached Cerf, then a professor at Stanford, to assist him in designing this new network. Cerf and Kahn soon worked out a preliminary version of what they called the ARPA Internet, the details of which they published as a joint paper in 1974. Cerf joined Kahn at IPTO in 1976 to manage the office's networking projects. Together they produced TCP/IP, an electronic transmission protocol that separated packet error checking (TCP) from issues related to domains and destinations (IP).

Cerf's work on making the Internet a publicly accessible medium continued after he left DARPA in 1982 to become a vice president at MCI Communications Corporation (after 1998, WorldCom, Inc.). While at MCI he led the effort to develop and deploy MCI Mail, the first commercial e-mail service to use the Internet. In 1986 Cerf became a vice president at the Corporation for National Research Initiatives, a not-for-profit corporation located in Reston, Va., that Kahn, as president, had formed to develop network-based information technologies for the public good. Cerf also served as founding president of the Internet Society from 1992 to 1995. In 1994 Cerf returned to WorldCom as a senior vice president, and in 1998 he became the first chairman of the Internet Corporation for Assigned Names and Numbers, the group that oversees the Internet's growth and expansion.

In addition to his work on the Internet, Cerf served on many government panels related to cyber-security and the national information infrastructure. A fan of science fiction, he was a technical consultant to one of author Gene Roddenbury's posthumous television projects, *Earth: Final Conflict*. Among his many honours is the National Academy of Engineering's Charles Stark Draper Prize (2001).

IAN WILMUT

(b. July 7, 1944, Hampton Lucy, Warwickshire, Eng.)

Sir Ian Wilmut is an English developmental biologist who was the first to use nuclear transfer of differentiated adult cells to generate a mammalian clone, a Finn Dorset sheep named Dolly, born in 1996.

Education and Cryopreservation Research

Wilmut was raised in Coventry, a town in the historic English county of Warwickshire, and he attended the Agricultural College at the University of Nottingham. In his undergraduate studies, Wilmut initially pursued his lifelong interest in farming, particularly in raising animals such as sheep. However, he soon turned his attention to animal science and basic research. In 1966, his final year at Nottingham, he received a scholarship to conduct research for a summer under English biologist Ernest John Christopher Polge in the Unit of Reproductive Physiology and Biochemistry, then a division of the Agricultural Research Council at the University of Cambridge. During this time, Wilmut performed basic experiments on animal embryos. Following his graduation from Nottingham in 1967, he returned to Cambridge, where he pursued a doctorate under the guidance of Polge, whose research was focused on improving methods of embryo cryopreservation. In 1971 Wilmut was awarded a doctorate by Darwin College, Cambridge; the title of his thesis was "Deep Freeze Preservation of Boar Semen." Wilmut remained at Cambridge and conducted extensive research on the cryopreservation of embryos. In 1973 he successfully implanted into a surrogate cow a calf embryo that had been cryopreserved. The embryo was carried to term, and Wilmut named the first-ever "frozen calf" Frostie.

Genetic Engineering and Cloning Research

Pharming

In 1973 Wilmut was appointed senior scientific officer at the Animal Breeding Research Organisation (ABRO;

renamed Edinburgh Research Station of the Institute of Animal Physiology and Genetics Research in 1985 and finally Roslin Institute in 1993), a government-supported research facility located in Roslin, Scot., just south of Edinburgh. At the ABRO facility, Wilmut studied embryo development and became interested in the underlying causes of embryo death in mammals. However, in the early 1980s, changes in ABRO leadership and a shift in the focus of government research projects forced Wilmut into the realm of genetic engineering. The new goal of ABRO was to generate sheep genetically engineered to produce large quantities of human proteins that would be suitable for therapeutic uses, a pursuit that came to be known as "pharming." Although Wilmut had little experience with genetic engineering and had limited enthusiasm for the project, he used his knowledge of developmental biology to obtain zygotes (one-celled embryos) from sheep and developed techniques to inject DNA into the zygote pronucleus (a haploid nucleus occurring in embryos prior to fertilization). This work eventually led to the generation of a sheep named Tracy. Tracy was created from a zygote genetically engineered through DNA injection to produce milk containing large quantities of the human enzyme alpha-1 antitrypsin, a substance used to treat cystic fibrosis and emphysema.

NUCLEAR TRANSFER

Wilmut's initial forays into cloning began in the late 1980s with embryonic stem cells. Wilmut and his colleagues were interested primarily in nuclear transfer, a technique first conceived in 1928 by German embryologist Hans Spemann. Nuclear transfer involves the introduction of the nucleus from a cell into an enucleated egg cell (an egg cell that has had its own nucleus removed). This can be accomplished through fusion of the cell to the egg (the technique that Wilmut used in all his later cloning experiments) or through the removal of the nucleus from the cell and the subsequent transplantation of that nucleus into the enucleated egg cell (a technique refined in the early 2000s). In 1989 Wilmut and Lawrence Smith, a graduate student conducting his thesis research at Roslin, generated four cloned lambs by using embryonic cell nuclear transfer, in which the nucleus from an embryonic stem cell was inserted into an enucleated egg. This research led Wilmut and Smith to an important discovery—namely, that the stage of the cell cycle (the sequence through which

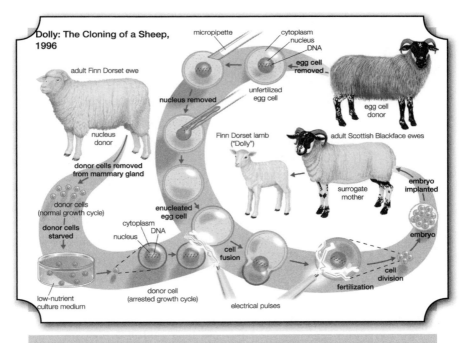

Dolly the sheep was successfully cloned in 1996 by fusing the nucleus from a mammary-gland cell of a Finn Dorset ewe into an enucleated egg cell taken from a Scottish Blackface ewe. Carried to term in the womb of another Scottish Blackface ewe, Dolly was a genetic copy of the Finn Dorset ewe. Encyclopædia Britannica, Inc.

293

each cell progresses from one cell division to the next) at the time of nuclear transfer determined the success or failure of the experiment. They realized that the four clones they had generated happened by chance.

In 1991 Wilmut hired English biologist Keith Campbell (Smith had left the research centre in 1990), whose knowledge of the cell cycle proved instrumental in advancing the technique of nuclear transfer developed at Roslin. Wilmut and Campbell's first major success came in 1995, with the generation of two cloned Welsh mountain sheep, Megan and Morag. The following year Wilmut, Campbell, and their team of scientists decided to test a new theory based on the idea that the age or the stage of differentiation of a donor cell did not matter in nuclear transfer. Prior to this theory, nuclear transfer was believed to work only if the nucleus used as the donor for nuclear transfer came from a cell that was totipotent—i.e., having the ability to differentiate into any type of cell in the body and therefore possessing no characteristics of differentiation itself. However, observations from laboratory experiments and from Megan and Morag, who were produced using nine-day-old embryonic cells, which are presumably less totipotent than younger embryonic cells, indicated that an enucleated host egg could somehow reverse the differentiation of the donor cell nucleus, converting it back to a state of totipotency or pluripotency (slightly more differentiated than a totipotent cell). This led to the idea of using the nucleus from an already differentiated adult cell as a donor nucleus.

DOLLY AND POLLY

During the winter of 1995–96, Wilmut was involved in three pivotal cloning experiments conducted at Roslin. In the first, Wilmut and his team of scientists performed embryonic cell nuclear transfer by using cultured embryonic cells that were nine days old. This was similar to the experiment that led to the creation of Megan and Morag. However, the new experiment involved a different sheep breed; the cells used for nuclear transfer came from a Poll Dorset sheep. This first experiment resulted in the birth in 1996 of four Poll Dorset clones: Cedric, Cecil, Cyril, and Tuppence. In the second experiment, the team used fetal fibroblasts isolated from sheep fetuses after 26 days of development; these cells served as nucleus donors for transfer into an enucleated egg. This experiment resulted in the birth of two clones, Taffy and Tweed. In the third experiment, the scientists isolated adult cells (in this case, mammary gland cells) from a six-year-old ewe and used these cells as nucleus donors for transfer into egg cells; this technique inspired the later development of a procedure called somatic cell nuclear transfer (SCNT). Wilmut and his team constructed 277 embryos containing adult cell nuclei that were implanted into 13 surrogate mothers, only one of which became pregnant. This pregnancy was carried to term successfully. The Finn Dorset lamb, born on July 5, 1996, was Dolly.

In 1997, following the publication in the journal *Nature* of a summary of their research leading to Dolly, Wilmut, Campbell, and the Roslin Institute instantly became known for having opened the door to a new era of controversial cloning research. The cloning of Dolly generated speculation in the media and in the scientific community about the possibility of cloning humans. Wilmut considered human cloning impractical for both ethical and scientific reasons. From his work with sheep, he knew the dangers of cloning; many embryos died following implantation, and those embryos that survived and developed to term as full-grown fetuses sometimes died immediately following birth or were born with birth defects.

Wilmut was not interested in cloning simply for the sake of producing cloned animals, and neither was his team of scientists at Roslin. They still had problems to solve concerning their work on pharming. In 1997 Wilmut and his colleagues generated Polly, a Poll Dorset clone made from nuclear transfer using a fetal fibroblast nucleus genetically engineered to express a human gene known as *FIX*. This gene encodes a substance called human factor IX, a clotting factor that occurs naturally in most people but is absent in people with hemophilia, who require replacement therapy with a therapeutic form of the substance. Polly—along with two other sheep engineered to produce human factor IX that also were born in 1997— represented a major advance in pharming. The successful birth of Polly marked Wilmut's last major cloning experiment.

LATER CAREER

Throughout Wilmut's career at Roslin, he had been slowly moving away from research relying on embryonic stem cells, primarily because culturing embryonic stem cells from sheep embryos was extraordinarily difficult and impractical in terms of cost and time. In 2000 Wilmut was promoted to head of the department of gene expression and development at the Roslin Institute, and his research interests shifted from animals to humans. He was particularly interested in uncovering the genetic mechanisms that control embryonic development and the role that these mechanisms play in human disease. In 2005 he accepted a position as chair of reproductive science at the University of Edinburgh. He maintained a relationship with the Roslin Institute, acting as a visiting scientist. Wilmut also directed the Medical Research Council's

Centre for Regenerative Medicine, located in Edinburgh, and led research efforts into cellular reprogramming.

Wilmut received several awards during his career, including the Ernst Schering Prize in 2002 and the Paul Ehrlich and Ludwig Darmstaedter Prize in 2005. Wilmut also was made fellow of the Royal Society of Edinburgh in 2000 and of the Royal Society of London in 2002; he was knighted in 2007. In addition to papers published in high-ranking journals such as *Nature* and *Science*, Wilmut also published several books, including *The Second Creation: Dolly and the Age of Biological Control* (2000; with Keith Campbell and Colin Tudge) and *After Dolly: The Uses and Misuses of Human Cloning* (2006; with Roger Highfield).

RODNEY BROOKS

(b. Dec. 30, 1954, Adelaide, South Australia, Austl.)

Rodney Allen Brooks is an Australian-born computer scientist, artificial intelligence scientist, and designer of mobile autonomous robots.

While attending Flinders University in Adelaide, where he received his bachelor's (1975) and master's degrees (1978) in pure mathematics, Brooks was given access to the university's mainframe computer for 12 hours each Sunday. This experience with computers was enough to convince Brooks to come to America to study with the artificial intelligence (AI) pioneer John McCarthy at Stanford University, California. Brooks chose a traditional AI problem for his doctoral research (1981), which he subsequently expanded and published as *Model-Based Computer Vision* (1984).

By the time Brooks had finished his doctorate and moved to the Mobile Robotics Laboratory at the Massachusetts Institute of Technology (MIT) in 1984, he had become discouraged with AI research, especially with the field's top-down approach to problem solving. The top-down approach, which dominated the field at that time, presupposes that a computer must first be supplied with an internal representation of the "essential" features of the world in which it operates—an immensely difficult framework problem for all but the very simplest tasks. Brooks turned this approach on its head, arguing that research should focus on a bottom-up approach—that is, on action and behaviour rather than on representation and function. Brooks began by building basic robots that could perform the simplest "insect-like" actions. Although no one claims that insects have sophisticated brains, they can engage in rather elaborate behaviours. Similarly, building on a few simple actions and the premise that learning comes from interacting with the real world rather than any model, Brooks's robots displayed surprisingly complex behaviour.

In 1997 Brooks became director of the MIT Artificial Intelligence Research Laboratory, where he continued to push AI in this fundamentally new direction. His influential and accessible essays were collected in *Cambrian Intelligence: The Early History of the New AI* (1999). What initially had appeared heretical to traditional AI eventually became a new orthodoxy, complete with industrial and military applications. Brooks and his students designed robots to explore Mars, as well as for more mundane tasks such as clearing minefields.

Brooks went on to the project of "raising" a robot "child" named Cog—a clever allusion to cognition and gears. Ironically, in abandoning AI's traditional attempts to model human intelligence, Brooks and Cog hold out the possibility of redefining what it means to be human and intelligent.

STEVE JOBS AND STEPHEN WOZNIAK

respectively, (b. Feb. 24, 1955, San Francisco, Calif., U.S.); (b. Aug. 11, 1950, San Jose, Calif., U.S.)

L
ike the founding of the early chip companies and the invention of the microprocessor, the story of Apple is a key part of Silicon Valley folklore. Two whiz kids, Stephen G. Wozniak and Steven P. Jobs, shared an interest in electronics. Wozniak purchased one of the early microprocessors, the Mostek 6502, and used it to design a computer. When Hewlett-Packard, where "Woz" had an internship, declined to build his design, Jobs suggested that they could sell it together. The product, which they called the Apple I, was actually only a printed circuit board. It lacked a case, a keyboard, and a power supply. To raise the capital to buy the parts they needed, Jobs sold his minibus and Wozniak his calculator, and they set up production in Jobs's parents' garage. From these beginnings sprang one of the leading personal computer companies in the world. In 1980 Apple Computer, Inc., announced its first public stock offering, and its young founders became instant millionaires.

STEVE JOBS

Steven Paul Jobs, cofounder of Apple Computer, Inc. (now Apple, Inc.), is a charismatic pioneer of the personal computer era.

FOUNDING OF APPLE

Jobs was raised by adoptive parents in Cupertino, Calif., located in what is now known as Silicon Valley. Though he was interested in engineering, his passions of youth varied.

He dropped out of Reed College, in Portland, Ore., took a job at Atari Corporation as a video game designer in early 1974, and saved enough money for a pilgrimage to India to experience Buddhism.

Back in Silicon Valley in the autumn of 1974, Jobs reconnected with Stephen Wozniak, a former high school friend who was working for the Hewlett-Packard Company. When Wozniak told Jobs of his progress in designing his own computer logic board, Jobs suggested that they go into business together, which they did after Hewlett-Packard formally turned down Wozniak's design in 1976. The Apple I, as they called the logic board, was built in the Jobses' family garage with money they obtained by selling Jobs's Volkswagen minibus and Wozniak's programmable calculator.

Jobs was one of the first entrepreneurs to understand that the personal computer would appeal to a broad audience, at least if it did not appear to belong in a junior high school science fair. With Jobs's encouragement, Wozniak designed an improved model, the Apple II, complete with a keyboard, and they arranged to have a sleek, molded plastic case manufactured to enclose the unit.

Though Jobs had long, unkempt hair and eschewed business garb, he managed to obtain financing, distribution, and publicity for the company, Apple Computer, incorporated in 1977 — the same year that the Apple II was completed. The machine was an immediate success, becoming synonymous with the boom in personal computers. In 1981 the company had a record-setting public stock offering and, in 1983, made the quickest entrance (to that time) into the *Fortune* 500 list of America's top companies. In 1983 the company recruited PepsiCo, Inc., president John Sculley to be its chief executive officer (CEO) and, implicitly, Jobs's mentor in the fine points of running a large corporation. Jobs had convinced Sculley to accept the position by challenging him: "Do you want to sell sugar water for the rest of your life?" The line was shrewdly effective, but it also revealed Jobs's own near-messianic belief in the computer revolution.

INSANELY GREAT

During that same period, Jobs was heading the most important project in the company's history. In 1979 he led a small group of Apple engineers to a technology demonstration at the Xerox Corporation's Palo Alto Research Center (PARC) to see how the graphical user interface could make computers easier to use and more efficient. Soon afterward, Jobs left the engineering team that was designing Lisa, a business computer, to head a smaller group building a lower-cost computer. Both computers were redesigned to exploit and refine the PARC ideas, but Jobs was explicit in favouring the Macintosh, or Mac, as the new computer became known. Jobs coddled his engineers and referred to them as artists, but his style was uncompromising; at one point he demanded a redesign of an internal circuit board simply because he considered it unattractive. He would later be renowned for his insistence that the Macintosh be not merely great but "insanely great." In January 1984 Jobs himself introduced the Macintosh in a brilliantly choreographed demonstration that was the centrepiece of an extraordinary publicity campaign. It would later be pointed to as the archetype of "event marketing."

However, the first Macs were underpowered and expensive, and they had few software applications—all of which resulted in disappointing sales. Apple steadily improved the machine, so that it eventually became the company's lifeblood as well as the model for all subsequent computer interfaces. But Jobs's apparent failure to correct the problem quickly led to tensions in the company, and in

1985 Sculley convinced Apple's board of directors to remove the company's famous cofounder.

NeXT and Pixar

Jobs quickly started another firm, the NeXT Corporation, designing powerful workstation computers for the education market. His funding partners included Texan entrepreneur Ross Perot and Canon, Inc., a Japanese electronics company. Although the NeXT computer was notable for its engineering design, it was eclipsed by less costly computers from competitors such as Sun Microsystems, Inc. In the early 1990s, Jobs focused the company on its innovative software system, NeXTStep.

Meanwhile, in 1986 Jobs bought Pixar Animation Studios, a computer-graphics firm founded by Hollywood movie director George Lucas. Over the following decade Jobs built Pixar into a major animation studio that, among other achievements, produced the first full-length feature film to be completely computer-animated, *Toy Story*, in 1995. Also in 1995, Pixar's public stock offering made Jobs, for the first time, a billionaire.

Saving Apple

In late 1996, Apple, saddled by huge financial losses and on the verge of collapse, hired a new chief executive, semiconductor executive Gilbert Amelio. When Amelio learned that the company, following intense and prolonged research efforts, had failed to develop an acceptable replacement for the Macintosh's aging operating system (OS), he chose NeXTStep, buying Jobs's company for more than $400 million—and bringing Jobs back to Apple as a consultant. However, Apple's board of directors soon became disenchanted with Amelio's inability to turn the company's finances around and in June 1997 requested Apple's prodigal cofounder to lead the company once again. Jobs quickly forged an alliance with Apple's erstwhile foe, the Microsoft Corporation, scrapped Amelio's Mac-clone agreements, and simplified the company's product line. He also engineered an award-winning advertising campaign that urged potential customers to "think different" and buy Macintoshes. Just as important is what he did not do: he resisted the temptation to make machines that ran Microsoft's Windows OS; nor did he, as some urged, spin off Apple as a software-only company. Jobs believed that Apple, as the only major personal computer maker with its own operating system, was in a unique position to innovate.

Innovate he did. In 1998, Jobs introduced the iMac, an egg-shaped, one-piece computer that offered high-speed processing at a relatively modest price and initiated a trend of high-fashion computers. (Subsequent models sported five different bright colours.) By the end of the year, the iMac was the nation's highest-selling personal computer, and Jobs was able to announce consistent profits for the once-moribund company. The following year, he triumphed once more with the stylish iBook, a laptop computer built with students in mind, and the G4, a desktop computer sufficiently powerful that (so Apple boasted) it could not be exported under certain circumstances because it qualified as a supercomputer. Though Apple did not regain the industry dominance it once had, Steve Jobs had saved his company, and in the process reestablished himself as a master high-technology marketer and visionary.

REINVENTING APPLE

In 2001 Jobs started reinventing Apple for the 21st century. That was the year that Apple introduced iTunes, a computer program for playing music and for converting music to the compact MP3 digital format commonly used in computers and other digital devices. Later the same year, Apple began selling the iPod, a portable MP3 player, which quickly became the market leader. In 2003 Apple began selling downloadable copies of major record company songs in MP3 format over the Internet. By 2006 more than one billion songs and videos had been sold through Apple's online iTunes Store. In recognition of the growing shift in the company's business, Jobs officially changed the name of the company to Apple, Inc., on Jan. 9, 2007.

In 2007 Jobs took the company into the telecommunications business with the introduction of the touch-screen iPhone, a mobile telephone with capabilities for playing MP3s and videos and for accessing the Internet. Later that year, Apple introduced the iPod Touch, a portable MP3 and gaming device that included built-in Wi-Fi and an iPhone-like touch screen. Bolstered by the use of the iTunes Store to sell Apple and third-party software, the iPhone and iPod Touch soon boasted more games than any other portable gaming system. Jobs announced in 2008 that future releases of the iPhone and iPod Touch would offer improved game functionality. In an ironic development, Apple, which had not supported game developers in its early years out of fear of its computers not being taken seriously as business machines, was now staking a claim to a greater role in the gaming business to go along with its move into telecommunications.

HEALTH ISSUES

In 2003 Jobs was diagnosed with a rare form of pancreatic cancer. He put off surgery for about nine months while he tried alternative medicine approaches. In 2004 he underwent major reconstructive surgery, known as the Whipple operation. During the procedure, part of the pancreas, a portion of the bile duct, the gallbladder, and the duodenum are removed, after which what is left of the pancreas, the bile duct, and the intestine is reconnected to direct the gastrointestinal secretions back into the stomach. Following a short recovery, Jobs returned to running Apple.

Throughout 2008 Jobs lost significant weight, which produced considerable speculation that his cancer was back. Perhaps more than those of any other large corporation, Apple's stock market shares are tied to the health of its CEO, which led to demands by investors for full disclosure of his health. On Jan. 9, 2009, Jobs released a statement that he was being treated for a hormonal imbalance and that he would continue his corporate duties. Less than a week later, however, he announced that he was taking an immediate leave of absence through the end of June in order to recover his health. Having removed himself, at least temporarily, from the corporate structure, Jobs resumed his stance that his health was a private matter and refused to disclose any more details. In June it was reported that Jobs had received a liver transplant the previous April. Not disclosed was whether the pancreatic cancer he had been treated for previously had spread to his liver. Jobs came back to work on June 29, 2009, fulfilling his pledge to return before the end of June.

STEPHEN WOZNIAK

Stephen Gary Wozniak, an American electronics engineer, was cofounder, with Steven P. Jobs, of Apple Computer, Inc., and designer of the first commercially successful personal computer.

Wozniak—or "Woz," as he was commonly known—was the son of an electrical engineer for the Lockheed Missiles and Space Company in Sunnyvale, Calif., in what would become known as Silicon Valley. A precocious but undisciplined student with a gift for mathematics and an interest in electronics, he attended the University of

Colorado at Boulder for one year (1968–69) before dropping out. Following his return to California, he attended a local community college and then the University of California, Berkeley. In 1971 Wozniak designed the "Blue Box," a device for phreaking (hacking into the telephone network without paying for long-distance calls) that he and Jobs, a student at his old high school whom he met about this time, began selling to other students. Also during the early 1970s Wozniak worked at several small electronics firms in the San Francisco Bay area before obtaining a position with the Hewlett-Packard Company in 1975, by which time he had formally dropped out of Berkeley.

Wozniak also became involved with the Homebrew Computer Club, a San Francisco Bay area group centred around the Altair 8800 microcomputer do-it-yourself kit, which was based on one of the world's first microprocessors, the Intel Corporation 8080, released in 1975. While working as an engineering intern at Hewlett-Packard, Wozniak designed his own microcomputer in 1976 using the new microprocessor, but the company was not interested in developing his design. Jobs, who was also a Homebrew member, showed so much enthusiasm for Wozniak's design that they decided to work together, forming their own company, Apple Computer. Their initial capital came from selling Jobs's automobile and Wozniak's programmable calculator, and they set up production in the Jobs family garage to build microcomputer circuit boards. Sales of the kit were promising, so they decided to produce a finished product, the Apple II; completed in 1977, it included a built-in keyboard and support for a colour monitor. The Apple II, which combined Wozniak's brilliant engineering with Jobs's aesthetic sense, was the first personal computer to appeal beyond hobbyist circles. When the company went public in 1980, its market value exceeded $1 billion, at the time the fastest rise to that milestone in corporate history, and Wozniak's stock in the company made him an instant multi-millionaire.

During these years, Wozniak designed new hardware components, such as the 3.5-inch (8.9-cm) floppy disk drive for the Apple II, and various components of the Apple operating system and its software applications. This work ended in 1981 when he crashed his small airplane, leaving him temporarily with traumatic amnesia (unable to form new long-term memories), and he was forced to go on a sabbatical. He soon decided to return to Berkeley, under the pseudonym of Rocky Clark, in order to finish the computer science and electrical engineering courses needed to earn those degrees. Although he dropped out again, he eventually was given credit for his work at Apple, and the school awarded him a bachelor of science degree in electrical engineering in 1987.

Wozniak returned to Apple in 1982, though he resisted efforts to involve him in management. He finally retired as an active employee in 1985, immediately after being awarded, along with Jobs, a National Medal of Technology by U.S. Pres. Ronald W. Reagan. Wozniak spent the ensuing decades engaged in philanthropic causes, especially involving the education of children, and in volunteer work teaching computer enrichment classes to preteens.

Although Wozniak was semiretired after leaving Apple, he kept up with the computing world by funding various business ventures and occasionally serving as an adviser or board member for different companies. In 2009 he became the chief scientist at Fusion-Io, an American company that produces high-capacity, solid-state storage devices. Wozniak was serving on the company's board of directors when he decided to become a full-time employee.

In 2006 Wozniak published his autobiography, *iWoz: Computer Geek to Cult Icon: How I Invented the Personal Computer, Co-Founded Apple, and Had Fun Doing It.*

TIM BERNERS-LEE
(b. June 8, 1955, London, Eng.)

English computer scientist Tim Berners-Lee is generally credited as the inventor of the World Wide Web. In 2004 he was awarded a knighthood by Queen Elizabeth II of the United Kingdom and the inaugural Millennium Technology Prize (€1 million) by the Finnish Technology Award Foundation.

The computer scientist Tim Berners-Lee wrote the software for the first web server and is often credited as the inventor of the World Wide Web. Getty/Catrina Genovese

Computing came naturally to Berners-Lee, as both of his parents worked on the Ferranti Mark I, the first commercial computer. After graduating in 1976 from the University of Oxford, Berners-Lee designed computer software for two years at Plessey Telecommunications, Ltd., located in Poole, Dorset, Eng. Following this, he had several positions in the computer industry, including a stint from June to December 1980 as a software engineering consultant at CERN, the European particle physics laboratory in Geneva.

While at CERN, Berners-Lee developed a program for himself, called Enquire, that could store information in files that contained connections ("links") both within and among separate files — a technique that became known as hypertext. After leaving CERN, Berners-Lee worked for Image Computer Systems, Ltd., located in Ferndown, Dorset, where he designed a variety of computer systems. In 1984 he returned to CERN to work on the design of the laboratory's computer network, developing procedures that allowed diverse computers to communicate with one another and researchers to control remote machines. In 1989 Berners-Lee drew up a proposal for creating a global hypertext document system that would make use of the Internet. His goal was to provide researchers with the ability to share their results, techniques, and practices without having to exchange e-mail constantly. Instead, researchers would place such information "online," where their peers could immediately retrieve it anytime, day or night. Berners-Lee wrote the software for the first Web server (the central repository for the files to be shared) and the first Web client, or "browser" (the program to access and display files retrieved from the server), between October 1990 and the summer of 1991. The first "killer application" of the Web at CERN was the laboratory's telephone directory—a mundane beginning for one of the technological wonders of the computer age.

From 1991 to 1993 Berners-Lee evangelized the Web. In 1994 in the United States he established the World Wide Web (W3) Consortium at the Massachusetts Institute of Technology's Laboratory for Computer Science. The consortium, in consultation with others, lends oversight to the Web and the development of standards. In 1999 Berners-Lee became the first holder of the 3Com Founders chair at the Laboratory for Computer Science. His numerous other honours include the National Academy of Engineering's prestigious Charles Stark Draper Prize (2007). Berners-Lee is the author, along with Mark Fischetti, of *Weaving the Web: The Original Design and Ultimate Destiny of the World Wide Web* (2000).

BILL GATES

(b. Oct. 28, 1955, Seattle, Wash., U.S.)

American computer programmer and entrepreneur William Henry Gates III cofounded Microsoft Corporation, the world's largest personal-computer software company.

Gates wrote his first software program at the age of 13. In high school he helped form a group of programmers who computerized their school's payroll system and founded Traf-O-Data, a company that sold traffic-counting systems to local governments. In 1975 Gates, then a sophomore at Harvard University, joined his hometown friend Paul G. Allen to develop software for the first microcomputers. They began by adapting BASIC, a popular programming language used on large computers, for use on microcomputers. With the success of this project, Gates left Harvard during his junior year and, with

Allen, formed Microsoft. Gates's sway over the infant microcomputer industry greatly increased when Microsoft licensed an operating system called MS-DOS to International Business Machines Corporation—then the world's biggest computer supplier and industry pacesetter—for use on its first microcomputer, the IBM PC (personal computer). After the machine's release in 1981, IBM quickly set the technical standard for the PC industry, and MS-DOS likewise pushed out competing operating systems. While Microsoft's independence strained relations with IBM, Gates deftly manipulated the larger company so that it became permanently dependent on him for crucial software. Makers of IBM-compatible PCs, or clones, also turned to Microsoft for their basic software. By the start of the 1990s he had become the PC industry's ultimate kingmaker.

Largely on the strength of Microsoft's success, Gates amassed a huge paper fortune as the company's largest individual shareholder. He became a paper billionaire in 1986, and within a decade his net worth had reached into the tens of billions of dollars—making him by some estimates the world's richest private individual. With few interests beyond software and the potential of information technology, Gates at first preferred to stay out of the public eye, handling civic and philanthropic affairs indirectly through one of his foundations. Nevertheless, as Microsoft's power and reputation grew, and especially as it attracted the attention of the U.S. Justice Department's antitrust division, Gates, with some reluctance, became a more public figure. Rivals (particularly in competing companies in Silicon Valley) portrayed him as driven, duplicitous, and determined to profit from virtually every electronic transaction in the world. His supporters, on the other hand, celebrated his uncanny business acumen, his flexibility, and his boundless appetite for finding new ways to make computers and electronics more useful through software.

All of these qualities were evident in Gates's nimble response to the sudden public interest in the Internet. Beginning in 1995 and 1996, Gates feverishly refocused Microsoft on the development of consumer and enterprise software solutions for the Internet, developed the Windows CE operating system platform for networking non-computer devices such as home televisions and personal digital assistants, created the Microsoft Network to compete with America Online and other Internet providers, and, through Gates's company Corbis, acquired the huge Bettmann photo archives and other collections for use in electronic distribution.

In addition to his work at Microsoft, Gates was also known for his charitable work. With his wife, Melinda, he launched the William H. Gates Foundation (renamed the Bill & Melinda Gates Foundation in 1999) in 1994 to fund global health programs as well as projects in the Pacific Northwest. During the latter part of the 1990s, the couple also funded North American libraries through the Gates Library Foundation (renamed Gates Learning Foundation in 1999) and raised money for minority study grants through the Gates Millennium Scholars program. In June 2006 Warren Buffett announced an ongoing gift to the foundation, which would allow its assets to total roughly $60 billion in the next 20 years. At the beginning of the 21st century, the foundation continued to focus on global health and global development, as well as community and education causes in the United States. After a short transition period, Gates relinquished day-to-day over-sight of Microsoft in June 2008—although he remained chairman of the board—in order to devote more time to the Bill & Melinda Gates Foundation.

It remains to be seen whether Gates's extraordinary success will guarantee him a lasting place in the pantheon of great Americans. At the very least, historians seem likely to view him as a business figure as important to computers as John D. Rockefeller was to oil. Gates himself displayed an acute awareness of the perils of prosperity in his 1995 best seller, *The Road Ahead*, where he observed, "Success is a lousy teacher. It seduces smart people into thinking they can't lose."

LINUS TORVALDS

(b. Dec. 28, 1969, Helsinki, Fin.)

Finnish computer scientist Linus Torvalds was the principal force behind the development of the Linux operating system.

At age 10 Torvalds began to dabble in computer programming on his grandfather's Commodore VIC-20. In 1991, while a computer science student at the University of Helsinki (M.S., 1996), he purchased his first personal computer (PC). He was not satisfied, however, with the computer's operating system (OS). His PC used MS-DOS (the disk operating system from Microsoft Corp.), but Torvalds preferred the UNIX operating system he had used on the university's computers. He decided to create his own PC-based version of UNIX. Months of determined programming work yielded the beginnings of an operating system known as Linux. In 1991 he posted a message on the Internet to alert other PC users to his new system, made the software available for free downloading, and, as was a common practice among software developers at the time, he released the source code, which meant that anyone with knowledge of computer programming could modify Linux to suit their own purposes.

Because of their access to the source code, many programmers helped Torvalds retool and refine the software, and by 1994 Linux kernel (original code) version 1.0 was released.

Operating Linux required a certain amount of technical acumen; it was not as easy to use as more popular operating systems such as Windows, Apple's Mac OS, or IBM OS/2. However, Linux evolved into a remarkably reliable, efficient system that rarely crashed. Linux became popular in the late 1990s when competitors of Microsoft began taking the upstart OS seriously. Netscape Communications Corp., Corel Corp., Oracle Corp., Intel Corp., and other companies announced plans to support Linux as an inexpensive alternative to Windows. In addition to Linux being free, its source code can be viewed and freely modified by anyone, unlike a proprietary OS. This means that different language versions can be developed and deployed in markets that would be too small for the traditional companies. Also, many organizations and governments have expressed security reservations about using any kind of computer software that contains code that cannot be viewed. For all of the above reasons, localized versions of Linux have become common in China and many other non-Western countries.

In 1997 Torvalds took a position with Transmeta Corp., a microprocessor manufacturer, and relocated to California. Six years later he left the company to work as a project coordinator under the auspices of the Open Source Development Labs (OSDL), a consortium created by such high-tech companies as IBM, Intel, and Siemens to promote Linux development. In 2007 OSDL merged with the Free Standards Group to form the Linux Foundation.

SERGEY BRIN AND LARRY PAGE

respectively, (b. Aug. 21, 1973, Moscow, U.S.S.R. [now Russia]);
(b. March 26, 1973, East Lansing, Mich., U.S.)

On Aug. 19, 2004, Sergey Brin and Larry Page went from being promising computer science graduate students to multibillionaire technology mavens when Google, Inc., the online search engine company they had founded in 1998, issued its much-anticipated initial public offering (IPO). By creating the easy-to-use hyper-text search engine Google, one of the most successful applications in the history of the Internet, Brin and Page had provided World Wide Web browsing at its simplest

This photo shows Google founders Sergey Brin and Larry Page at the 2004 Frankfurt Book Fair, preparing to unveil their new Google Print project. John MacDougall/AFP/Getty Images

to millions of ordinary computer users and had added a new verb, *to google*, to the English language.

SERGEY BRIN

Sergey Brin's family moved from Moscow to the United States in 1979. After receiving degrees (1993) in computer science and mathematics at the University of Maryland, he entered Stanford University's graduate program, where he met Page, a fellow graduate student. The two were both intrigued by the idea of enhancing the ability to extract meaning from the mass of data accumulating on the Internet, and together they began working to devise a new type of search technology that leveraged Web users' own ranking abilities by tracking each site's "backing links"— that is, the number of other pages linked to them. Brin received his master's degree in 1995, but he went on leave from Stanford's doctorate program to continue working on the search engine.

In mid-1998 Brin and Page began receiving outside financing, and they ultimately raised about $1 million from investors and from family and friends. They called their updated search engine Google—a name derived from a misspelling of the originally planned name, googol (a mathematical term for the number 1 followed by 100 zeros)—and created the corporation Google, Inc. Brin became the company's president of technology, and by mid-1999, when Google received $25 million of venture capital funding, the search engine was processing 500,000 queries per day. Google then became the client search engine for Yahoo!, one of the Web's most popular sites, and by 2004 users were accessing the Web site 200 million times a day (roughly 138,000 queries per minute). On Aug. 19, 2004, Google, Inc., issued its IPO, which netted more than $3.8 billion dollars for Brin.

In 2006 Google acquired YouTube, the Web's most popular site for user-submitted streaming video, for $1.65 billion in stock. The move reflected the company's efforts to expand its services beyond Internet searches. That same year Google was criticized for agreeing to comply with the Chinese government's censorship requirements—blocking Web sites extolling democracy, for example, or those covering the 1989 demonstrations in Tiananmen Square. Brin defended the decision, saying that Google's ability to supply some, albeit restricted, information was better than supplying none.

LARRY PAGE

Lawrence Edward Page, whose father was a professor of computer science at Michigan State University, received a computer engineering degree from the University of Michigan (1995) and entered into the doctorate program at Stanford, where he met Brin. Working from Page's dormitory room, they began to devise their revolutionary search engine technology, which they initially dubbed BackRub. Most search engines simply returned a list of Web sites ranked by how often a search phrase appeared on them. Brin and Page incorporated into the search function the number of links each Web site had—i.e., a Web site with thousands of links would logically be more valuable than one with just a few links, and the search engine thus would place the heavily linked site higher on a list of possibilities. Further, a link from a heavily linked Web site would be a more valuable "vote" than one from a more obscure Web site. Meanwhile, the partners established an idealistic 10-point corporate philosophy that included "Focus on the user and all else will follow," "Fast is better than slow," and "You can make money without doing evil." In 1990 the two founded Google, with Page the new company's president of products. Google, Inc.'s, IPO in 2004 netted Page more than $3.8 billion.

GLOSSARY

agronomy The science of soil management and field crop production.

anesthesiologist Physician specializing in the administration of anesthetics.

antivivisectionism Opposition to dissecting or cutting into a live body.

apocryphal Of doubtful origin or authenticity.

apotheosis Elevation to a preeminent or exalted rank.

artillery Large but transportable projectile-firing guns or missile launchers.

auscultation Listening to the body as a method of diagnosis.

automata theory The study of machines and the problems they are able to solve.

ballast Used to give balance or change the center of gravity in ships or planes.

baronetcy The rank of a baron, the lowest form of nobility.

cathode The source of electrons in an electrical device.

centrifugal Moving outward from the center, or directed in such movement.

chassis The frame, wheels, and machinery of a motor vehicle.

chromatic aberration Colour distortion in an image produced by a lens that results from the inability of a lens to bring all the colors of light to focus at a single point.

circumscribe In geometry, to draw a figure around another figure so as to enclose the original figure and touch as many points of it as possible.

coagulant A substance that aids a liquid in becoming thicker.

compendium A brief treatment or account of an extensive subject; concise treatment.

congenital Relating to a condition present at birth.

consortium An association, union, or partnership.

cowl-flap Moveable doors on an airplane that control the amount of air flowing through the engine compartment to help cool the engine.

cystic fibrosis A disease of the exocrine glands that affects the pancreas, respiratory system, and sweat glands when glands produce an abnormally viscous mucus.

determinism Philosophical doctrine in which all events are inevitable consequences of previous conditions and not the result of free will.

duodenum The first portion of the small intestine; connects to the stomach.

emeritus Retaining a title after honorably retiring from duties.

emphysema A chronic disease of the lungs in which the air sacs become stretched and enlarged, decreasing the capability to supply oxygen to the blood.

epochal Significant.

eunuch A castrated man, employed by Middle Eastern and Chinese rulers from remote antiquity as a harem guard or palace official.

geometer An expert in geometry, also known as a geometrician.

haberdasher A retailer of small wares, particularly men's accessories.

hydrodynamics The study of fluids in motion.

hydrolysis The decomposition of a compound caused by its reaction with water.

hydrostatics The branch of hydrodynamics that deals with the pressure of liquids.

improvident Lacking foresight, unwary.

isotope One of two or more atoms with the same atomic number (number of protons in the nucleus) but with different atomic weights (numbers of neutrons in the nucleus).

iterative Repeating; making repetitions.

macerate To form into a pulp by steeping in liquid.

magnum opus Great work; a masterpiece.

microprocessor An integrated computer circuit that contains a processor (CPU).

necropolis A cemetery or burial ground of an ancient city.

ophthalmia Inflammation of the eye or surrounding areas.

oscillate To swing or to move to and fro, as a pendulum.

paradigm Something that serves as a pattern or model, a touchstone.

piscatorial Of or pertaining to fish.

polymer A chemical compound made of smaller, repeating molecules linked together.

prototype An original model on which something is based.

quantum theory The study of reactions between matter and radiation.

radiocarbon dating Determining the age of organic objects by measuring the radioactivity of their carbon content.

roulette A game of chance.

sobriquet Nickname.

subterfuge A deception to escape a rule or its consequences.

superconductivity A property of some materials in which their electrical resistance goes to zero and they can carry electrical current with no energy loss.

syntax Rules of patterns for forming grammatical sentences.

thermion An emission from an incandescent bulb.

thermonuclear Involving the fusion of atomic nuclei at high temperatures.

transistor An electronic device that can transform weak electrical signals into strong ones, acting as an amplifier.

treatise A formal exposition in writing, generally longer and more specific than an essay.

vellum The skin of a lamb, calf, or kid (baby goat) treated for use as a writing surface.

venerate To revere or regard with reverence.

vizier A high official or executive of state.

vulcanize To treat rubber with sulfur and heat to increase its strength and durability.

zenith The highest point or point of culmination.

For Further Reading

Austin, Guy. *Contemporary French Cinema: An Introduction*. Manchester, England:Manchester University Press, 1996.

Brown, David E. *Inventing Modern America: From the Microwave to the Mouse*. Cambridge, MA: The MIT Press, 2002.

Carey, Charles W. *American Inventors, Entrepreneurs, and Business Visionaries*. New York, NY: Facts on File, 2002.

Evans, Harold, Gail Buckland, and David Lefer. *They Made America: From the Steam Engine to the Search Engine: Two Centuries of Innovators*. Boston, MA: Back Bay Books, 2004.

Fagan, Brian M. *The Seventy Great Inventions of the Ancient World*. New York, NY: Thames & Hudson, 2004.

Franklin, Benjamin. *The Autobiography of Benjamin Franklin & Selections From His Other Writings*. New York, NY: Modern Library, 2001.

Goodchild, Peter. *Edward Teller, the Real Dr. Strangelove*. Cambridge, MA: Harvard University Press, 2004.

Harrison, Ian. *The Book of Inventions: How'd The Come up with That?* New York, NY: National Geographic Society, 2004.

Jonnes, Jill. *Empires of Light: Edison, Tesla, Westinghouse, and the Race to Electrify the World*. New York, NY: Random House, 2003.

Klein, Maury. *The Power Makers: Steam, Electricity, and the Men Who Invented Modern America*. New York, NY: Bloomsbury, 2008.

Man, John. *Gutenberg: How One Man Remade the World with Words*. New York, NY: John Wiley and Sons, 2002.

Mellor, C. Michael. *Louis Braille: A Touch of Genius*. Boston, MA: National Braille Press, 2006.

Newman, Paul B. *Daily Life in the Middle Ages*. Jefferson, NC: McFarland, 2001.

Sale, Kirkpatrick. *The Fire of His Genius: Robert Fulton and the American Dream*. New York, NY: The Free Press, 2001.

Seifer, Marc. *Wizard: The Life and Times of Nikola Tesla*. Secaucus, NJ: Citadel, 2001.

Shulman, Seth. *The Telephone Gambit: Chasing Alexander Graham Bell's Secret*. New York, NY: W. W. Norton, 2008.

Silverman, Kenneth. *Lightning Man: the Accursed Life of Samuel F. B. Morse*. New York, NY: Da Capo Press, 2003.

Smith, Roger. *Inventions and Inventors*. Pasadena, CA: Salem Press, 2002.

Stross, Randall E. *Wizard of Menlo Park: How Thomas Alva Edison Invented the Modern World*. New York, NY: Three Rivers Press, 2007.

Webster, Raymond B. *African American Firsts in Science and Technology*. Detroit, MI: Gale, 1999.

Watts, Steven. *The People's Tycoon: Henry Ford and the American Century*. New York, NY: Vintage, 2005.

Wood, John C., and Michael C. Wood, eds. *Henry Ford: Critical Evaluations In Business and Management*. New York, NY: Routledge, 2005.

INDEX

Runaway Mine Ride, 279
Ruska, Ernst, 281

S

safety elevator, 99–100
Sanger, Frederick, 14, 264–270
Sarnoff, David, 202, 203
Saturn, rings of, 31, 32
Saturn space boosters, 261
scanning tunneling microscope,
  280–283
Schawlow, Arthur, 262
Schöffer, Peter, 30
Schrieffer, John, 256
Schrödinger, Erwin, 228
Scott, Léon, 134
Sculley, John, 300–301, 302
secondary-emission
  multiplier, 203
*Second Creation: Dolly and the
  Age of Biological Control,
  The*, 297
Sekhmet, 20
Selden, George Baldwin, 166
*Select Works of A. van
  Leeuwenhoek, The*, 38
Sematech, 278–279
Senefelder, Alois, 12, 69–70
Shannon, Claude, 228
Shockley, William, 253–257,
  276–277
shortwave wireless
  communication, 187
Sikorsky, Igor, 12, 197–201
Single Action Army Model 1873
  revolver, 105
Skeleton Dance, 221
sniperscope, 203
snooperscope, 203

*Snow White and the Seven
  Dwarfs*, 222
somatic cell nuclear transfer
  (SCNT), 295
"Some Aeronautical
  Experiments," 176
sonic depth finder, 170
*Sortie des ouvriers de l'usine
  Lumière, La*, 162
Soundex, 208
space launcher, 260–262
Spectator, The, 39
Spemann, Hans, 292
Stalin, Joseph, 159
stamps, 89
Standard English Braille,
  grade 2, 96
Starley, James, 106–108
Starley, John Kemp, 108
steamboat, 61–65, 136
Steamboat Willie, 221
steam engine, 48, 49–52, 116, 122
steel plow, 91–92
steel roller coaster, 279–280
Stephenson, George, 75–77
Stephenson, Robert, 75–76
Stereometrica, 24
stethoscope, 71, 73–74
Stevens, John H., 115,
stone tools, 14, 17–18
store, 86
stored-program digital
  computer, 228, 231
Story of the Winged-S, 201
Stratocaster, 252
stroboscopic photography, 149
submarine, 62, 63, 123–124, 139, 170
superheterodyne principle, 170,
  204, 206